Opening Doors

Opening Doors

Reimagining the American Musical

John Doyle

With a Foreword by Patti LuPone

methuen | drama
LONDON · NEW YORK · OXFORD · NEW DELHI · SYDNEY

METHUEN DRAMA

Bloomsbury Publishing Plc, 50 Bedford Square, London, WC1B 3DP, UK
Bloomsbury Publishing Inc, 1359 Broadway, New York, NY 10018, USA
Bloomsbury Publishing Ireland, 29 Earlsfort Terrace, Dublin 2, D02 AY28, Ireland

BLOOMSBURY, METHUEN DRAMA and the Methuen Drama logo are trademarks
of Bloomsbury Publishing Plc

First published in Great Britain 2026

Copyright © John Doyle, 2026

John Doyle has asserted his right under the Copyright, Designs and Patents Act, 1988,
to be identified as author of this work.
All music and lyrics of Stephen Sondheim reprinted courtesy of the
Stephen J. Sondheim Trust. All rights reserved.

Cover Design by Lara Himpelmann
Cover image © Gremlin via Getty Images

All rights reserved. No part of this publication may be: i) reproduced or transmitted
in any form, electronic or mechanical, including photocopying, recording or by means
of any information storage or retrieval system without prior permission in writing from
the publishers; or ii) used or reproduced in any way for the training, development or
operation of artificial intelligence (AI) technologies, including generative AI technologies.
The rights holders expressly reserve this publication from the text and data mining
exception as per Article 4(3) of the Digital Single Market Directive (EU) 2019/790.

Bloomsbury Publishing Plc does not have any control over, or responsibility for,
any third-party websites referred to or in this book. All internet addresses given in
this book were correct at the time of going to press. The author and publisher
regret any inconvenience caused if addresses have changed or sites have ceased
to exist, but can accept no responsibility for any such changes.

No rights in incidental music or songs contained in the work are hereby granted
and performance rights for any performance/presentation whatsoever must
be obtained from the respective copyright owners.

A catalogue record for this book is available from the British Library.

A catalog record for this book is available from the Library of Congress.

ISBN: HB: 978-1-3505-0852-1
ePDF: 978-1-3505-0855-2
eBook: 978-1-3505-0854-5

Typeset by RefineCatch Limited, Bungay, Suffolk
Printed and bound in Great Britain

For product safety related questions contact productsafety@bloomsbury.com.

To find out more about our authors and books visit www.bloomsbury.com
and sign up for our newsletters.

FOR ROBBIE AND BECCY

Contents

Foreword by Patti Lupone ix
Acknowledgements x
Preface xi

1   A Boy of No Importance 1

2   The Only White Guy on the Bus 17

3   The Early Artistic Director Years 33
    TIE-UP Theatre company 1975–1980 33
    Worcester Repertory Company 1980–1985 39
    Cheltenham Everyman Theatre 1985–1989 45

4   The Later Artistic Director Years 53
    Liverpool Everyman Theatre 1989–1993 53
    York Theatre Royal 1993–1997 59
    Classic Stage Company, Off-Broadway 2016–2022 63

5   Thinking Out of the Box 73

6   Why God Was a Woman! 93

7   Then Along Came Steve 107

8   Building The Box Set 127

9   Give My Regards to Broadway 143
    Number One: *SWEENEY TODD*, Eugene O'Neill Theatre, 03 November 2005 – 03 September 2006 145
    Number Two: *COMPANY*, Ethel Barrymore Theatre, 29 November 2006 – 01 July 2007 147

Number Three: *A CATERED AFFAIR*, Walter Kerr Theatre, 17 April 2008 – 27 July 2008 154

Number Four: *THE VISIT*, Lyceum Theatre, 23 April 2015 – 14 June 2015 156

Number Five: *THE COLOR PURPLE*, 10 December 2015 – 08 January 2017 160

10 Now I Was Driving the Bus! 163

11 From the Met to Sydney Opera House 179

12 Opening Doors 195
    to the storytelling of politics in the theatre 195
    to "essentialism" in theatre-making 198
    to those who have not been given a fair opportunity 200
    to collaborating with artists from different cultures 202
    to William Shakespeare 205
    to rethinking cast-sizes and methods of casting 206
    to the next generation of theatre artists 208
    to the rehearsal room 210
    through music 214
    to myself 215

Notes 217
Bibliography 219
Shows by Chapter 221
Index 229

Foreword by Patti LuPone

I first met John when he was casting the 2005 Broadway revival of *Sweeney Todd*. He flew to Portland, Oregon where I was working to meet me. I was so moved by that gesture. I saw a gentleman sitting in the lobby of my hotel and I instantly knew it was him. We shared a meal and a stroll where we were simply two fellow travelers negotiating a strange city. He eventually cast me as Nellie Lovett, opening a door which led to my Broadway debut in a Sondheim musical.

As a director he is a Master. The rehearsal process was specific, deeply informative, creative and ultimately more fun than the dark subject of the musical should have been. During the course of our rehearsals in New York, another door swung open that ushered in our long friendship, sharing Thanksgivings, teas, dinners, swims, gossip, complaints, and most of all joy in each other's company.

I've only worked with John twice, *Sweeney Todd* on Broadway and the Brecht/Weill musical *The Rise and Fall of the City of Mahagonny* with the LA Opera. I would be elated beyond description to be in a rehearsal room with him again. That experience is one of constant learning, from his knowledge of stage craft to his wisdom into the human soul to his courage in speaking truth, be it political, societal, or spiritual. I'm extremely fortunate to have this human being in my life. I don't see him enough, but I treasure the theatrical lessons I've learned from John and the friendship that has forever enriched my life. Now with this incisive, deeply personal, and entertaining book, John continues to open doors that will inspire and enlighten his readers just as he has for me.

Patti LuPone, February 2025

Acknowledgements

My love and thanks to those good people who raised me.

My respect to all the composers, writers, actors, designers, musicians, and collaborators I've had the good fortune to meet on my journey.

My gratitude to those who have encouraged me to write it all down.

My sincere thanks to Dom and the team at Bloomsbury for their care and guidance.

My deep love and gratitude to my husband for putting up with the endless hours of absence when I've been glued to my computer – and when I've been living in my past.

Preface

It was very early in November 2005. A Press Preview of the Broadway Revival of *Sweeney Todd*. The night Ben Brantley, the feared *New York Times* critic, was in the house. The one man, at that time, who could make or break your future. I'm standing in the little curtained-off vestibule situated between backstage and the auditorium of the delightful O'Neill Theatre on Manhattan's 49th Street. I've just left Patti LuPone's dressing room. Everybody was trying to appear relaxed, but secretly knowing it had to be a really good show! Beside me, leaning side by side against the old New York radiator, is the man who single-handedly changed the face of the American Musical Theatre, Stephen Sondheim. He turned to me and said quietly, *"Well, John, this is Broadway!"* There we were waiting to slip in when the house went dark and we were equally afraid. The question in the forefront of my mind was, as Steve said in *Merrily We Roll Along*, *"How did you get to be here, what was the moment?"*[1]

1
A Boy of No Importance

Quite recently I found myself lying for many days in a bed in St Thomas' Hospital, London. I'd had a medical emergency which left me somewhat incapacitated. Before going any further, I should make it clear that I've recovered. However, it was an enforced period of stopping, though probably not the most predictable way of allowing myself to take a break. Probably like so many of you, I have always just kept going. A career in the arts has meant the need to stay on track, sometimes to the detriment of self and all around. So, here I was, two weeks of lying still. Two weeks of retrospection. Plenty of time to take stock. If this was how it was going to end, had I achieved what I set out to achieve? Did I even know what it was that I set out to achieve? That question is certainly problematic in a profession so driven by opportunity and, most certainly, by a modicum of luck.

So, how do I look back? How do I give those memories and observations any sort of form? When I'm rehearsing stories for the theatre, I seldom start the process at the beginning, rather I start with key moments in the story and work forward and backward from there. I could indeed do that with looking at my life and work, but to give things some clarity and some context, and to save you from becoming totally confused, I think that starting at the beginning is the best way for me to write it all down. To paraphrase TS Eliot in his great series of poems *The Four Quartets*, "In my end is my beginning". So let's see.

I've only recently become comfortable with looking back. It must be a symptom of what Shakespeare would have called the Seventh Age. From the very beginning I was encouraged to put yesterday behind me. I come from a family dominated by tough women who had no interest in what happened yesterday. There was no time! They had to survive. They got through two World Wars. They'd lost more than I will ever understand. Perhaps it was too hard to look back? Generally Scottish people – and I'm a proud Scot – are known for being sentimental. Known for enjoying reflecting upon past glories. I do hold some of that same sense of reflection, but it seldom manifests in sentimentality. It's the difference between being sentimental and wallowing in sentimentality, the latter, where I come from, being perceived as a weakness. Perhaps because of that familial insistence on living in the present, I have only a small store of memorabilia and few papers to prove what I've done. I do have some boxes in the attic full of theatre programmes and press cuttings, but I never look at them. In fact, I'm not quite sure what they're in that attic for. For my daughter and grandchildren? I don't think so. For me? If I'm totally honest, possibly.

Having been raised in a very Scottish Presbyterian manner, I would have been reprimanded for boasting about what I had achieved. Ridiculed for resting on my laurels. *"Stop showing off"* was a familiar childhood admonishment. I didn't like it at the time but I'm grateful for it now. It keeps you on track and reminds you that you are only as good as the work you are doing today. So to now ask oneself *"Was it worth it?"* or *"Have I made a difference?"* is, to say the least, unnerving. Another childhood question ringing in my ears is *"Who do you think you are?"* My family were staunchly lower middle class and very proud of it. We were, as the title of this chapter suggests, "of no importance". However, there was no shame in that, far from it. My family were decent hard-working people who married, attended church, did what they could to save a little, and who supported and enjoyed each other.

When I started my career in the theatre, I had three aims: to keep working (which I'm amazed to say, I have achieved); to have the respect of my peers (well, you'd have to ask them, but I remain hopeful); and to make a difference (though I'm not sure I knew what that difference was). Perhaps this somewhat uncomfortable exercise in retrospection will help me find out? I certainly had a gut feeling, more than fifty years ago, that theatre could help to change the world. The communion of an audience sitting together could make our world a better place. The story being told, if a worthwhile story, could inspire change. For all the ups and downs, and even though we live in an imperfect world,

I still believe it. Nothing shakes my faith in the fact that theatre can have a profound effect upon our lives and how we live them.

I was born in Inverness in the Highlands of Scotland. It was 1952, the year a beautiful young Queen Elizabeth came to the throne. It was only seven years after the end of World War Two, and times were still hard. Some foods remained rationed. I can clearly remember the tall blue and white tin of powdered milk that sat in my granny's kitchen, fresh milk being hard to come by. It was a world free of supermarkets and food deliveries. A time when your mother would shop for the needs of the day and not for the week. When she knew the butcher by name and he saved her the inexpensive "cuts". When she had her own little book at the grocer's shop, in Highland slang known as "the chitty", in which the grocer would notate how much money she owed for the week, a debt that was paid every Friday after "pay day". Indeed "pay day" was a focal event of the week, when the brown wage packet would be opened and the cash divided into small piles on the kitchen table. My granny even had her own funeral fund, a penny a week, as there would have been great shame in not being able to pay for your own coffin.

I was fortunate to know my great-grandfather throughout my childhood. A wonderful connection with a very real past. His first job had been to drive a coach and horses, and many years later I sat with him to watch man landing on the moon. It was the only time I ever saw him cry. Every week he would look in our weekly newspaper, the "Inverness Courier", to see who had died. My grandmother, his daughter, would look to see who was getting married. Attending funerals and weddings were two of the most exciting aspects of my childhood, even if I was only standing on the street to watch the bride enter the church, or standing outside a house to see the coffin leaving. I actively looked forward to Saturday morning wedding-watching and to the moment when the father of the bride threw lucky coins to the children outside the church. Early memories. Early rituals.

There was another important ritual that I shared with my great-grandfather. When school was on holiday, every Wednesday throughout the summer he would take me to the cattle market, known locally as "The Mart". A magical circular brick building. Grandad had been a farm-hand for most of his working life and local farmers still sought his advice on the quality of their pigs. On the table where my Tony Award sits, there is also a fading presentation box that houses an engraved silver coin. Grandad won it at the Royal Northern Agricultural Show for breeding the Best Female Pig! Two prizes, generations apart. Both for different kinds of "shows". He and I would sit together on those tiered bleacher seats, thoroughly enjoying sharing the smell of the cattle. The big doors would open at the back of the "ring", and the animals, or the "beasts" as he called them, came charging out. The auctioneer would speak at a thrilling pace that made it sound like a whole new exciting language. I loved it. It was probably one of my first experiences of theatre. We all showed up, we sat in seats, we watched an event, we went home satisfied. Something had happened.

When my cousins and I went out to play in the back garden, always the back garden never the front, we played "British and Germans", and, unsurprisingly, the British always won. I was aware that my father and his twin brother had "come back". For a long time I was never quite sure where they had come back from, because, oddly enough, such a life-changing experience was never actually talked about. On becoming an adult I asked my father to tell me about it, to tell me what he could remember. He did. He told me in detail about his experience on a Royal Navy mine-sweeper in what was then known as the Java Straits. Only on hearing those awful remembrances did I understand why it wasn't spoken about.

I was an only child, though I had no sense of the loneliness often associated with being the only one. That's probably because my entire family lived within a few streets of each other. I had seventeen younger cousins, five of whom lived in a building only two doors along. Our home was in fact a flat, a tenement really. They weren't called apartments in those days. To live in a flat was perceived as meaning that you couldn't afford a house. Not only that, but we rented our flat. Even more of a social stigma. It was a one-bedroom, with my parents sleeping on the pull-out sofa in the sitting room. We had no bathroom but considered ourselves fortunate in having an inside toilet. I can still smell the gas lamps in the hallways, lit by the lamplighter who came round every day as the evenings drew in. I remember Salvadori's, the Italian ice cream shop across the street, which served a rather exotic white coffee with froth on the top. I remember the wool shop, where my mother bought one ball of wool at a time and where they reserved the others until she could afford them. I remember the sweetie shop, where you could buy four chewy sweets for a penny. You could play on the street outside the house safe in the knowledge that everybody knew everybody else. Laundry was hung in the communal back "green" and the budgie was in its cage in the kitchen. Eventually we moved from that flat to a modern house, with a blissful bathroom! There was then a further move to a house with a small garden. My parents never owned any of these properties, they were council-owned and in areas of town that identified you as being of inferior status. The wonderful thing is that nobody felt aggrieved by that class structure.

My father and his twin brother were inseparable. Sundays after church were always spent at my Granny Doyle's house, where the adults played card games. There seemed to be a certain secrecy to the card sessions, after all you didn't want the neighbours to know that you were gambling on the Sabbath. My cousins and I were banished to that back garden to play. As the eldest, I was always in the position of being "in charge" of the play activities. So, "in charge of" was ingrained even then. I taught some of the cousins to read and write and I took the blame if they were badly behaved. I'm not sure that I was particularly playful myself but I certainly enabled all of them to play. Do you see the pattern? I always thought of myself as luckier than the cousins. After all, at the end of those long family afternoons I could go home to my own room, to my own books and to the security of my own imagination! I'm sure that explains a large part of who I am and of the job I do.

In that bedroom, which was probably much smaller than I remember, there was a double-fronted wardrobe housing clothes for me and for my parents. It had a wooden veneer front and to me there were faces in the wood. There was a small set of bookshelves which housed the books my mother received monthly in the mail, from what I think was called the National Book Club. I can still see the coloured covers on those books. In fact I still have a few of them. I have no recollection of her ever reading them, so perhaps they were just a symbol of the fact that we may have been poor but we weren't uneducated. My mother was a smart woman, who, if life had offered different opportunities, would probably have gone into one of the professions. My father was a quieter person, gentle by nature, who unfortunately was progressively overwhelmed by what was somewhat judgementally called the "Demon Drink". This made life harder than it might otherwise have been. Also on those shelves were some "plays" which came from my mother's involvement, before she was married, in amateur drama. I loved those plays. I read them again and again. It's interesting that reading plays doesn't hold such pleasure for me now. Exploring them does, reading them, no. I fear there was more discipline in the seven-year-old me than there is in the person that seven-year-old became.

There was also a box of toys in the room. Not many, but much loved. My generation of Scottish children didn't have the expectation of numerous Christmas and birthday gifts. The highlights of our Christmas stocking were an apple and an orange. Nothing to feel sorry for though. I can still see the two teddy bears. I wonder what happened to them? I have a feeling that my mother may have given them away when she thought I was too old for that "nonsense". After all, teddies after a certain age were sissy items, particularly for boys. To this day I bring books into the rehearsal room. I bring in visual stimuli and things to play with. I still see the stage as the bed I once played upon. Then there was the piano. A black wooden upright. It stood between my bedroom and the window of the sitting room. I can remember banging away on those keys from a very early age, remember opening the door below the keyboard and plucking the exposed metal strings. I loved to open the lid at the top of the piano and still recall the joy of speaking into it and hearing the echo. It being a black piano still fascinates me, as in those days almost every piano was brown. One abiding memory of the piano belongs to a certain awful day in world history, 22 November 1963. The assassination of President John F. Kennedy. Everybody says "*I remember where I was when I heard. . . . .*" Well, I was standing beside the black piano. My mother told me what had happened. I didn't fully appreciate the enormity of the event but I did understand that something dreadful had taken place. As Stephen Sondheim wrote in *Assassins*, "*Something just broke*". To contextualise what I mean by "enormity", bear in mind that at school we practised getting under our desks in case those Russians dropped "The Bomb". The more I think about it, the more extraordinary our early life experiences are. Opening oneself to those experiences and putting them into one's work are exactly the things I have spoken to actors about throughout my career. It may be worth my noting that most actors know a great deal about my personal life by the end of a rehearsal period. I always say to them that my telling my story does not mean they have to share theirs.

However, it does encourage some personal recall, kept safely private, which I believe greatly enriches the work we make together.

We had no television for the first seven years of my life, for which I am now deeply grateful, even though not having a television was another outward sign of being poor. I avoided talking about the "TV" at school. No, the radio was where we found all our home entertainment. Listening to the radio was a family event. Sitting down on a Saturday evening and facing the radio, or wireless as we called it then, to all listen to Saturday Night Theatre will always be a rich and happy memory. I'm grateful because, with radio, you have to use your imagination, and the visualisation of the story comes from you. A theme as I write will be my deep sense that we are denying our audiences the opportunity to imagine. We still haven't evaluated what our access to the Internet will do in terms of how we visualise. We no longer need to make our own pictures as they are available to us with the click of a keyboard.

When we did get TV, there was only one channel available, The BBC. I was allowed to watch the hour between coming home from school and the Six O'Clock News – Children's Hour. Then when the news came on, you sat silently in fear of being yelled at for disrespectfully intruding upon the grownups' concentration. A couple of years later I first experienced what we called 'Independent' or 'Commercial' Television, The ITV. It was a Sunday evening. "Sunday Night at the London Palladium." I can still sing the theme tune and still see the magic of the revolving stage at the end of the show. An innocent magic and one I have strived to recreate in so many ways.

My primary school was quite near our home. Wooden floors, a gas cooker in the classroom for making the staff cups of tea, every teacher a woman. Little bottles of free milk for break, warm in the summer and frozen in the winter! In fact, everything was frozen in the winter, including your knees in those dreaded school shorts. I had one set of clothes for school, one set for church on Sunday. I will forever despise a particular teacher who one day examined the collar of my shirt and admonished me, saying that I had to wear a clean shirt to school every day. It really wasn't that easy!

Probably the most central influence on my young life was music. The black upright piano with the piano stool filled with sheet music. Joining in the school choir, and later the church choir. Piano lessons, even cello lessons at school, my lowest moment being my inept playing of the bagpipes – not a proud failure for any Scottish boy! Music, and indeed dance, were very much part of my life. My grandmother told a lovely story about Saturday Dance Nights at the Northern Meeting Rooms. Her parents' generation would gather on the ground floor and dance traditional Scottish dances, her generation would gather in the middle floor and waltz or foxtrot, and my mother and her generation would be on the top floor doing the jive and any other dances they learned from the American GIs who were based in town during the war. The charming thing is that at the end of the evening all three generations would meet outside the building and walk home together. Forgive my divergence, but the sense of community that story conjures for me is in itself a pure act of theatre.

During my childhood I loved the annual occasion where my mother and father would dress up and go with their siblings to the "Bobby's Ball", a charity dance in aid of the local police force. The ladies' dresses, that always seemed to be shiny and to stick out at the side, were just thrilling! Dad and my uncles were in their "demob suits", the somewhat formal wear they were given by the authorities on returning from the war which helped them be respectable when going for a job interview, or even for getting married. Dressing up, being somebody you weren't for an evening. I hope you can see the themes emerging.

My first memory of singing was with my grandmother. She ran a boarding house and there were numerous beds to change every morning. She encouraged my help by saying we would change the sheets and sing as we worked. I can't quite equate this with her threat of *"dying in the poorhouse if you sang before midday"*, but I suppose one will do anything to get necessary peace and quiet. To this day I associate singing with work. I don't sing much at home, don't even listen to much music, but the moment I walk into a rehearsal room I start to sing. Singing was certainly a major part of my teenage years. Let's start with singing in church. Church was central to life. I went to three services every Sunday, long services with sermons lasting forty minutes. I remember a lot of Hellfire and Damnation, not much joy, and a great deal of asking forgiveness for our sins. However, it did provide some form of order, ritual and discipline. In fact, throughout my teenage years, before I found theatre, it was my full intention to go to university to read Divinity. I even studied Ancient Greek in high school and I was, unsurprisingly, the only student in the class. I eventually joined the church choir and was always happy to sing the solos at the Christmas carol service.

I attended the Inverness Royal Academy. I wasn't a bad student, though perhaps a little undisciplined and lazy. Never top of the class, never did the homework I should have done. Some things just never change. I became a more enthusiastic student when I found music classes. I'm sure we all have people from our education to whom we are grateful. Well, our small music department was headed by a young teacher called Ian Bowman. Mr Bowman had only recently lost his wife and was left as the single parent of two young children. This didn't stop him putting his energies into us, his students. Perhaps we were the positive experience in his saddened life? He certainly was a rich and lasting influence upon me. He provided my first introduction to orchestral music and my first experience of Opera, a form that I certainly didn't grasp at the time, but which has always intrigued me. Ian Bowman gave us experiences of seeing live Opera – going to the Edinburgh Festival to see Scottish Opera do "The Magic Flute". The image of the Queen of the Night suspended high above the stage on a floating moon remains with me to this day. Little did I know that many years later I would be directing that prestigious company.

Some of my fellow music students were really great singers, much better than me. In fact their skills quickly made me realise I would have to come at things from a different angle. Janis Kelly and Harry Nicoll went on to have significant opera careers. Again, as coincidence or life would have it, Janis and I were at the New York Metropolitan Opera at the same time. We all remain friends to this day. Mr Bowman created a production of Mozart's *Cosi Fan Tutte* for us. What a remarkable thing it was to see the potential in young students and to follow it through with hard work and dedication to our journeys. Hard work was totally fundamental to the culture I was raised in. The Protestant work ethic was what was expected of us and was the cornerstone of how we led our lives. To this day I believe that my "work is the rent I pay for the space I take up on the earth". Right or wrong, I've lived by that philosophy.

Our school was on a hill above the town and we were always led to believe that the hill was the site of Macbeth's castle. As I'm sure you know, William Shakespeare wrote a rather successful play about this notorious Scottish King and so understandably our teachers felt encouraged to ask us to study the play. Indeed we studied it with annual regularity, and even staged a production. My friend Harry was in it alongside me. I played King Duncan and wasn't at all happy to be killed at the end of the first act. Harry played my son Malcolm and we also co-designed the costumes, looking spectacular in gold and silver respectively. I'm not quite sure about everybody else! My next experience of designing costumes was for my 2005 production of *Sweeney Todd* on Broadway! *Macbeth* wasn't my first experience of being in a play, that was in primary school, probably as a six-year-old. I played the Mayor of Wytchwood and my one line was *"I'm the Mayor of Wytchwood, and I've come to thank you all for catching the dragon."* I was then to present a medal to the hero. Oh the humiliation! I'd forgotten the prop. I can feel that humiliation to this day.

Unquestionably my mother was a big influence on my choice of career, though she'd probably never have admitted it. She had been involved in competitive festivals where a number of church and community drama groups were judged against each other for the best play, best actress et cetera. My mother Molly was a member of the Blue Triangle Players. Like so many women of her generation, she stopped her work and her other activities early in her marriage. However, all the way to her death at eighty-six years of age she met for a monthly coffee with her fellow "drama girls".

I also joined a drama society, the Inverness Opera Company, which had been established for many years and which staged an annual musical. This was my first practical experience of the theatrical form that would become the bedrock of my professional life. I discovered the Opera Company by attending shows in the Inverness Empire Theatre. I think the first musical I saw was *The Desert Song*, though it may have been *Rose Marie*. Fortunately these are musicals that you no longer see in the popular canon. My mother and I went to see the show together early in the week of performances. I asked if I could make a return visit later in the week. Money was tight, but my parents always did their best and so they gave me the two shillings and sixpence for a ticket. I sat there in the stalls on a Saturday evening knowing nobody around me. I still love the experience of going to the theatre by myself. I couldn't have articulated it as a fifteen-year-old, but it's something about participating in a common experience but yet being alone. I can still remember the smell of The Empire

Theatre, which to me, in the late 1960s, was a heaven on earth. You could almost smell all the performers and performances that had happened there. Like every theatre, it was a church where great songs had been sung and great stories had been told. In the interests of what is deemed Civic development, that old theatre has been replaced by a somewhat sad hotel.

So, I joined the Inverness Opera Company. I've never found new groups of people easy, and to this day I'm fearful of that first day of rehearsal and the obligatory "meet and greet". Somehow though, when I did join, I knew I was "home". Everybody was very friendly toward the enthusiastic fifteen-year-old, and I will always be grateful to that group of friends for teaching me about the need to show up prepared and ready. Coincidentally we held our rehearsals in what had been my primary school. I look back with joy on the memory of being back in that room where the once-big desks had somehow shrunk. However, there was still a sand-pit in the corner of the room, used for the children to play in when the weather was inclement outside, as is so often the case in the chilly but beautiful Scottish Highlands. Being somewhat awkward I never wanted to step into the box, though I do remember that I liked to help the other children to go in. Perhaps that's where it all began?

My first role with the Opera Company was – wait for it – Og The Leprechaun in *Finian's Rainbow*. Fortunately there are no known photographs to tell the tale. I had to wear a strange green outfit, which dismantled piece by piece during the show until the mystical character became a human. Like so many musicals, a bizarre concept, but it did have a great score. My one somewhat egocentric memory is that at the end of the show I climbed out of a "well" that was centre stage, just as the best Irish leprechauns do. All I could hear was applause. They'd liked me! Applause! So odd that something to which I've had deep ambivalence for so long was right there at the beginning. During my career I've built a reputation for cutting off applause at the end of songs, preferring to hold the tension of the story and keep the audience intently involved. It can take actors time to understand the breaking of this long-held tradition, but the audience's pent-up excitement at the end of the event makes it all worthwhile. To this day I hate being in a theatre for applause at the end of any show of mine. It embarrasses me. Yet that's the one thing I remember from that formative *Finian's Rainbow* experience. Somehow, though, the pleasure of applause conflicts with the "*Who do you think you are?*" culture. Maybe when I get the answer to this conundrum, I may finally be able to stop making theatre!

Some years after my debut as that Irish sprite I revisited the soon-to-be-demolished Empire Theatre, a sad haunted temple empty of its audience. To this day I still love walking into an empty theatre. So full of stories that have been told or that are waiting to be told. I also love the experience of sitting in a theatre on closing as the set is being dismantled. I relish telling the story and yet I'm relieved to see it disappear.

Being taken to the theatre was not a regular occurrence. We were much more likely to go to a concert of Scottish music – if we went anywhere at all. However, one of the benefits of being the eldest of all those grandchildren was that my grandmother took me on my first trip to London, representing a rite of passage. A long train journey. Seeing the sights of that amazing city for the very first time. The eleven-year-old in me will be forever grateful to have seen a Brian Rix farce at the Whitehall Theatre. The Brian Rix company was dedicated to preserving the skills of the British farce, even presenting farces on live television. Seeing the curtain rise at the beginning of one of those live television performances was thrilling, and here I was seeing them in real life. Many years later, the Whitehall Theatre became the Trafalgar Studios, which was the initial London home to my production of *Sweeney Todd*. I would often stand at the back of that theatre and sense again my childhood excitement at seeing that plush red curtain going up!

My mother unknowingly introduced me to the notion that you could earn a living from your talent. I learned to sing for my supper, as part of a concert party entertaining American tourists in the Northern Meeting Park. We were on a small tartan-clad stage in the middle of a field with the audience sitting under the shelter of the stand from where you would normally have watched athletics, or the school sports. My mother accompanied me on the piano as I stood in my kilt singing Scottish songs. After each show I was given my payment in a small brown envelope. My very first wage packet. I don't know if my memory serves me correctly, but I'm fairly sure my mother took the envelope. Momma Rose eat your heart out! A few years later I was still singing for my supper, this time at the F&F Ballroom on Argyll Street in Glasgow. Singing every Friday night at the intermission of the Bingo, the "*Ave Maria*" to audiences of up to 2,000 gambling women! I don't recommend it, but it certainly helped pay my way through Drama School.

Glasgow was a very different city to the gentle Inverness. Scotland's second city, always the poor relation to Edinburgh, it had been one of the great industrial centres of the former British Empire. Its buildings are impressive, the art gallery quite wonderful, and the people unique. A big, grimy, wonderful, working-class city. Remember, I'd spent my early years surrounded by Highland beauty, with a river flowing through town and mountains all around. Like many young people though, I couldn't wait to get out. That idea of becoming a minister had been upstaged by my desire to go to drama school, in that big vibrant city, full of so many wonderful temptations. That Leprechaun has a lot to answer for!

Now, to be honest, I'm not sure I knew what drama school was going to mean. I auditioned and was awarded a place at the then Royal Scottish Academy of Music and Drama, now the Royal Conservatoire of Scotland. I was excited to wave goodbye to my parents as I left on the train. I remember looking at my mother as we pulled out of the station and feeling a little sad. To me she looked like she was getting old. It was only some years later that I did the math and realised that she was indeed only thirty-eight. The arrogance of youth.

It was 1970. Drama school at seventeen years of age. Far too early, although I loved it. This was before the days of taking a gap year and it was expected that young people would go straight from school into further education. I don't regret going to the RSAMD when I did, but if I had my time again I would have planned it differently and would have done a little growing up first. Mine was a conservatoire training of the sort I would recommend to any young person who may be exploring their choices. Students often ask me should they go to university or to a conservatoire, the former being a little more academic, the latter more practical. I think it really is horses for courses but inevitably I lean toward the practical training.

I was with forty other young people who all wanted to study the same thing. Three years of immersing oneself in something I had fallen in love with was a remarkable privilege. I will be forever grateful to the UK socialist government of the time. Every young person of my generation had the right to four years of fully-funded further education. If I hadn't had that, I don't believe I would have had my career or the life I have today. I see what students pay, the burden of student loans, the terrifying costs for the students I taught at Princeton. Not only were my fees paid, but I also received a government grant to cover my living expenses. My parents did have to commit to contributing a modest weekly figure, which probably wasn't always easy to find, but on the whole we were so very lucky. It saddens me that so many young people today don't get the experiences they deserve because of the unattainable cost it would mean to them and to their families.

Undeniably I look back and question some of the things we were taught. Did we really need fencing? Was "period movement" ever going to be of any use? After all, we only have literature, paintings and other inanimate objects to refer to when considering a period or an era. What *was* wonderful was the daily voice classes, the regularity of movement classes, the practical study of technical aspects of the theatre, the putting on of numerous plays, the scene study and most importantly, the growing up. I wouldn't have exchanged it for the world. Of my graduating class I think I was the only one to go on to be a director. Some had excellent teaching careers, some long and fulfilling acting careers, some just simply went off and did something else. Whatever happened, I do believe each and every one of us had an experience we will never forget.

At the end of my first year I and three other students drove through Europe in a little car. I'd never had a passport and had never used foreign currency. We motored down through France, through part of Switzerland, visited various Italian cities, then over to Athens, and finally some of the Greek Islands. We slept under trees, ate with the aid of a primitive camp stove, probably didn't change our clothes very much, drank retsina for the first time and had a wonderful fearless experience. I recall the awe of first visiting one of those ruined Greek theatres and standing in a central point of the stage to make a whisper that could be heard at the back of the enormous arena. Gosh, we really have gone backwards. No sound consoles for them, and of course those Greek actors made their own music.

During my Glasgow life one important aspect was regularly attending the Glasgow Citizen's Theatre. The "Citz" as it was affectionately known, is situated in an area called the Gorbals, at that time a very rough neighbourhood considered unsafe at night. This old theatre stood alone in what was then very real dereliction. As students, we were extremely fortunate to get free access to shows by using our Student Card. There were three Artistic Directors: designer Philip Prowse, writer Robert David MacDonald and director Giles Havergal. I'd never heard the term Artistic Director before this triumvirate. Together they led that company for a remarkable thirty-three years. I vividly remember my first visit. There was Giles, draped in a long cloak, welcoming each patron as they came through the doors. I saw *Hamlet*, which I remember as having an abundance of nudity. I'm not sure I understood it, but I saw it three times that week! The repertoire at The Citz was extraordinary, with many European playwrights being featured. The work itself was visually stunning and it was there I saw that a play could be done on an empty stage, red plush curtain abandoned, often to remarkable effect. How lucky I was that my formative theatregoing was so progressive and so theatrically dangerous. Years later, while directing at San Fransisco's famous American Conservatory Theatre, I had the pleasure of meeting Giles, who was there doing some work with the students from their theatre school. It felt very special to be able to thank him for the influence he had upon me as a young theatremaker. He seemed surprised, which was somehow very touching.

Of all my memories of that time, one stands out above all the others. It was Graduation Day. I remember I was walking through the corridors of the school with one of my friends. We had just graduated and were feeling very pleased with ourselves. We were met by John Groves, the curmudgeonly deputy director of the school. Johnny stopped us and playfully punched my friend in the stomach! I said "*Mr Groves, that wasn't very fair.*" His response – "*Who ever said it was going to be fair?*" The greatest lesson of my three years. I was entering a profession that isn't fair. One that favours the brave and most certainly the fortunate. A profession where many hugely talented people don't get the opportunities they deserve. What did those forty young kids from Scotland have in common? A love of an art-form that has hopefully endured for us all, and not only for those who were dealt the fairest cards!

So the question then was, "What's next?" A question that repeats itself again and again in a career in the theatre. You spend three intense years at a prestigious school and then you leave with no idea of how you are going to use any of it, even if given the opportunity. For me, well I saw an advertisement on the school notice board. I applied for a scholarship that was going to change my life!

2

The Only White Guy on the Bus

Some fifty years on I still remember my first sighting of the Manhattan skyline as seen from an airplane window. Such a glorious exhibition of the hubris of mankind. There was a time when cathedrals were our tallest buildings, now it's apartment blocks and financial centres. However, if you're lucky enough to fly into New York with the evening sun shining over it, it remains extraordinarily beautiful. I remember the twenty-hour Greyhound bus journey that was a turning-point in my life. The Greyhound was and still is the ordinary man or woman's inexpensive mode of cross-country travel in the United States. People are astounded when I say I once rode the Greyhound. Well – I was the only white guy on the bus! Bear in mind, I'd never met a person of colour. Scotland in 1973 was a very different place. So was Georgia.

To take you back a step, I applied for that scholarship not really knowing what it would entail or what I would be letting myself in for on the slim chance that I should be awarded it. I had to submit a couple of recorded audition pieces and to answer some questions, all on an old reel-to-reel tape recorder. After Glasgow graduation I returned to Inverness and got a summer job in the bakery where my dad worked, standing on one side of a conveyor belt putting cakes into boxes. Six assorted cakes per box. One of the great gifts of that conveyor is that I was standing opposite a co-worker who was profoundly deaf. If we were to be there together for three months we had to somehow be able to communicate. She taught me basic sign language and we had a lot of fun. I waited to see what the scholarship application might bring, with little or no expectation of success, though if it didn't work out I had nothing else on the horizon. Maybe I would go to Jordanhill College of Education in Glasgow and get an official qualification to teach? That's what a number of my fellow students were doing. To this day I don't know how the choice was made, but I was indeed successful. I'd earned a scholarship to undertake post-graduate study on a Master of Fine Arts programme at the University of Georgia, beginning a life-long love affair with the United States of America. I'd earned my place without a meeting or even a phone call. The study was funded by the Rotary Clubs of America and I believe that the vision behind the annual Scholarship was that students from all over the world, each coming from a different discipline, would be awarded a place at an American university. The place of study was determined by the body that distributed the scholarships, so you had no choice over where you would be going. I was to be the Junior Artist in Residence at the University of Georgia, Athens, Georgia, USA.

So, let's start with that flight into New York City. Bear in mind my only previous international travel was in that old car through Europe, so I'd never been on an airplane and certainly had never travelled long distance. The scholarship funded everything – accommodation, tuition and financial support. Everything, that is, except the costs of travel. My parents weren't in a position to cover any expenses and indeed, why should they? This was, after all, the beginning of my professional journey. It was my responsibility and the conveyor belt would only manifest enough financial resource to pay for an inexpensive flight. This was long before you went onto a website to shop around for travel and I'm sure the sole travel agent in Inverness wasn't used to booking flights to the United States of America. Maybe I could have flown into Atlanta, but bear in mind I didn't even know where Georgia was. I flew from Prestwick, on the West Coast of Scotland, and was seen off by my then fiancé Jacquie. Thank goodness for those blue folding airmail letters or we'd never have married and never eventually have had our lovely daughter Beccy.

The flight landed into John F. Kennedy Airport and I still feel exactly the same sense of excitement every time I fly into the city. Many years later I recall flying over Manhattan and looking at the mass of buildings below and thinking, "Gosh, I have a musical playing in a theatre down there!" However, let's take it one step at a time.

I have no recollection of how I made my way into Manhattan from Queens. To this day I'm nervous when I climb into one of those yellow taxi cabs and I can only imagine that they were comparatively expensive even then. So it was either a bus or the subway, memory fails me so I'll never know. I got myself to what must have been the Port Authority Building, even then the world's busiest bus terminal. I find it terrifying now, so what was it like then? I remember seeing 42nd Street for the first time, a thoroughfare that would become so familiar in years to come. There was the Empire State Building on the skyline and that extraordinary Chrysler – my favourite to this day.

I got on the bus to Athens, Georgia. The bus slowly filled up with passengers and it was then that I realised something different was happening in my life, something unnervingly unfamiliar. I was becoming a minority. It was 1973! I would ask that you contextualise my youthful reactions by considering the small Highland town I grew up in and the people who raised me. Now I must acknowledge that as a child I felt virtuous about the fact that my mother had befriended the only person of colour in Inverness, for whom she found housing and therefore safety from an abusive marriage. The Asian corner stores, or Pakistani shops as they were then called, were the only ones open on a Glasgow Sunday. Chinese restaurants were becoming popular. Harry and I always felt very grownup when we met in the Chinese restaurant on Inverness High Street, the only one in town. However, I had no opportunity to meet a person whose skin was actually black, even during three years at drama school. I'm now ashamed to say that I experienced a gradually increasing fear as that bus filled with people who quite simply didn't look like me.

As we drove the twenty hours down through Maryland and across Tennessee I was too scared to get off the bus to use a toilet. I fervently held my luggage close to me, afraid to go to sleep. One clear memory is of looking out of the steamy window in the middle of the night and there it was – The White House! The experience of that journey was fundamental to my development. I wasn't going to feel this irrational fear again. I was going to exist in a different, perhaps more complicated world than I had known to this point. I duly arrived in Athens, Georgia.

The University of Georgia is known as a "Greek" University, the buildings having faux Corinthian columns, many of them fraternities and sororities. In total there were over 20,000 students at UGA when I went there. It seemed an enormous number to me, but I was later to learn it was one of the smaller American universities. As the Junior Artist in Residence, I was to be an adjunct Faculty member, attending staff meetings and sharing ideas. Being on a Graduate programme, I had to do some mentoring and advising of individual undergraduate students, work which I absolutely loved and which gave me my first taste of teaching. However, for most of my time I was attending classes, meeting people from different life experiences and thoroughly enjoying myself. On many weekends I visited Rotarian host families, which meant being invited to speak to the Rotary Club members, while enjoying wonderful Southern hospitality. It alarmed me that so often the Rotarians or their wives would say *"Could you say that again?"* After some time I realised that it had nothing to do with lack of clarity, but rather that they liked the sound of my Scottish voice. That same soft voice that has got me through many tense theatrical situations.

Georgia was hot! Like, really hot! I'd never experienced humidity, after all you seldom get extreme heat in Scotland. The air conditioning, when it was available, was somewhat primitive. I was allocated accommodation in a Halls of Residence, sharing my twin-bedded room with another student. In the first few days I experienced that until now unfamiliar feeling of excitement and sadness mixed together. Excitement for what was to come and sadness for not being near my loved ones. Remember there was no FaceTime, no mobile phones and International Calls were most certainly cost-prohibitive. I did learn the phrase "Call Collect", but the folks back home were never happy to hear those words. It expected them to collect the cost and was very expensive. There were just those blue folding airmail letters.

Being away from home is one of the occupational hazards of a career in the theatre. It could be an out-of-town tryout, a National Tour or directing an Opera on the other side of the world, and it can be hard to simply live in the moment and enjoy the experience, because you miss the security of your home and of your loved ones being around you. I provide you with this context because the young man with whom I shared that dorm room seemed sad. Very sad. One day I asked him if he would like to go for a walk, which felt like a rather grownup thing to do. I enquired if anything was wrong and he started to cry and admitted that he was feeling overwhelmingly homesick. He came from Tennessee, the neighbouring State! I don't share this story to in any way belittle his emotional experience, rather to say this was a step in the learning process of living what was going to be a somewhat transient life. The sense of loss wasn't about distance, it was about people. I love that a Broadway dancer is referred to as a "gypsy". This is not intended to be derogatory. In fact I know many such dancers who are proud to be "gypsies". No, it means people who go from place to place, town to town, state to state, looking for the next encampment in which they can set up shop and sing, dance or act their stories. I have a close colleague who likens our job in the theatre to being itinerant grape-pickers, needed when the crop is good, not so much in the lean seasons.

Something that very quickly struck me when I arrived in the US was a sense of scale. It really is a country made up of a collective of countries, bound by one somewhat unwieldy political and financial system. In comparison to my home country, America was enormous. Scotland could probably have fitted into the State of Georgia twice! Because it was a Graduate Programme, this meant that students had sought out this particular course of study. They had earned their undergraduate degrees from schools that were probably in or near their home state. Having found the most appropriate Graduate Programme for them meant they had to travel further afield and so my contemporaries came from Illinois, Michigan, Arkansas, maybe even California.

Let's take a moment to recall some key events of 1973. President Richard Nixon was in the White House, the Vietnam War was drawing to a sad close, and Watergate was becoming a cornerstone of our political vocabulary. Only five years earlier the Reverend Martin Luther King was assassinated in Memphis, Tennessee. The State of Georgia had begun desegregation in schools in 1961, starting with the University of Georgia, and the state's legal desegregation ended in the early 1970s. This may give you some sense of the conversations that were taking place within the student body. Every student feels they have the most progressive voice in the politics of their day. I know this first-hand from my time teaching at Princeton University. There is something thrilling and humbling about working with students who perceive themselves as being at the centre of our political turmoil, especially when they confidently believe they have the answer. Well, our 1973 University of Georgia body of students was no different. On the funny side of things, this was the era of the "Streaker" and I clearly remember hundreds of naked students running through campus. The following year, 1974, was the pinnacle of streaking's pop culture significance and that crowd streak I witnessed was the largest group streak on record. It was on 7 March 1974 and had 1,543 simultaneous streakers!

It's interesting and indeed disturbing to note that my recollections don't include a significant proportion of students of colour attending our classes. Maybe it was difficult for the theatre department to break through to the African-American Community, perhaps it was too near the final days of desegregation. It takes a long time to change a culture. I don't remember any Black students in any of our productions, I don't recall any programming that would have encouraged participation, and I don't believe the school was supporting the telling of their stories. Now, bear in mind that in those days we were still being taught, in theatrical make-up classes, how to transform ourselves into characters of different races. Shocking when you think of it now, but we didn't question it at that time. As privileged white students we expected that we would be asked to play people who didn't look like us! Equally shocking was when I went to watch a production of Noel Coward's *Private Lives*. It was being performed by five African-American students, I think as an independent study project. Whether as a reaction to the habits of the time, or simply to justify their performing this very white text, the actors had gone into "whiteface". It was disturbingly disorientating and threw up a plethora of unanswered questions. The experiences of my career have told me that many of those questions remain unanswered.

It was when in Georgia that I started to become aware of the true function of a director. I had by this point directed a couple of projects, *The Glass Menagerie* with some fellow students in Glasgow and, one summer back home, an amateur production of *The Prime of Miss Jean Brodie*. I was probably quite organised; after all I was trained by a long line of super-organised women. My mother became the manager in a local Doctor's practice and was a very dedicated local politician. My grandmother had the traditional routines that gave life structure, dusting on a Tuesday, laundry on a Wednesday, polishing on a Thursday, all leading to a day of rest on the Sabbath. Probably because of their example, I was disciplined, proficient at scheduling, and to this day I encourage rehearsal routine and relish the human need for repetition. I was probably OK with making it look and sound good, I possibly still am, but it took some time before I started to analyse what a director's function could be, and even longer before I found my own style and process. It all started with three particular Professors at UGA. Interestingly, and I don't say this to denigrate so many fine American educators, all three of these Professors were European.

Dr John Reich was Austrian-born and had been trained by the great European director Max Reinhardt. Reinhardt was famous for his radical avant garde staging and John Reich had been part of some of his most epic productions. I remember he told us about the famous *A Midsummer Night's Dream*, which was for one performance only. It was perfectly timed so that when Puck came in the Casement Window for the final scene, the real window of a chateau in this case, the full moon was directly behind his head. Extravagant, somewhat rarified, but certainly inspiring to a young student of directing. Reich came to the United States and was made Artistic Director of the Goodman Theatre in Chicago. In 1957 he wrote a famous adaptation of Schiller's *Mary Stuart*, which was directed on Broadway by the great Tyrone Guthrie. Dr Guthrie started the now world-famous Shakespeare Theatre in Stratford, Ontario, where I was very fortunate to work many years after my time in Georgia. I think our greatest gift from John Reich was to have access to his knowledge of the depth of work in the non-English-speaking European repertoire, much of which had influenced the American theatre during and after World War Two. To this day those companies in Germany, and particularly in what we now know as Eastern Europe, produce work that is given longer rehearsal periods than we Western artists would ever know. Most of those theatres are heavily subsidised at State level and the "process" through which the work is made is possibly prioritised above the eventual "product". Almost the antithesis of how we make work in the UK and the US today. Our rehearsal periods have been dangerously retracted, all because of economics, and financial success has become imperative, sometimes to the detriment of the creation of good work and even good taste. Dr Reich showed us that it is the work in the rehearsal room that matters. Of course one wants audiences to enjoy what you have made, and of course the bills need to be paid, but these needn't be the sole artistic objectives. He was thorough in his approach, rigorous in his attitude toward text and inspiring in his seriousness about all he tried to achieve. Those artists who escaped persecution in their own countries brought with them a determination and unique vision that one simply can't learn.

There was one key thing that I did take from John Reich. Never be afraid of the experiment. Don't hesitate in taking text out of its natural place and looking at it from a different viewpoint. I remember he was working on the balcony scene from *Romeo and Juliet*. Rather than the generic balcony with Juliet above and Romeo on the street below, he explored it as if they were in two separate prison cells. Each actor sat on a chair as if tied to it, sitting back to back. They had to pretend that there was a small crack in the imaginary wall that separated their two cells, and had to connect and deliver the text through that crack. The tension of knowing that a prison guard could come along at any moment, just as the Nurse does in the original play, raised the stakes and somehow the two students no longer had to "act". They just had to "be". He then took them back to the original balcony scenario and they were able to draw very naturally and honestly from the tensions of the scene as they had explored it. It was absolutely brilliant. That for me is the essence of rehearsing. Exploring. I say to students all the time that if they have four weeks, rehearse for the first three and then practise in the fourth. By week four you will understand what it is that you need to practise. You will know the intended interpretation of the production you've built, and will be able to polish what you know. Please don't start on week one with the polishing. Differentiate between a) the process of rehearsing; and b) the product-based part of the journey when you refine everything you have learned in the process. I have always tried to follow John's example. Certainly as my career has developed, I have even become less and less interested in the element of practising in week four and have discovered that if you've truly, rigorously rehearsed, you don't really need to practise. More later!

Dr Aleksander Bardini visited from Warsaw, where he was a lecturer in the Theatre Academy. Polish-Jewish, he had an extensive career in film and theatre in his own country. Through him I first heard of an artist who would have a profound influence on my own work, Bertolt Brecht. Brecht was arguably the greatest of the European theatremakers, who went on to form the famous

Berliner Ensemble. His output was extensive, writing many of the plays studied in schools and universities today. Importantly, Brecht developed his own unique way of working, creating a study in theatremaking, that of putting the actor first in the process, and centring politics at the heart of the work. Many years later I would direct *The Rise and Fall of the City of Mahagonny*, his epic Opera which he wrote with his long-time collaborator Kurt Weill. Bardini had worked with Brecht's Ensemble, and with us he staged a production of *The Resistible Rise of Arturo Ui*, a Brecht play based on the rise of the Third Reich but told with humour and irony. We put together a large production, the antithesis of the one I would make in New York many decades later.

Bardini was a real character and used his ebullient personality to make every rehearsal fun. He didn't try to be anybody other than himself as a director, which is surely the essence of how to make good work. You are all you have. What I take away from my time with Bardini was about the actor's exploration of "the truth". He directed from the point of view of an actor. I remember he was working with a student actor and was exploring how we demonstrate "shock" onstage. Not the shock of special effects but rather the shock a character experiences when they hear or see something disturbing or life-changing. He tried everything he knew to encourage my fellow student, Taylor Pope Lawrence, to show a truthful reaction to a shocking situation. Taylor was a Southern gentleman, a wonderfully larger-than-life character, and quite the performer. Bardini worked with him on this moment in a text where he needed to show how he was experiencing a shocking event. Taylor worked hard to be convincing, pulling a number of faces along the way. Bardini, who was quite liberal in his criticism, was never convinced. He said, about Taylor, "*Too many bad movies!*" He stood at the front of the class and Taylor was standing beside him, when suddenly, whilst engaging Taylor in conversation, Bardini dropped his trousers. A shocking moment indeed and very naughty on the part of a glinting Bardini! Taylor was totally still, almost ashen, and it was the most convincing his shocked reaction had been throughout the session. It was the stillness, the lack of "acting", that proved most truthful. The art of acting is centred in "reacting". I don't recommend young directors to follow Bardini's technique. You may get yourself in serious trouble. However it does point to the fact that actions are sometimes stronger than words in the directorial process. What I now realise is that he was teaching us about how film acting had influenced theatre acting. Many years later I directed a movie with famous screen actors and I saw again that need for simplicity, for letting the camera do the work. There is no question in my mind that the camera has gone on to influence how we make theatre. Not in special effects, or the modern obsession with live camera work onstage, but rather in encouraging us to tell theatrical truth.

Another memorable anecdote was his description of the way in which the Polish theatre advertised a production. You rehearsed the play, and only when it was ready did you announce the Opening Night, put up the posters and start to advertise the show. Can you imagine that today in our Western theatre? We put tickets on sale long before rehearsals begin. On the first day of rehearsal producers love to tell you how many tickets have sold, which creates undue pressure and is really of no value to a productive rehearsal period. The method Bardini spoke of would cause a major societal panic but who knows, it might actually work?

Bardini left us early. I have a feeling that America was too much for his Polish sensibility. He was replaced by the third of those Professors, one of his former students, Helena White. Helena had by this point emigrated to Philadelphia. She was a young mum and gave us a quite different perspective to the two preceding gentlemen. We did some exciting work with her, and she approached things in a much gentler and very focussed manner. She was also unafraid of the word "exploration". Maybe even "improvisation". Now, I was terrified of improvisation at drama school. Not for me, pretending to be a tree! I suppose the vulnerabilities it brought out and the sense of the unknown that it engendered made me panic. However Helena didn't use improv in a threatening way. Rather she created situations based on reality and asked us to explore what we had learned in order to then use it onstage. I suppose one could say that this was my first foray into "process". I recall one particular example. My friend Michael O'Brien and I were working on a scene involving King Henry II and Thomas Becket. It may have been a scene from *Murder in the Cathedral* but I'm no longer sure. Anyway, Helena thought it would be a useful exercise for Michael and I to experience such a scene as it might really have happened – on horseback. So, one Sunday, we went to a beach, we two on horseback, with Helena directing us. We rehearsed our scene accordingly and what had been a rather stilted piece of classical text suddenly became a living breathing experience, affected by weather, different use of distance, being outdoors and, of course, the horses. An exercise in theatremaking. For me, the first of many. Look at the reality and then examine how to represent that reality. Thank you Helena White!

I now know that the experimental side of my theatremaking had its roots in that time in Georgia. Each student had to direct the opening scene of a play. I believe opening scenes were asked for because they lay out the rules of the play and also during that scene the audience needs to become familiar with the style you are using to tell the story, so these scenes were a good exercise in how to be clear and how to communicate your approach. I have no memory of which play I chose. However, I do remember doing an independent study where I directed three fellow students in a production of *Huis Clos*, an existentialist 1944 play by Jean-Paul Sartre, often known as *No Exit*. It is a depiction of the afterlife in which three deceased characters are punished by being locked in a room together for eternity. At that time I was searching for unique methods of audience interaction. I think I'd been reading a lot about the Off-Broadway Avant Garde Movement, which sadly no longer exists. I only allowed twenty-four audience members to watch the play. They were locked in the room just like the characters in the play, and we performed it in the round, something that was new to most of us. It was probably all rather pretentious, but to us it felt very important. As far as I can remember we didn't even ask their permission to lock them in! Somebody could have been claustrophobic! Anyway, it was all about being different and wanting to shock. Thank goodness I got over that phase. However, I now see that it started for me a journey of exploration in how to experiment in the theatre, a journey that is never over.

I'm often asked who my mentors were and I never quite know how to answer. There have been too many. What I do know is that at the University of Georgia I studied with extraordinary professors, and worked with students who have become life-long friends. Yet the greatest gift was not studying with the professor who had been in the Berliner Ensemble with Bertolt Brecht, nor with the gentleman who had been Max Reinhardt's student, or even the lovely young woman who started my fascination with theatrical "process". The gift was the exposure to a different world. A world of weekend horse-riding in America's wide open spaces; six-packs of beer and Dunkin' Donuts; my twenty-first birthday in New Orleans; and my one and only experience of dope with Roberta Illg in her trailer, her lava-lamp swirling between us. Seeing *The Exorcist* with Marcia Elvidge, in its first week of performances, a week in which people literally had heart attacks in cinemas whilst watching that ground-breaking movie. Many years later I would direct both a film and a play with the great Ellen Burstyn, who had so brilliantly played the mother in that iconic film. I would also direct the world premiere of a theatrical adaptation of *The Exorcist* in Los Angeles, starring Brooke Shields and the late Richard Chamberlain. Who knew? Many fellow students and professors from that magical time in Georgia have gone on to be a major part of my life. Dr Jackson Kesler, who later invited me to join his faculty at Western Kentucky University, where I directed a series of productions. Dr Charlotte Headrick, who, many years later, came to observe my work at the Liverpool Everyman and later invited me to Oregon State University to teach a series of master classes. And of course my dear Michael O'Brien, who can remember more about that time than I've forgotten.

So, it was time to go home. I returned to Scotland, and immediately had an interview for a job at the newly-formed Ochtertyre Theatre, near Crieff in Perthshire. Off the plane in the early morning and secured the job by lunchtime. Did I realise how lucky I was? It all seemed so easy then! Ochtertyre House was a beautiful eighteenth-century Scottish stately home owned by Sir William Keith Murray. He had the passion to turn one of the spaces on his property into a theatre, a passion which eventually destroyed him financially and broke him spiritually. Sadly he took his own life when his dream went wrong. However, he had a couple of memorable seasons with some of Scotland's greatest actors gracing his stage and I will forever be grateful to him. My function in the season was as the male Acting/Assistant Stage Manager. As the role probably doesn't exist anymore I ought to explain. I swept the rehearsal room daily, often stage managed the shows at night and understudied all the male actors in the season. A workload which didn't phase me in the least. Bear in mind I was understudying men of all ages, so thank goodness I never had to go on! I did have a tiny role in Neil Simon's *Barefoot in the Park*, playing The Delivery Boy. I had one offstage line, "*Lord and Taylor!!!*" I also did some serious acting when playing the spotty Prince John in James Goldman's *The Lion in Winter*. My mother in the play was one of Scotland's great actresses of her generation, Edith MacArthur, from whom I learned so much. In those days rehearsal rooms were formal. She was always called Miss MacArthur. However she was a wonderful example of how to maintain the formality and yet have fun at the same time. I still love the fun and, if I'm honest, I miss a little of the formality. Not that I'd want to say Mr or Miss, but to always find ways of appropriately respecting those from whom you can learn. I ought to take a moment and say that whilst I am fascinated by actors and have spent my life working with and admiring them, I never found much joy in acting myself. I don't think I was necessarily bad, but I hated the nightly repetition and wasn't much interested in learning the lines. I was always meant to be on the outside looking in. Always meant to be outside that sand-box. Always happy to have a great rehearsal period and then leave them to it.

The resident director at Ochtertyre was a wonderful woman by the name of Ann Stutfield. Ann had been artistic director of a theatre in Newcastle and was, at that time, one of the UK's very few female directors. It was unquestionably a man's world. From her I learned about important qualities like being positive, being kind, being clear, organised and pleasant. During our season, she directed a whole series of contrasting plays, all with two-week rehearsal periods: *Private Lives* – very different this time; *Barefoot in the Park* by the marvellous Neil Simon – a hero of mine. I met him many years later, which I'll tell you about in due course; *Ghosts* by Henrik Ibsen, my introduction to a playwright whose work I now love; and of course that *Lion in Winter*, another play about King Henry II and, this time, his wife Eleanor of Aquitaine. As a director, one very seldom sees another director direct and so I've little idea of the different ways in which it's done. What did strike me about Ann is that she didn't sit behind a table. She was active. She was almost in it with us. She was alive and not sitting in judgement. That was my greatest lesson and it provided a way of working and communicating that I've followed ever since. What else about that wonderful time? Meeting Amanda Jacobs, my fellow acting-ASM, a lovely English girl who would become a life-long friend. We worked hard together, we shared the same apartment in the local town, and we sat in the theatre bar at the end of the day, Mandy chatting and me singing Scottish songs.

Something remarkable happened toward the end of that Ochtertyre season. Another Ann, this time Ann Rye, the Administrator of the theatre, asked me if I'd *"like to have lunch"*. I hardly thought she knew who I was, though she'd probably had to endure those songs! It was the first time in my career that I had a lunch meeting and I was shocked. She was important and I literally swept the rehearsal room floor. She asked me if I was interested in directing. Heck, I was twenty-one years old, I was interested in anything!

Anyway, how did she know that? I wasn't sure that I knew it myself! She asked if I would like to direct the play after next in the season. Every career needs an angel, someone looking out for you, someone who's unafraid to give an opportunity to an unknown. That was Ann Rye. She'd been a successful actress. She was strong and determined. She moved into the steadier world of theatre administration because she had a young son to raise. She was another woman carving a path in a man's world. I learned a lot from her.

One of Ann's most memorable pieces of advice was about auditioning. I was put on the train and sent to London where most auditioning happened, and in fact still does. I was looking for an actress to play opposite the well-known Russell Hunter in this new two-person play that I was to be directing. Ann said, *"John, ask for whoever you want to be in your play. Never think that anybody is too big or too famous. They may have been out of work for months and need a job!"* More importantly she said, *"Never forget, it is your responsibility to make the audition a worthwhile experience for the actor. This may be their only audition this year and they may not have been able to afford the bus fare to get to it!"* I've practised her advice on every audition I've participated in during the last fifty years, advice I've passed on to students. We need to take responsibility for infusing care and consideration into what can be an uncaring and inconsiderate profession.

Sweeter Than All the Roses was that first play. Written by the late W. Gordon Smith, a well-known Scottish writer. Kay Gallie played opposite Russell Hunter. The play was, somewhat bizarrely, set in the staff office between a ladies and gents public convenience! Was I scared or intimidated? Not a bit of it! It was as easy as going down a ski-slope. How come it got more difficult as one went on? Why is it scarier now than when I was young and green and in my salad days? I was paid the grand total fee of £50 for the entire job. Somewhere or other I still have the contract. I thought I'd hit the big time! I remember we rehearsed in a barn. I remember that Mandy was the stage manager. I remember we had two weeks of rehearsal, and that I was very diligent. I sat at home with a floor plan and little coloured counters working out the "blocking" in advance of the next day's rehearsal! Those days have long gone. I was unafraid of challenging these wonderful actors, but I also probably thought I had to have all the answers and that my final decision was the one that mattered. Also an approach that is long gone!

Within a year I had directed *Jock*, a one-person play by the same playwright, for the Edinburgh International Festival. I was so fortunate to have a working relationship with a writer so early in my career, working on a series of four exciting World Premieres. I'd also directed for the Scottish Society of Playwrights. I'd directed another famous Scottish actor, Iain Cuthbertson, in Stravinsky's *The Soldier's Tale*, with the Scottish Chamber Orchestra, which I suppose was my first foray into the world of Opera. In between directing jobs I stage-managed a tour and a pantomime. I taught at my alma mater for a term. I've never done a "day job". I've always looked to the theatre to pay the bills. Sure, I've sometimes done plays that I didn't really want to do. The gas bill had to be paid! I judged drama festivals, the sort my mother had participated in – even when they were performed in Gaelic. To be clear, I don't speak Gaelic! I applied for an Arts Council of Scotland Trainee Director placement and wasn't accepted. As Fate would ironically have it, the following year I was invited to be one of the judges. I think through all of these invaluable experiences, I was searching. Searching for my next step. Even though I didn't really know what it involved, I sensed I wanted to become an Artistic Director. Careful what you wish for. That's indeed what I would be doing for the next twenty years.

3

The Early Artistic Director Years

I've been an Artistic Director six times: one touring company, four UK repertory theatre companies and finally a New York Off-Broadway Company. That journey was life-changing for me, in so many ways. I learned how to lead, how to plan, how to budget, and how to bring my own hopes and aspirations to the work I was making. Perhaps some readers may aspire to taking on the role themselves and hopefully they may find something useful, or even forewarning, in these next two chapters. I'd like to lead you through the journey by taking a look at each theatre, three in one chapter, three in the next, doing my best to share my experiences, good and bad.

TIE-UP Theatre Company 1975–1980

In my earliest days working in the theatre, politics and education were at the heart of artistic programming. Companies were set up with the sole purpose of sharing their political viewpoint with the audiences they served. For example, there was a prolific company that worked in Scotland called 7:84 Theatre Company. Their name tells you their philosophy in that they wanted to constantly draw their audience's attention to the fact that seven percent of the population owned eighty four percent of the wealth. Their body of work explored why that was happening and that something needed to be done about it. The work was robust, involved the audience, included a lot of music and song and was highly entertaining, and most importantly, provocative. One of their most celebrated pieces looked at the pillaging of Scotland's natural resources, particularly at the hands of the English. It was called *The Cheviot, the Stag, and the Black, Black Oil*. It's interesting to note that political theatre of the 60s and 70s was happening at the same time as the emergence of Theatre in Education. This was a very strong movement in that almost every theatre had its own T.I.E. company, the premise being that theatre be taken into schools for young people of all ages. By using the word theatre, I don't mean long-established plays, but rather devised pieces, written around subjects that were relevant to the young person watching. Importantly the student should participate in some way, and the work be undertaken in a familiar space. Sadly Conservative governments of the 1980s gradually weakened the funding of these companies. After all, political and educational theatre meant that questions were being asked, and they didn't want any of that!

TIE-UP Theatre Company was a touring company that I helped form in 1975 with the mission of taking theatre to the Highlands of Scotland. I had a dream of giving audiences in small rural communities the experience of live theatre, one that I myself hadn't had in any substantive way. Here's how it happened. Jacquie and I hadn't long been married and we were at a party in Glasgow. There I met up with Christine Redington, an acquaintance who had been Artistic Director of the Glasgow Citizen's Theatre In Education Company. During our conversation at that party, Christine and I determined that we wanted to find colleagues to help us create a small company that would take T.I.E. into schools and theatre spaces in the North of Scotland. As the name of the company suggests, it would also be for audiences upward of school age. The dream was that a young person could experience the company in their school during the day and then they and their family could go to their local community space or theatre and see a more formal play at night.

Within a few months of planning and making suitable contacts we were joined by Mandy Jacobs, my friend from Ochtertyre, who I knew was interested in making the kind of theatre that had meaningful social purpose. We were also joined by Iain Lauchlan, who had been in the year following me at the Royal Scottish Academy and who, as a good musician and with great practicality, I sensed would be perfect for the work we hoped to do. Off we went to Inverness, back where things felt so very familiar, full of aspiration and an overwhelming amount of naivety. We didn't even know how we were going to earn a living. Before we left Glasgow, Christine and I had connected with an enthusiastic Arts Officer in the Aberdeen area and he put us in touch with numerous schools throughout Inverness-shire and Aberdeenshire. We prepared two short shows, suitable for quite young children. Charging each school £25 per performance, we presented four performances a day, moving between schools over lunchtime. It was exhausting, and we stayed at modest Bed and Breakfasts to keep the costs down. We secured a £2000 grant from Aberdeen Education Department, which meant that our weekly wage of £18 per person could be achieved. Iain sourced a small van that had been owned by the Post Office, where his Mum worked. It had the grand purchase price of £5. There was just enough room to get three black wooden boxes into the back of the van, to transport our costumes and props, and those boxes also formed the basis of the furniture that represented any hint of a stage set. On some level, I think I've been working with those three boxes ever since. So with our small red van and with Christine's equally diminutive "Beetle" car, we took off to start a way of life that would, for some of us, last for the next five years.

Somehow it never entered my head that it wouldn't work. When asked by young directors and actors if they should start their own companies I usually say – "*Why not?*" After all, I did it. Having said that, I do stress that I think it was much easier then. The political world was a different one. The UK Socialist Government of the 1970s sought to proactively fund the arts and wanted to support companies focussed on theatre that functioned within and for the community. They were particularly interested in providing funding that concentrated on areas of the country that weren't already being served, and that was most certainly the case with our project. The Scottish Arts Council in Edinburgh became aware of our work and within six months of our launch they offered us a new 12-seater mini-bus and gave us an annual grant of £20,000. I have no memory of making an application for those resources. I'm quite sure it was simply a strategic and generous gesture from a government department that believed in the importance of the arts. Sadly I believe I'm right in saying that this was probably the greatest act of governmental commitment I have seen in many years of leading theatre companies. To be given without having to ask is the essence of generosity. As the years went on and the political landscape altered, that generosity was eroded, perhaps not totally but certainly substantively. Art needs financial support or it becomes exclusive, potentially elitist and only available to the rich. Financial support creates an environment where artists can take risks. Great art comes from risk and a belief in the right to fail, seeing failure not as a negative but rather as a step toward something that may work under different circumstances. An opportunity to learn and to grow, without which we will never achieve true success.

In starting our own company we had to work out each of our individual functions, knowing that in order to be successful we would need some sort of organisational structure. Christine didn't stay with us for long, but she did set up the administrative aspects of the company and really taught the rest of us the values of theatre in an educational setting. Iain and Mandy took on responsibilities which included set-building, costume making, writing music and even the tasks that would usually be taken on by a Company Manager, such as finding accommodation for visiting artists. They were both interested in performing, me less so. I was the local boy who had many contacts and a sense of context for the company in a community that tended to resist folk coming in from the outside. Also I had an ability to create budgets, to schedule rehearsals and plan seasons, an ability that has stood me in good stead throughout my career. The combination of these skills led to my eventually becoming Artistic Director. My wife, although herself an excellent actress and teacher, initially took on a proper job, which helped subsidise the journey we were undertaking. I'm so proud of the fact that we were always paid, in cash in those little brown envelopes. I don't know how we did it, but there was always a bottle of wine on the table at the end of a long week. The travelling was extensive and often exhausting. In those days, before the bridges were built in the Highlands, you had to travel long distances to get to nearby places. You may have been able to see the village where you were going to "play", but you had to go all the way round the loch to get there.

Gradually more actors joined us from other parts of Scotland and from London. Some joined for one project, some stayed longer and made a much greater commitment. We found an office space, the garage of my rented house was our workshop, we managed to pay for some secretarial help, and although we didn't have a formal Board of Management there were key people from the community who helped and supported us. Eventually we joined forces with Eden Court Theatre, a new and very impressive theatre complex that had been built in Inverness. Joining that new theatre gave us credibility and of course provided us with exciting spaces in which to rehearse and to perform. Let me share a few memories that may give you some sense of the challenges we faced and the fun we had.

We opened our production of *Macbeth* at Cawdor Castle. All that study at school had to be good for something! The production was played by seven actors, including ladies playing men's roles, with nobody changing costume. I now see it was the beginning of some of the fundamental approach I take in almost all of my work. An Opening Night in a haunted castle made for a thrilling evening. Shakespeare's Thane of Cawdor performing for the very much alive Earl of Cawdor is something I won't forget. I will also forever remember a performance of the play in a hall in Oban on Scotland's West Coast. When we arrived to set up, we discovered there was no "black-out" in the hall and the sun was streaming in the windows. Also, there were no chairs, so I invited the audience to sit in a circle on the floor. Then I explained that although we couldn't use our small set-up of theatre lights – I think we toured with six – we would still like to perform the play for them in daylight. I clearly remember a moment in the play when Fleance says to his father, when asked what time it was – "*The moon is down, I have not heard the clock.*" Shakespeare's indication of an ominous night of darkness. The actress playing Fleance did what she always did and, during the line, looked up to the sky to see where the moon was. At that moment of simple action, the entire audience also looked up. Now remember, the room was full of daylight. So that audience, along with the character, was pretending. In that moment I saw the simple, ordinary but in fact extraordinary power of the theatre. I will forever remain grateful to that hall in Oban with no black-out! Let's also remember that Shakespeare's own audiences were experiencing the plays in daylight, so he certainly knew the power of great words in the journey of the imagination. I believe that one of the things that is having a detrimental effect on theatre today is our underestimation of the audience – audiences have imaginations! They can join the world of make-believe. Should helicopters really be landing on stages?

Then there was a performance of *Toad of Toad Hall* in a remote community centre. My mother, who often took days off from her proper job in order to be our Musical Director, was playing our invaluable electric keyboard. She was half way through one of the songs when the keyboard gradually ran out of sound, our few theatrical lights started to flicker and everything went to darkness. The sight of Ratty, Mole and Badger groping around trying to find fifty pence pieces to feed the meter and eventually getting some from audience members – well, it had to be seen to be believed.

It was the incredibly hot summer of 1976 and we had travelled to Dunvegan on the beautiful Isle of Skye to perform a musical revue called *The Spirit of Scotland*. I was performing in it as well as running the box office and doing front-of-house duties. It came time to let the public into the venue. I opened the wooden doors of what could euphemistically be called "the lobby". Now, if any of you know the roads on the West Coast of my beautiful country, you will know that there are animals everywhere, wandering free. So, I opened those doors and in stepped two sheep! Sadly they were the only mammals to show up on that hot summer's evening. We sought solace in the pub and a good time was had by all.

The Skye Gathering Hall is a small community hall in the delightful town of Portree. The hall was packed for the aforementioned production of *Macbeth*. It came to the great final scene where MacBeth and MacDuff fight for the glory of Scotland. In this production they were fighting with traditional Scottish broadswords. A woman in the front row looked pleadingly at MacDuff and shouted out "*Kill him! Go on kill him.*" She had never seen the play, had never seen a Shakespeare, and so didn't know the pompous rules. She believed it! It was one of those moments that can only happen in the live theatre and I truly believe that The Bard would have been proud.

Dornoch in Easter Ross provided a very wonderful learning opportunity. We were presenting our production of *The Glass Menagerie*. Five folks showed up, constituting one family. Well, there were only four actors in the play but we always followed the old theatre rule that you only cancel if there are more of you than there are of them. We did the play. As it finished, the father of the family stood up during the curtain call and invited us back to their home for supper. We delightedly had a late-night feast of scrambled egg! He asked me if we would please come back to Dornoch. I indicated that it was hard if there was no audience interest. He said, "*If you come back I promise you will have an audience.*" So we did return with our next play and he fulfilled his commitment. There were 200 people in the hall, which was a huge percentage increase in a small community. It was the perfect example of the power of "word-of-mouth". Audience development in a living and active way, involving nothing other than human communication. This was years before marketing and press departments. You printed and put up the posters yourself. Our new friend told his neighbours they had to be there, and in doing so opened up a whole new enterprise for us. We found a similar representative in each place we visited and called them our "pilots". They brought in our audiences. Very simple, very human and very inexpensive. Much more meaningful than a series of "likes" on Facebook!

Five years after starting the company we were all ready to move on. We were in our mid-twenties and probably, if I'm honest, rather ambitious. Sadly we hadn't the experience to set up a Board structure that guaranteed any form of longevity and so gradually the work of the company faded away. However, I have no regrets about that wonderful time. I know we touched and entertained audiences who wouldn't otherwise have seen live theatre. And I learned the greatest lesson of all – from that lady in the front row!

Worcester Repertory Company 1980–1985

We have a weekly trade newspaper, *The Stage*, where, in those days anyway, available jobs were listed. I saw an advertisement for the position of Associate Director at Worcester Repertory Company. Worcester is a middle-sized town in the centre of England surrounded by wonderful countryside including the famous Malvern Hills. I applied, travelled down from Inverness to have an interview, and got the job. We packed up our lovely home in Scotland, and I went on ahead of my wife and small daughter to take up the position, find somewhere to live, and all the usual things that theatre gypsies have to do. Leaving Scotland wasn't easy. Not only because of leaving the family, although I knew that was temporary. No, it was the actual leaving Scotland itself that was unsettling. Leaving home. I loved the Highlands, but I'd never felt part of the rest of the Scottish theatre scene, which at that time was very much based around Edinburgh and Glasgow. It was somehow "angrier", more macho than suited my personality. So, I emigrated to England. Those childhood games in the back garden could just as easily have been about the Scots fighting the English. Though in truth, the English nearly always won! Many years later, I still feel the same sense of displacement that I felt on first working in England. I don't want you to think I am a "Nationalist". I believe in the Union of the countries that make up the United Kingdom. However, I am Scottish to my soul. Much as I enjoy many aspects of living in England, I've always felt as if I was living abroad. Hence when I eventually started working in the United States, I felt quite comfortable. I was simply going from one foreign country to another.

I enjoyed Worcester though. It was a community that loved its theatre – this one being affectionately called "The Swan". The Swan Theatre, home of the Worcester Repertory Company, was built in the early 1960s and is situated very near the Worcester Race Course. It's an intimate space, having tiered seating, which makes for an excellent actor/audience relationship. It was a repertory theatre, meaning it presented a number of plays in an annual season, often with a permanent company of actors and a resident team of designers. Musicals, contemporary plays, Shakespeare, pantomime were all part of what made audiences come and keep coming.

My family joined me, we settled in, and for my first eighteen months in Worcester I was the Associate Director. This meant that, as the title suggests, I was answerable to the Artistic Director. I worked with him creatively, but didn't hold the final responsibility. I directed a reasonable proportion of the work in the season, and certainly was provided with the opportunity to practise my craft. I had the invaluable opportunity to learn the art of making strong stage pictures, learning how to make the story clear, learning how to make the work visually engaging usually on very limited budgets, and, as the old theatre adage goes, learning how to prevent actors bumping into the furniture. I joke, but I do wish directors today could have more opportunity to practise their art in a practical way. Great staging, or blocking as it may be called, is powerful. I think of seeing the inaugural production at the Barbican

Theatre, London in 1982. It was *Henry IV, Part One*, and was directed by Trevor Nunn. I recall sitting there and drifting off slightly, as most of us probably do now and again when watching those plays. However I didn't lose the story because the pictures he created, the physical interrelationships between actors, made everything totally clear. You knew exactly who to look at, exactly who was important to any given moment of the story. Good staging carries with it an element of audience manipulation. You're telling your audience where to look, indicating what to feel, all rooted in craft. There is no better way to learn that craft than directing play after play in a season. I was so fortunate that the repertory system was still going strong when I started and I feel sad that young artists today find it hard to access similar opportunities. These repertory companies were a breeding ground for the great theatre artists of the future. My fellow Associate was the designer Mark Thompson, who has gone on to have a stellar design career in theatres all over the world. After those eighteen months, there was a change of management and I was invited to become Artistic Director of the company, my first directorship of a building-based organisation. I was running an English regional theatre at the age of twenty-nine.

So, what exactly does the role entail? Crudely, you're the leader, the boss, you guide the Mission of the company and you're where the buck stops. The person who programmes the season, casts the plays, creates and manages the budgets, and in those days anyway, directed a high percentage of the programme. Much has changed since I started and the relationships with staff and artistic colleagues today are much more collaborative. Theatres have HR departments. When I took over at Worcester it was expected that the director would be in overall charge of every activity, in what I like to think of as a benevolent dictatorship!

There were two companies working in the building, one professional and one amateur. The former making work through which they earned their living, the latter local people who were making theatre purely for the love of it. The interaction of those two groupings was occasionally challenging but most of the time the model worked beautifully. As well as mounting their own plays, the amateur company also provided many of the volunteers who manned the box office, served behind the bar, did all front-of-house duties, helped in the costume department and even worked backstage. It was, even then, a rather unique concept which would probably be very hard to recreate in our contemporary world. There were up to 200 volunteers supporting the professional company in one way or another. I had to get to know them all and had to remember who was related to who, who was divorced from whom, and of course whose children were succeeding at school et cetera. It was gruelling but challenging work, taking all of my time and sadly having a somewhat detrimental effect on my private life. Finding a balance between professional life and home life has always been challenging to me, on which I continue to work!

I directed up to twelve pieces in any one year, including main house and studio shows, lunchtime plays and late-night cabarets. I recall one day where there was a lunchtime play in the bar area, two performances of *Romeo and Juliet* to follow, and the day ended with a late-night show. Starting after the main house show it was staged in the theatre's restaurant and was called *Simply Simon*, my having created it around the works of the great American writer Neil Simon. That show was accompanied by food – "chicken in a basket" suppers. Not only did I devise and direct the programme, I was also in it. And, I cooked the suppers!

The sheer output of work meant that you had little time to do any research – perhaps that's why I'm still not very good at doing lots of work before I hit the rehearsal room? You opened a show on a Tuesday evening and did the read-through for the next play on the Wednesday morning, with or without a hangover. We had two-week rehearsal periods, one day of technical rehearsal and opened to press and public on the same night. It was fast but it wasn't always bad. In fact, I think sometimes it was really quite good. I certainly don't advocate short rehearsal periods, but these were with actors who knew each other very well, having performed play after play together. Their learning muscle was well honed, one didn't need to use up any time "bonding" and everybody was totally unafraid. Your audiences had seen you be really good in your last role, so they would forget some questionable choices on the current one.

My own working style at this time was probably much more based in "product" than it was in "process". The aims were to be efficient, to plan a detailed schedule before you begin rehearsal (something I do to this day), to help actors be in the right place at the right time, and maybe to help a little on characterisation. I don't remember there being much psychological character study, and very few discussions. You just had to get the job done with as much repetition of the material as you could manage. I hope it's true to say that you would hear much more discussion and character study in my rehearsal room today, but my work is always rooted in repetition. Repetition builds confidence and confidence allows everybody, actor and audience, to relax. There were some special actors in Worcester who really understood what was expected of them and who never let their egos stand in the way of the work. I learnt a wonderful objective from one particular actor, Terry Wale. Terry had a good career, working with most of the UK's best companies. On stage he spoke beautifully, was clear, and was almost musical in his approach to text. I remember one day he said to me *"Always Cherish the Words"*. I have upheld that maxim to this day. Words are after all the root of almost all theatre. Language giving form to often complex thoughts, written by great playwrights. There's nothing better. I had no awareness of terms like "minimalist" and "essentialist" when I was at Worcester. I was young and doing my thing. Staging musicals and plays that were sometimes fun, sometimes challenging. Programming in a "two for them, one for us" pattern. By that I mean you did two successive shows that you felt strongly would sell tickets, then one that was simply for yourself, that you would grow from, that was a box-office risk. I can think of so many amusing situations.

I recall the aforementioned production of *Romeo and Juliet*, which was not one of my highlights. We were at the end of the play and the actress playing Juliet was lying on a tomb downstage centre, supposedly dead of course. We used my mother's wedding veil to cover her. Suddenly she had a little coughing turn which got progressively louder. In an attempt to save the day the actress playing the Nurse jumped on top of her and wrapped herself in the veil! A winded Juliet lay on the tomb while Lady Capulet and Lady Montague were seen to be rocking backward and forward, not in painful grief but rather in fits of laughter.

Then there was a production of *Side by Side by Sondheim* which I didn't direct but in which I played the male singer. Joined by my old friend Ginni Barlow, who I'd known since college days and by Karen Mann, who years later would play Mrs Lovett in my West End production of *Sweeney Todd*, we set about learning all those complicated songs that make up Stephen Sondheim's repertoire. As Steve writes in *Pacific Overtures*, "I Was Younger Then". Many years later I was able to show him a photograph of the production. Bear in mind, I was forty years younger! He took one look at it, made some wry Sondheim comment, and laughed aloud. That made it all worthwhile.

I smile as I remember a production of Neil Simon's *Last of the Red Hot Lovers*, where one of the actresses cut a whole chunk of her scene. Instead of leaving well alone, she tried to put it back in. Her scene partner was in a state of shock when the actress then started again going round and round in a circle, adding about ten minutes onto the evening. It was on the Opening Night, and although I don't think the audience even noticed, it was an experience that has made me do all I can to avoid sitting in an auditorium to watch any Opening Night ever again.

And then my final show at The Swan was *Sweet Charity*, by Cy Coleman and Neil Simon. It was right up my street! I've always been fascinated by American comedy, from *I Love Lucy* to *The Golden Girls*. It amazes me that I've only ever done this show once, as I'm so fond of it. It has a wonderful score and a brilliant book. Originally directed by Bob Fosse, its virtuoso central role has been played by Gwen Verdon, Chita Rivera and Donna McKechnie to name but a few. At Worcester it was played by Liz Whiting. Playing opposite her was Alan Radcliffe – father of Daniel! There is a famous scene where Charity and Oscar are trapped in an elevator. I worked out that there were approximately seventy laugh lines in the scene. There was time to study the potential laugh points because, after all, there was no real blocking to do. They were standing side by side in an elevator. When we opened they were getting roughly forty of the laughs. I set them new targets every night and eventually they hit – all seventy. I think I so enjoy *Charity* because it is a perfect example of a well-crafted "book" musical. A musical where the enjoyment lies as much in the text as it does in the music. It's an ideal "musical-comedy", written by a terrific jazzy composer and a very funny American playwright. I've built a reputation for doing dark intense pieces. The fact is though, I love to make audiences laugh. Comedy is a technique and probably the hardest thing to do. To get laughs in an honest, non-mugging way is challenging and thrilling.

There are many more memories. I only share those to let you see that it isn't all serious and scholarly and political. It's often silly and joyous and a means of survival! I met and worked with many remarkable people in Worcester. I had the privilege of giving a first directing opportunity to Phyllida Lloyd, who has gone on to be one of our finest contemporary directors. I was introduced to my favourite musical collaborator Catherine Jayes, one of the UK's first female musical directors and orchestrators. She and I have done so many projects together over our lengthy careers, and you will read more of her in future chapters. Then there was Rufus Norris. He was a boy in the Youth Theatre that I had started there, and I believe operated Follow Spot on our production of *Cabaret*. Rufus went on to be Artistic Director of the Royal National Theatre. It was the sort of company environment where, if you didn't have a part in the current play, you would spend your evening being babysitter for the family of one of your fellow actors. Many of that company have left this earthly world, many are now parents and grandparents. We loved it and I do think that on the whole our audiences loved us.

It was time to move on. You may wonder why the tenures were not for longer periods of time? Very few directors of my generation stayed for long. That was the usual practice in the United Kingdom, and was very much encouraged by the Funding Bodies. I have always been surprised by the long tenures of Artistic Directors in the United States. I understand that the creative continuity of a long-term curatorship can be wonderful for the organisation but, deep down, I don't think it's a good idea! We should move on. Maybe artists are meant to move on? Maybe audiences need challenge and change? Staying for a long period can create a personal and organisational comfort that I believe can be detrimental to the growth of a theatre company and to the artist at the centre of it. Anyway, whether right or not, I kept moving on!

Cheltenham Everyman Theatre 1985–1989

Cheltenham is not much more than twenty-five miles from Worcester. This Gloucestershire city had once been extremely affluent due to its being a spa town, a place where wealthy Victorians came to "take the waters" and enjoy restorative cures. It is still a beautiful city with fine architecture and elegant streets. In the early 1980s almost every town or city in the United Kingdom still had its own repertory theatre. The Cheltenham Everyman had been designed and built in 1891 by the great Frank Matcham, who specialised in the design of theatres and music halls. Indeed during his forty-year career he designed some ninety theatres, many still standing!

Time had taken its toll on this gem of a building and Cheltenham City Council decided it was time to completely refurbish it. They protected the auditorium by enclosing it in what can only be described as a giant bird-cage, knocking everything down that surrounded and supported it. New lobbies, dressing rooms, offices, workshops, stage and fly tower were all part of the plan. The Arts Council of Great Britain saw this as the perfect opportunity to dismantle a long-established artistic directorship and staff, seeking to make a totally fresh start when the new building was launched. However, the changing of Artistic Director didn't meet with local approval and so the job was never going to be easy for anybody who succeeded. Running theatres always involves local politics with both a large and a small "p".

I applied for the job and was a little disappointed that my application wasn't successful. Rejection is a familiar sensation for anybody who works in the arts and without becoming accustomed to it, one would never survive. However, I then received a call from a colleague at the Arts Council in London. *"Why hadn't I applied?"* I was a little confused, explained that I had, and she said to leave it with her. Within a matter of days I was called to an interview and very shortly afterward I was offered the job. I'm not sure that I totally approve, but I do know that it doesn't hurt to have friends in high places. What this did make me realise was that taking on this job was going to be somewhat complex. A new Board of Management had been formed, who planned to create real and meaningful change, but they were having to negotiate disapproving voices from the community. A Patron had been appointed in the person of a member of the Royal Family. The building project was severely behind schedule and it needed an Artistic Director to come in and push things forward with real haste. I tell you all this to demonstrate that the role is often about being an arbitrator, a politician and, in this particular case, somebody who could read and understand architectural drawings. I spent a highly enlightening year on a building site, wearing a yellow hard hat. I had many lunches with local dissenters, building relationships with those who doubted the appropriateness of my very existence. So, my second building-based theatre, in my early thirties, was undoubtedly going to be character-building.

I could write an entire book about that first year at Cheltenham. Taking financial risks in the 700-seat main house was going to be concerning, and I wanted to develop a challenging programme. To achieve this, I encouraged that one part of the design became a second space, a studio theatre. I was responsible for building a business structure, both in terms of staff structure and financial plan, that was to sustain this beautiful auditorium's existence for another hundred years. Battles with contractors and builders ensued, it being in their contractual interest to create one delay after another.

One of the treasures of the theatre space was the beautiful painted ceiling of the auditorium. I was having one of those "lunches" on a Friday when I received a call at the restaurant. It was a member of my staff asking me to return to the theatre as quickly as I could. I ran, and when I arrived I saw fire engines and emergency vehicles outside. Working above the suspended ceiling, a workman had left a blow-torch running during his lunch break. You can imagine the rest of the story! The fire officers had to pump tons of water in through the roof above. I was told it would be Monday before we would know whether they could save the ceiling. That beautiful painted ceiling was one of the primary reasons for keeping the auditorium! It was one of the longest weekends of my life. Well, the ceiling was saved, the auditorium was finished, I'd helped design the layout of the dressing rooms to ensure a comfortable environment for performers, the lobbies and bar areas were nearly ready, we opened a box office, and on 20 March 1986 *My Fair Lady* had a glamorous Opening Night. The theatre was formally opened by Her Royal Highness the Princess Royal, whose support and encouragement certainly confirmed my being a dedicated royalist!

Just before we opened the main auditorium we launched the studio. I named it after the great actor Ralph Richardson, who was born in Cheltenham. Rehearsals were spent with pneumatic drills thumping outside the studio doors. Our opening production was *Peer Gynt* by Henrik Ibsen. Ibsen has always been one of my favourite writers. Perhaps my coming from the North of Scotland makes me feel close to the darkness so prevalent in his Nordic repertoire. During the technical rehearsals of the production I had a call telling me that my rather young father had died suddenly and I had to urgently fly back to Scotland. I had to go North, just as Peer does in the Fifth Act of that great play. Peer goes home to die, I had to go home to deal with death. The play really is about death. There is even a funeral reenacted. I went home, and organised a real funeral. Luckily Phyllida Lloyd was by now my Associate Director and she finished the job of the technical rehearsals and the very few previews. I flew back and saw the Opening Night of *Peer Gynt*. I found it too hard to watch the play. My relationship with my father was always complex. Art and life meeting isn't easy. Sometimes though, it is exactly why one is an artist. It is the job of the artist to look at your own "stuff" and express it through the work you make. I do believe that the journey of my career has been a perpetual exploration of who I am. Good theatre can help us understand the human condition. It powerfully demonstrates our "sameness".

The three-year period I enjoyed as an artist at the Cheltenham Everyman Theatre was hugely enriching, and once again, it might be fun to highlight a few highs and lows.

Let's start with the production of *Anyone Can Whistle* in my first season. This was one of those Sondheim musicals that has never truly worked, and it had a disastrously short Broadway run. We were to be doing the UK Premiere. A musical about corruption, set around the inmates of a lunatic asylum! Really? Great score though and I wanted to see if I could make it work. Did I? Who knows, but what I do know is that people came from far and wide to experience what had been deemed a failure in 1964 when it originally starred Angela Lansbury and Lee Remick. Many years later, I was sitting at the bar in Joe Allen's in Manhattan, that much-loved theatre restaurant that has walls covered in framed posters of "flop" shows, telling Stephen Sondheim about this production. In typical fashion, Steve said "*How many performances?*" I said "*twenty-nine*". He said "*twenty more than we got!!*" Life. One simply never knows! What I do know is, I'd love to have another go at *Anyone Can Whistle* . . .

Then there was *A Midsummer Night's Dream*, which Phyllida directed and had set in what had all the appearance of a nuclear bunker! I was standing in the box office one day (I've always loved to help sell the tickets, probably goes back to those early days in the Highlands) and I answered a call to an irate audience member who was screaming about the production. I asked her what she expected when she booked her tickets. Her response was *"Nineteen Thirties – with Fairy wings!"* Surely just as questionable as the nuclear bunker?

I clearly remember a production of *Hedda Gabler* in the studio, in which I was experimenting with the audience reaction to the more informal space, and so seated them on Victorian furniture as if they were sitting in the Norwegian house where the play is set. They could sit anywhere and the actors had to nightly adjust to not being able to play a scene on the seat they had planned to play it on. I love experiments in making theatre and the exploration of how to keep it "alive". Probably goes all the way back to that "locked in" audience in Athens, Georgia! Anyway, it was the second of two dress rehearsals and I knew that, because of a Board meeting, I wasn't going to be able to attend. I asked the actors to run the play anyway, just as if an audience were with them, but in the empty theatre without my presence. However, my meeting finished early and I did get there just in time for the start. I didn't want to disrupt the experience for the actors, and so I slipped into the lighting booth, which had the sort of glass where one could see out but the person on the other side couldn't see in. What I experienced that afternoon was remarkable. Probably the truest, most honest performance I have even seen. Why? Because I wasn't there. The actors weren't trying to please Daddy! Nothing was standing between them and the telling of the story.

Also in my Opening Season I directed the Regional Premiere of a play called *Tom and Viv* by Michael Hastings, which examines the complicated relationship between TS Eliot and his wife Vivienne Haig-Wood. The two actors playing husband and wife were excellent. He was delightfully thoughtful about the work and she was more than a little wild. At one performance she did a somewhat unforgivable thing. She changed the staging. I should explain that there is an unwritten rule that once you're in performance, there are no substantive changes unless mutually agreed in advance with the director and with your fellow actors. In America they call it "freezing" the show. I'll always feel somewhat ambivalent about the rule. To me, things should keep growing even if that does involve a little risk. Anyway, at one performance the actress playing Viv entered from the opposite side to that which she usually entered from. Not only that, but she made the decision to enter crawling on her hands and knees. Bear in mind Viv Eliot was suffering from severe mental health issues! The evening ended. The actor playing Tom was justifiably furious, after all it could have thrown him completely. He said to me *"You have to speak to her! You have to tell her she was wrong! She has to know it made no sense for the play!"* It was on the third point that I had to stop him. Yes, it may have been inappropriate of her to make her choices without consultation, but it made total sense for the play! In fact it was quite wonderful. It also made his reaction to her so much more interesting and alive. I did speak with her. I did tell her she was a little out of order. However I also said she must keep it in. I wished I'd thought of it myself. I have searched for safe ways to sustain that flexibility ever since.

Just to prove that I still hadn't found that "essentialism" thing, I look back on a Cheltenham production of Shakespeare's *Twelfth Night*. Set around a swimming pool, the design team had built a large deep pool into the stage. There was a wonderful moment when Malvolio comes to give Viola a ring. Now, Viola is dressed as a boy at this point in the play. Malvolio malevolently dropped the ring into the pool and left the scene. Then Viola had to strip off her boy's clothes – she had a bikini on underneath – and she dived in and retrieved the ring, speaking Shakespeare's verse all the way! Nothing minimalist about an onstage life-sized swimming pool! One of the things that I did love about that moment with that actress and that pool is that it could never be the same twice! It was perpetually "alive".

And finally one of my last productions in the main theatre, *Sweeney Todd*, again by Stephen Sondheim. This was the first of two productions of this musical masterpiece during my career. Later you will read much more about the second one, which was somewhat seminal in my body of work. For this first one though, well I think we made a good production, both respectful and respectable. It was great musically, with an orchestra in the pit. It was a smaller version of the usual setting that originated with the iconic Broadway director, Hal Prince. It was highly successful but, for me at least, not satisfying. I had to find an answer to why I was experiencing that lack of satisfaction. I didn't want to be depressed by the work I was making. What was it that was missing?

I realised there and then that I was no longer interested in making "copies". If I was to direct any more musicals, I had to develop my own way, my own voice. For now though, it was time to take a break from them, to give myself time to find out what that "way" was going to be. I needed to go somewhere where there wouldn't be any expectation of my directing a musical. Once again, it was time to move on.

4
The Later Artistic Director Years

Liverpool Everyman Theatre 1989–1993

I approach writing about this next engagement with some trepidation. My Artistic Directorship of the Liverpool Everyman Theatre, or the "Ev" as it's affectionately known, was fraught with difficulties and challenges, yet it was probably the most fulfilling assignment up to that point and certainly the most pivotal in terms of my artistic development.

Liverpool in 1989 wasn't easy. The city had been through major challenges. The Toxteth riots of 1981 arose from long-standing tension between the local police and the Black community. The once famous Liverpool docks fell into disrepair and the Conservative Prime Minister, Margaret Thatcher, went out of her way to be obstructive. This was a socialist city, led by an aggressively left-wing council, and she was going to dismantle it if she possibly could. I joined the company a few weeks after the awful events of the Hillsborough Football Stadium disaster, which happened on 15 April 1989. Liverpool fans were crushed into one area of the stadium, resulting in ninety-six people dying and hundreds more being seriously injured. This dreadful event had an intense effect upon an already alienated city, a city with huge unemployment figures and a profound lack of hope. How ironic that the theatre was sited on an inner-city street between the contemporary Roman Catholic Cathedral at one end and the huge Anglican Cathedral at the other. It was called – Hope Street.

My predecessors at the Everyman had done a wonderful job in attracting non-theatregoing audiences into the venue, often through the work of Liverpool playwrights such as Willy Russell, whose plays *Shirley Valentine* and *Educating Rita* went on to be international successes. Then my immediate predecessor, the daring Glen Walford, also presented a number of classics, as well as zany musical productions with actors making their own music. I think it's fair to say that the body of work before my tenure was exciting, rough in style and highly challenging of its audience. I'm not sure that I was quite the best person to inherit that body of work. A colleague, who knew the Everyman well, said to me at the time *"You will be good for The Everyman and the Everyman will be good for you."* I now know she was right about the latter but I'm not so sure about the former. I was in a major city, an unfamiliar experience that hadn't happened since my Glasgow days. Things were changing on so many levels, including personally. My marriage had come to an end, although I'm happy to say that Jacquie and I remain friends to this day. It was important to both of us to make this ending a new beginning, particularly because of the effect this change could have on our daughter. All was eventually well and we are now proud grandparents. Without going too deeply into this, I started living closely with another man. It's a little difficult to actually write about, not because I'm in any way ashamed of that new relationship or of life's new order but simply because I come from a generation of gay men for whom being able to share about your sexuality was difficult and potentially shameful. We didn't even use the word "gay", and we certainly didn't want to be known as "queer". That was then a derogatory word which I remember being yelled at me in the street. A word I can't use to this day. So much has changed, and I've now been happily married to a different man for over twenty-five years – more of that later. I only bring up these changes in my personal life to acknowledge how they again make me who I am, they are part of what makes the artist. I feel blessed to be part of a generation of change, a generation who, eventually, will no longer need to hide. No longer need to feel ashamed.

I want to take a moment to say how wonderful the Everyman space was. It was an old converted church, and with the audience on three sides it was a true thrust stage. This was where I first understood that the physical shape of the space directly influences the audience's participation in the story being told. In the Highlands my work had happened in all sorts of spaces, many of which weren't really theatres but rather church halls and social centres. Then I worked in two successive buildings with somewhat more formal configurations, though both very audience-friendly. To this day I find the smaller, less traditional spaces the most exciting in which to make theatre.

I found myself in the position of having to rather quickly prepare my first season for the theatre. I had two female associate directors, Catherine Jayes and Linda Dobell, which even in 1989 was considered progressive. Catherine was to write music for all the productions and Linda was to take care of the movement. It seems so bizarre to say this but for the first time I had a permanent company which included actors of colour. One male and one female in that first season. It feels disgracefully meagre now, but at that time it was a major step forward. During that season I made a co-production with the Talawa Theatre Company, a London-based Black company led by the formidable and visionary Yvonne Brewster. The play was called *The Gods Are Not To Blame*, an African adaptation of the Oedipus story, which formed part of a small season of Greek plays that I was programming. During the following year we again co-produced, this time on *Antony and Cleopatra* – the first UK production of Shakespeare by an all-Black cast. Thank goodness that so much has happened in so short a period of time. How shameful that it wasn't happening long before.

When I was planning my first season, one of my Board of Management suggested that, because of the recent event at Hillsborough, I should be doing a play about football. I responded – *"Do I look like a person who should be directing a play about football? Shouldn't we be doing a play about grief?"* That led me to opening my first season with the great Euripides play *The Trojan Women*. There is a moment in that ancient text when Hecuba, the matriarch of the defeated royal family, grieves the deaths of her son and grandson. At one performance, during Hecuba's great soliloquy about loss, I heard a woman in the audience howl out in mutual grief. An extraordinary moment when the pain of real life directly met the pain that we were acting out in the theatre. Tragic but vital.

Having that repertory company wasn't as easy as it had been in the past. Actors' reasons for making the work had somehow changed and there was an introduction of that unfortunate word we now use in everyday communication – "entitlement". Each actor thought they had the right to play a leading role. The expectation of each performer and their relationship to the work of the company was complex, and everybody's right to be heard resulted in company meetings and discussions that sometimes overwhelmed the work itself. Not necessarily a bad thing, and certainly an appropriate end to the "benevolent autocracy". I remember one such meeting where the young head of the marketing department started to share how, as a gay man, he felt alienated by other members of the organisation. I showed concern and assured him that I would do all I could to investigate this. He said to me *"It's all right for you. Your generation had it easy! Nobody cared whether you were gay or not!"* I said nothing. I smiled a little. He omitted to understand that when I was younger, homosexuality still had the possibility of being an imprisonable act. Perhaps ignorance really is bliss?

Budgeting for the theatre was getting harder. Funding was less plentiful during Thatcher's years, and her complicated relationship with Liverpool resulted in the tangible erosion of government support. The days of the Arts Council calling you up and asking what you needed had gone. I can even remember a year when they invited every company to tell them what they needed to make good work. Nobody asked for too much, nobody was greedy, and every company received what they'd asked for. I miss those days, but continue to believe that if that sense of fairness and balance was to come from our governments and our funding bodies we, as artists, would feel less vulnerable and therefore would respond more generously. One of the gifts of budgeting under such tight conditions meant that new ways of working had to be developed. We explored a method called "zero budgeting". This meant exactly what the title suggests. You start from zero. You know what you would like to allocate financially to a project but don't just dive in ready to spend that money. You start with the assumption that you may have to do it with no financial resource. You bring all your collaborators to the table and share with them your vision for the play or musical. You ask them what they think their departments might individually need to fulfil that vision. If it doesn't seem like a heavy project for costumes, ask that department if they would forgo a part of their usual budgetary allocation and pass it over to the lighting department.

And vice versa. Always remembering that everybody is working from a mutually agreed point of zero, and in doing so nobody can expect the impossible. After all it doesn't need expensive projections and fancy lighting rigs to make theatre. It doesn't need silks to make costumes or symphony orchestras to make music. It simply needs imagination. So, that was how we built our budgets and every time it worked. Everybody brought their creativity and their generosity to the table. None of the budgets exceeded any overall targets and everybody was happy with the work they were making. We turned things around from a deficit to a surplus situation, all the time doing challenging work. Common sense really, and yet somehow rather difficult to achieve.

I so often felt miserable in Liverpool. I felt I wasn't the right person for the job. I was shocked when a staff member said that I wouldn't understand Liverpool because I went to Public School (Private School for American readers). I asked why she thought I was privileged in that way and her response was, "*You wear a tie!*" On one particular day a senior staff member said "*How does it feel coming North?*" My response "*I come from somewhere three hundred miles further North than this, so you really don't own Northernness!*" I felt unwanted by the city. Sometimes the critics in that first season were offensive toward me personally, on a level that today would be totally unacceptable. I worked at it, took them to lunch, listened to them, never shouted back and eventually they turned around. Sometimes it felt like dancing with the devil and I'm relieved we didn't have Internet critics in those days.

Like all difficult times, there were also very positive experiences. One of these was spending time at the world-famous Moscow Art Theatre to develop two Russian plays for our Liverpool repertoire. There I worked with a young designer, Alexander Borovski. We communicated through a translator and for weeks we worked on the designs. He would ask me a question and I would respond by offering a solution to a problem. I would say, for example, "*We need a window.*" His response – "*But, what are you trying to say?*" "*We need a door.*" "*What are you trying to say?*" He drove me absolutely crazy, challenged everything about me, and thank God for him! He changed how I made my work. He made me realise that I didn't have to have the answers. That I had to have the vision and know what I was trying to say, but didn't have to provide the solutions. I had to have what the great Peter Brook called the "*smell*" of the production. My collaborators would help me find the answers. With them I would develop the "*concept*", the development of which is a step toward realising the "*vision*".

Then there were very special times in the rehearsal room, such as making a production of *The Caucasian Chalk Circle*. The play needs the presence of a little child, starting as a baby. Our props department made a beautiful baby which just didn't look right. Then they made a rag-doll puppet. Better, but not right. Then one day I came back from lunch and the actress playing Grusha, the child's protector, was sitting in a corner of the rehearsal room going over the lines where she was talking to the baby. She had an old pillow that she had squashed up to pretend it was the baby. Somehow this innocent, almost primitive image was perfect. Pure "let's pretend". So, that pillow became Michael, our child. At one of those audience talk-backs a lady was quite angry with me. She had found herself crying over the baby and she was sure she shouldn't be crying when she was watching a play written by Bertolt Brecht. I asked her why she thought she was crying? She said it was because the child was so "*real*". I gently pointed out that it was simply a pillow. At that moment she realised that the rest had been over to her imagination. Her very own "let's pretend". Her very own face in the wardrobe. I hope it was an important moment for her. It certainly was for me.

And then there were the many joyous moments, one such being at the end of our production of Shakespeare's *As You Like It*. We had removed almost all the seating in the auditorium, allowing the audience to sit where they liked. The empty tiered seating levels created a wonderful sense of being on a hill. So, the production was really festive and the relaxation of audience and actor took away any pressure of not being able to understand the play. There is a glorious Epilogue to the play where Rosalind, who has been disguised as a man for most of the evening, talks directly to the women in the audience and then to the men, telling them how she/he would relate to them. She says: "*If I were a woman, I would kiss as many of you as had beards that pleased me, complexions that liked me, and breaths that I defied not.*" Well, on one performance, as soon as she had said this line, a whole group of male students put on false beards. This wasn't set up. Somehow they knew about that line. So, our Rosalind was faced with what to do with this row of beards. She did indeed kiss them one by one and the audience went crazy. The word must have got out, because every performance thereafter there were rows of beards! For all the sadness and indeed anger that was in the city, there was also a powerful inherent sense of humour. When that humour was brought to the "Ev", it was like something you'd never experience anywhere else.

It came to my final show in Liverpool. The Board were not happy with me. In four years, I hadn't done a musical. I could have fought them on it but I didn't and decided I would "*show 'em*" by doing something that I thought was impossible. After all, I was leaving so I had nothing to lose. I suggested we do Leonard Bernstein's *Candide*. They liked the idea! The rest is history – a history I will share with you in an upcoming chapter.

York Theatre Royal 1993–1997

This was my final UK Artistic Directorship, and in many senses it was a relief to leave Liverpool. My then partner and I had gone our separate ways and starting again always seems a daunting prospect. York is a beautiful city, one of the most historic in the United Kingdom. The Theatre Royal is the second oldest repertory theatre in the country and is quite beautiful. Built in 1744, it was full of atmosphere and rather formal after the Liverpool theatre. On looking back, it was artistically a "safe seat" and probably a position I shouldn't have filled. Oddly, it was a terrific four years and I loved every moment of it.

During my many years in the role of Artistic Director, much had changed. The United Kingdom had been brainwashed into accepting the market economy of Margaret Thatcher. Many theatres had closed and the Arts Council was developing "Centres of Excellence" in the larger urban areas. Quite how you define "excellence" in any art-form is baffling to me. It was assumed that most families had a car so that meant that people could travel to a nearby theatre and so there was less demand for each city to have its own company. Marketing had become the cornerstone of success. I don't doubt the importance of developing a strategic approach toward how to attract audiences into a theatre, but I always look back to when in my Worcester days the government insisted that we use a proportion of our grant to employ a Marketing Director.

We did as we were told and our audience numbers initially dropped. Nobody's fault, she was totally great and given time she did turn things around, but the audiences didn't like being told what to do! Believe me, I know we can never turn back the clock, and I know that good thoughtful marketing and publicity is now fundamental to how our society works. I knew that over scrambled eggs that evening in Dornoch. I simply feel concerned that the more we utilise our resources on the organisational structures that overwhelm our budgets, the more vulnerable our theatre companies become. Explain to me why one should have a Fundraising department that basically raises money to pay for its own existence? I am quite certain that the more top-heavy our organisations become, the more cuts have to be made in the art itself. Productions have smaller casts, rehearsal periods get shorter and then real artistic vulnerability sets in. I was shocked during that visit to Russia to discover that the Moscow Art Theatre really did spend a year rehearsing a production. Excessive? By Western standards, yes. Effective? Most certainly. It made for rich work of great human depth, which was successful and so played for years. I saw a production of *The Seagull* there which had been in their repertoire for nine years and felt like it had opened yesterday.

One area of Thatcher's Theatre that had really changed was in the executive branches of the companies. For my first two companies, I created and managed the budget myself, untrained but with enough Protestant good sense to know that you don't spend money you don't have. At the next two, Cheltenham and Liverpool, we had administrators who managed the budget of which I had set the parameters, and who ran the business side of the company on a day-to-day basis. Excellent people who really cared about the work and saw their role as supporting the vision of the Artistic Director. In York, the tables had turned, following theatres throughout the country who were changing their business structures. More and more the budget was determining the art as opposed to supporting the art. Economic stresses before my arrival had determined that the company be led by an Executive Director, and that the Artistic Director was answerable to that Executive. A fundamental and fascinating change. I'm delighted to say that I had a good working relationship with Elizabeth Jones, who was my boss, and I rather enjoyed being number two. We were lucky in that we were mature people with reasonably healthy egos who worked together for a greater good. The freedom from committee meetings and budgeting sessions meant that I could concentrate on why I came into the theatre in the first place – to direct plays. Deep down and with real conviction I believe that the art should lead the money. "The Vision" should be what fulfils the mission and not the bank balance. I do believe that the Artistic Director should be an artist. Not necessarily a director, they could be a writer or a designer or an actor, but an artist. Whether it was because I didn't have the final sole responsibility, or because I was in an environment where it was a pleasure to walk to work in the morning I don't know, but I certainly rediscovered the sense of fun that makes for good work. The processes I had developed in Liverpool, of more rehearsal room freedom and experimentation, were with me forever.

Let me highlight a few productions that I dearly recall. I'm not going to include musicals, which we certainly produced quite successfully, nor am I going to highlight the largest event of my tenure, *The York Cycle of Mystery Plays*, as all of those will be given their proper place in later chapters. Rather I will focus on some plays that meant a great deal to me and that hopefully, for somebody, made a difference.

My first play at the Theatre Royal was something I would never have chosen myself. It had already been programmed by my predecessor and rather than rock any boats, I said I would take it on. *Charley's Aunt* is a beautifully constructed, very silly, middle-class comedy of the Victorian tradition. Not my cup of tea at all, I said to myself. Well – I loved it, and grew to appreciate its brilliance. Audiences were laughing at lines that had been similarly laughed at 100 years before. A clever design, inventive casting and a sense of play in the rehearsal room conveyed themselves to the audience in a wonderful way and got my tenure off to an excellent start. Interesting to note that many years later I did a musical version of the same story, *Where's Charley?*, as part of the estimable New York City Centre *Encores* Series. The same laughs prevailed and it too was a joyous experience.

Because of the ancient royal connection with York, I created a two-part adaptation of William Shakespeare's *Richard III* and *Henry VI parts 1,2 & 3* – *The Wars of the Roses*. Six hours of theatre with the same actors, over two evenings. Although I actually like my theatre experiences to be short, I've also been interested in how theatre has become more of an "event". Great productions of plays like *Nicholas Nickleby* at the Royal Shakespeare Theatre certainly led the way. Well, it was a thrill to work on those complex Shakespeare plays. It took chutzpah – or audacity – to put them on. Theatre needs a generous sprinkling of audacity every now and again.

And then there was a moment, not a specific production, that struck me deeply. *A Midsummer Night's Dream* was on in the theatre. On this particular night I wanted to go into the auditorium to watch a little of it. I was standing outside the Dress Circle doors listening to some of the play on the show relay that came into the foyer, waiting my opportunity to slip quietly in. I was standing beside a very nice usher who I had known for some time. It came to Titania's complex speech in Act Two, about the turmoil mortals create in nature. (Mr Shakespeare certainly was ahead of his time!) Anyway, my usher friend suddenly started joining in with Titania. Not in a showy way but very naturally and rather beautifully. She spoke that entire difficult speech with the actress, no script in hand. She knew it!!! I was gob-smacked. I asked her how on earth she could recite that fiendish text. She told me that as a child they had no radio or TV and sat as a family, a very ordinary working-class family, and read Shakespeare out loud. This led to her memorising great chunks of the plays. The lesson for me was: don't underestimate anybody. Don't categorise people or pre-decide their abilities. My friend knew it naturally, no fuss, no self-importance, in exactly the way the playwright would have intended.

I'd like to share one more anecdote about that same production of *A Midsummer Night's Dream*, to demonstrate a fun example of an experiment in theatremaking. It came in the joyous fifth act where the "Mechanicals" put on their play for the court. These characters are amateur actors, or rather "non-actors". It is traditionally great fun. I wanted the actors to have a real sense of not knowing what they were doing – hard to achieve with trained actors who have studied the roles they are playing. So, I rehearsed them individually. They each knew what they individually were going to do but had no idea about anybody else. Then, naughty as it was of me, I didn't let them perform it with each other as a group until they did it in front of the first night audience. What proceeded to happen was one of the funniest things I have ever seen on the live stage. The staring eyes, the terrified looks, the hysterical surprise – simply joyous. It was never as good as that first time, how could it be? However, it always had a freshness and aliveness that were quite wonderful. It was a wicked experiment on my part, one that could only happen with actors who trusted me. Yes, be safe – but be bold!

The year 1996 brought along a new relationship. I'd met the man who I would later marry and with whom I would spend the rest of my life. It was time to stop running theatres – for a little while anyway!

From 1997 until 2015, I would enjoy being freelance, never for a moment thinking I would become an Artistic Director again. I was enjoying the more flexible life of going to different places to make theatre, whilst having close relationships with companies such as the Watermill Theatre in Newbury. Things changed and without my seeking it out, along came another theatre that would mean a lot to me. Perhaps more than any of them.

Classic Stage Company, Off-Broadway 2016–2022

In many ways, it was all Stephen Sondheim's fault. Sometime in 2011, he asked me, with that familiar irony, if I would care to go on a date-night with him, to see some theatre and have dinner. He knew I'd seen a lot of what had been happening on Broadway and thought it was time I widened my horizons. There was a very successful production of *The Three Sisters* running at Classic Stage Company down on 13th Street on the Lower East Side. He got tickets, and off we went. He'd even booked a car! I don't think I'd ever been to the Lower East Side! I enjoyed the production very much, but I enjoyed the theatre space even more. It's a 200-seat gem of a room, with seats on three sides, just like the Liverpool Everyman, and very much reminding me of the Donmar Theatre in London. At that time, it was a "black box", which to explain the terminology is, as it suggests, a rather anonymous space painted black, getting rid of any character in the room that might stand in the way of the play. That had been very much the habit in those smaller theatres that had started in the 70s, as a response to the plush establishment theatres "uptown". I can remember thinking myself very smart as a student when I went to the Close Theatre Club at the Glasgow Citizens Theatre, which was their "black box".

The day after the infamous "date", I did something I never do. I called my agent and asked him if he could get me a "meeting" with the Artistic Director of CSC. I don't come from a generation of networkers, I never write to anybody to seek work, don't send out my reviews – in fact I now almost never read them! I'm extremely uncomfortable with the artifice of schmoozing at Opening Nights, so I wasn't sure that my request would be accepted. At that time, the Artistic Director of the company was a gentleman by the name of Brian Kulick. He graciously responded to my request and we started a conversation to see what I might be able to do in his theatre. I kept saying that I'd like to do a play. I'd by this time done so many musicals in America that I was concerned people might think I couldn't read words. After much back and forth I was to direct, guess what, a musical! A very special one, *Passion* by Stephen Sondheim and James Lapine. I suppose you could justify it as "classical". After all it was set in nineteenthth-century Italy and the ladies wore long frocks! Quite seriously I think you could comfortably argue that anything Sondheim wrote was a classic. I designed the set as well as directing, the wonderful Judy Kuhn played the curious and complicated leading character Fosca. It was a *New York Times* Critics Pick, was nominated for countless awards and was much loved by the public. It was the first of Steve's musicals that New York audiences would see in this intimate space and was a forerunner for many such revivals in other venues.

I entered into a loose relationship with the company, becoming the Associate Director, which involved directing one show a year. Then in 2016 things changed a little. Brian left and I was invited to take over the reins. I don't know a theatre artist who doesn't like to be "asked". I know hardly anybody who finds it easy to say "no". When I was asked, my head knew I should probably decline, after all I wasn't getting any younger and by now I also had a wonderful position as a Professor in Theatre at the highly renowned Princeton University. However, I also had to recognise that I felt "rootless" in the freelance world and missed having an artistic "home". I discussed it all with my husband Robert, and my heart won the day.

Boy were the next six years a learning curve – one I wouldn't have missed for the world. First of all there was the Board of Management. The system is totally different to the theatres I had run in the United Kingdom. It's always been interesting to me that the two systems identity themselves in such different ways. In the UK there is Subsidised Theatre (supported by the government) and Non-subsidised (profit being created by investment in the product). In the US there is Not-for-Profit (the equivalent of Subsidised) Theatre and Commercial Theatre of course – profit being the aim. Note that the negative – "Non" or "Not" – applies to opposite things on each side of the Atlantic and therein lies the challenge for the US not-for-profit movement that started as a reaction to profit-driven Broadway. There is comparatively little government subsidy in the States, and any non-earned income comes either from Foundations that cultivate the arts or from the kindness of strangers. Not a safe sustainable system it seems to me. The art in both countries is becoming more and more driven by the need for profit, which is in many senses not an achievable goal. To state the obvious, if you only have 200 seats then even your greatest hit at the box office isn't going to pay all the bills. Actors, crew and staff need to be paid, then there's the marketing, and the timber for the set, and the electricity bill, and even the rental costs of your space, which in New York City is usually very high. The good people who have the ultimate fiscal responsibility in the not-for-profit theatre are the Board of Management.

I was extremely fortunate during my six-year tenure, the longest in any of the theatres I led, that my board were always supportive and understanding of their role. After all, if they said that I couldn't do a certain project simply because they didn't like the idea, then as Artistic Director I would have to acknowledge that we were at odds and I would have to offer my resignation. That never happened. They went with me and worked so hard in so many ways to support my vision for the company. They were led by Board Chair Lynn Angelson, a remarkable woman who has gone on to be a dear friend. Lynn was generous with both her time and her resources, and she was a great listener. I truly think we led that organisation together, along with our brilliant executive director Toni Davis. I made it very clear when I agreed to take on the position that I could only do it if I was recognised as a "first among equals", in the belief that when push comes to shove it is the art that should have the final say when you are trying to fulfil a Mission. The biggest difference between the UK board and the US board is that the former is there to manage funds and the latter is there to provide them. UK boards are made up of genuine theatre lovers, representative of the audience and of the funding bodies, both national and local. In the US the board members themselves are a major part of the funding structure, each having to put a certain amount of their own money on the table every year. By the time I left CSC, board members each gave $25,000 minimum per annum. A truly extraordinary generosity. If you are lucky and if your board recognises what you are doing and understands their role in supporting your vision then it's great. However it's worth noting it doesn't always work out and those who can afford this level of financial commitment may have their own agenda, political or social.

Not only did the board give generously but it was expected that as part of my programming, I would stage a big fundraising Gala each season. These are usually dinners, where Board members can bring guests for hospitality and entertainment. Bear in mind that every not-for-profit in the community is doing the same thing and so theatres are in the position of being competitive as far as resources are concerned. Although I didn't agree that a chicken dinner should subsidise the arts, I made the pragmatic decision that it was useful to board members as a networking opportunity, and so we did an annual themed fundraiser, often honouring a renowned guest. I was able to bring wonderful artists along to give of their time and talent in order to make these evenings as memorable as I could. An example of the fact that the artists themselves are major contributors to the sustainability of the American theatre.

Every company has its own "development" department, some of them being very successful. I was confused when I met the small development team at CSC. I had assumed that "development" meant development of the work. I didn't realise it was a positive-spinning euphemism for "fundraising". Don't get me wrong, their input into the work of a successful non-profit company is crucial, otherwise the bills really can't be paid. Not only does this department have to raise money, but they are also responsible for developing relationships with those Foundations that are set up to support the arts. Many hours are spent writing grant proposals and finding new ways of getting funders to focus on the work of the company.

As you will have surmised from previous chapters, I have reservations about the place of Marketing in the theatre. However, I thought the department at CSC were excellent. They were very hands-on, very focussed on audience development and on making the event of attending a play as comfortable as possible, finding ways for audience members to not only enjoy CSC but also to enjoy their visit to the Lower East Side. They were non-formulaic in their approach and thought out-of-the-box as much as I did. We did all we could to maintain reasonable ticket prices, and this certainly paid off in terms of bringing young people into the theatre.

Then there was the theatre space itself. I loved the relationship between actor and audience that was intrinsic to CSC, but when I started I felt it was time to rid ourselves of the "black box". My friend, world-famous architect and theatre designer David Rockwell, sat with me in the auditorium and recommended that, as the artist that will be taking the lead, the nature of the theatre space should marry my aesthetic. It should be a space that reflects the stripped-back, bare, essentialist type of theatre that I had been making for some time. So, we rented a number of large dumpsters, stripped everything out of the space that was not in itself essential, eradicated the blackness and took it back to the beautiful bare brick underneath. In reality the brick was fragile and would have been vulnerable if we had "blasted" it all. So instead I hired a team of scenic artists, provided them with visual references, and they painted the underlying brick to look exactly like brick. Warm and very New York. People are still surprised when they're told that the brick is painted on top of brick, a great example of the mysterious artifice of theatre. We took everything we could out of the space above the acting area, opening up an "upper area" or "upper room" in Shakespearean tradition. We exposed all the beams in the roof above the space, originally a stable which had once been a carriage house for the rich families that had inhabited the neighbourhood. A sort of nineteenth-century car-lot! It was a thoroughly satisfying project, back in the yellow hard hat though this time on a more intimate scale. So now for the work itself.

One of the great challenges in working with a company that has "Classic" in its title, is – how do you define "Classic" or "Classical" in the world we live in today? Classic Stage is situated in Downtown Manhattan, which is a characterful, indeed colourful section of a multi-cultural city. The Lower East side was where many Europeans settled when they came in from Ellis Island. The US Trades Union movement started in that area – on Union

Square – so it was then and is now a part of the city that is progressive and political. How do you provide classical theatre for that audience? There's nothing wrong with having the white elite from the Upper East Side as a strong regular theatregoing base, but that can't be everything. Diversity is everything in Manhattan, just as it was in Liverpool. I often think of the great liners that used to sail between those two cities and the similar issues that both have inherited.

"Classic" can embody the higher ideals to which we all aspire. The Greeks, Shakespeare, the Jacobeans were all telling big stories that reflect the good, bad and indifferent of the audiences that were there in front of them. In early theatre the celebration of tragedy was as strong as the celebration of comedy. After all those two masks overlap and are the same size. We tend to be more comfortable with comedy in our modern world, but I do recall attending, all the way back in that student road-trip, an outdoor performance of a tragedy in a Greek Amphitheatre. At the end, all 17,000 audience members rose to their feet and started dancing together. A spontaneous recognition that tragedy is as crucial a storytelling form as comedy, perhaps even more so.

"Classical" theatre unfortunately brings with it a repertoire written by long-since-dead white men. Not representative of the world we live in today. It was my job, as the artistic leader of the company, to gradually break down that preconception. The plays didn't have to be old. They could and should feel relevant. Here follows a handful of examples of pieces that I programmed to fulfil the mission in a somewhat contemporary way.

In my first season, in a small step toward breaking the "*plays by dead white men*" preconception, I directed *Dead Poets Society*, the world premiere of a theatre adaptation of that great film that had made Robin Williams so famous. This time the inspiring teacher was played by Jason Sudeikis, who has gone on to an award-winning TV career for his role in *Ted Lasso*. He brought a real joy and magic to the man who teaches these teenage boys about Dead Poets and what makes them still worth reading. The audiences poured in, perhaps primarily because Jason was at that time a regular in *Saturday Night Live*. There is nothing wrong with working with actors from film and television, after all most of them started their careers in the theatre. Their recognition factor makes the audience excited and comfortable. The subject matter captured the imagination, and seeing the world though the expanding minds of the boys in the story was really very moving. For those boys, the "classics" were no longer boring!

To show that the greatest classics could be made accessible and exciting, I directed my fourth production of *Macbeth*, this one done with a cast of nine, racially integrated. It was interesting to present it at a politically challenging time. A play about a man who wanted to steal power. The King himself was played by the wonderful Corey Stoll, one of America's finest Shakespearian actors. He can deal with classical text in a virile manner, with the pace and energy that Shakespeare demands but doesn't always get. The great thing though is that he doesn't look like a rarified actor but rather more like a bloke you might meet on the subway. Interestingly Lady Macbeth was played by Corey's real-life wife, actress Nadia Bowers. Their chemistry was remarkable, so very real and down-to-earth. Lack of pretence is so vital and often so hard to find in what is, after all, a somewhat artificial world. I did the play with no intermission, made almost no cuts, and it ran a little over 100 minutes. Nobody would believe I hadn't taken the knife to it. Taking the language with the gallop it deserves is surely the answer. Even after the aforementioned school production, plus the productions with TIE-Up, Worcester, York and CSC, I'd still do that great play again in a heartbeat.

Dracula was adapted by Kate Hamill, a young American female writer, who very much puts her own feminism at the centre of her work. Kate was also a performer in the production, not a usual situation with a writer. However I do believe that being in the first productions of her plays puts her closely in touch with the rhythms of what is or is not working in her work. The production was performed in repertoire with a new adaptation of *Frankenstein*, which was directed by Timothy Douglas with a wonderful African-American actress, Stephanie Berry, in the title role, which gave a very new take on the story. The exciting thing was that, because of the repertoire, you could see these two very different productions both in the same week. It's interesting to note that the idea of doing plays in "repertoire" was seen as being a very novel experiment! How times change!

Then there was *Mies Julie*, an African adaptation of Strindberg's vicious and angry play, directed by Shariffa Ali, a young African theatremaker.

Contemporary and intense, it really was a terrific interpretation of that terrifying text. It was depressing to have to recognise that surprisingly few women had directed at Classic Stage during the fifty years it had then been in existence, and certainly no Black African women! It makes me happy that we were taking some important steps. That production ran, again in repertoire, this time with Strindberg's *The Dance of Death*, again directed by a woman, Broadway star Victoria Clark. Two very different "takes" on two plays by the same great playwright.

Sometimes work can be hugely successful even if not particularly popular with an audience. One such at CSC was *The Cradle Will Rock*, a play in music by Marc Blitzstein. It was written for the Federal Theatre Project and was originally directed by Orson Welles. Set in Steelstown USA, it's a Brechtian allegory of corruption and corporate greed and there was no better time for Classic Stage to be doing a new production of it. The closeness of the audience made the political message of the play disturbingly powerful and impactful. The piece follows the efforts of Larry Foreman to unionise the town's workers in order to combat the powerful industrialist Mr Mister, who controls the factory, the press and the church. It is as terrifying now as it was when it was first produced in 1937. Interesting to note that the Federal Theatre Project was created during the Great Depression as part of the New Deal, in order to help fund live theatre in America. Their motto was "*We let out these works on the vote of the people*". It was a visionary project which sadly is now almost forgotten. *Cradle* is a vibrant piece of theatre. I think it's a good example of a contemporary classic – a play or musical that was written in a past century but which is still reading in a vital way for the modern audience, as if the text had been written only yesterday. I've always believed that it's my responsibility to have an effect, even if only on one member of an audience. One engaged and challenged viewer makes it all worthwhile. At least *Cradle* was seen and enjoyed by more than the two sheep!

A thrilling project was *Fire and Air*, a new play about the world of Diaghilev and the Ballet Russes. The late Terrence McNally was one of America's finest and most important writers, particularly with his commitment to writing about what it meant to be gay. He was a true artist, a wonderful friend, and I miss him enormously. I remain thrilled that we were able to stage the World

Premiere of his final play. Not so much a classic, but dealing with an aspect of classicism, this time through dance. There were many great actors in that small cast. It was the last appearance of Broadway star Marin Mazzie. It was led by the brilliant British actor Douglas Hodge. It also featured Oscar nominee Marsha Mason, muse of the great Neil Simon. The play dealt brilliantly with how dance and theatre have influenced each other, and also with the complex personalities of the geniuses who make great art.

My final production at CSC was possibly the most personally meaningful. *A Man of No Importance*. The one musical I will mention for now. Again by Terrence, with music and lyrics by the wonderful Lynn Ahrens and Stephen Flaherty. The leading role was played by Jim Parsons, one of the most famous faces on television. It's set in a church hall in Dublin, where Alfie Byrne, a bus conductor, is trying to direct his humble troupe of players in a production of Oscar Wilde's *Salome*. When the secret of his sexuality is exposed it would appear that his sister, played by the magnificent Mare Winningham, and all the ordinary people in his modest life, will reject him. I knew those people in this story. I could identify with the central character. I was once so afraid of what might happen if my gayness was exposed. It really is looking at "*the love that dare not speak its name*" and was a mirror up to nature – in this case my own. His family don't deny him, in fact through their shared love of the power of theatre, they embrace him. The world has changed – never enough but certainly in a positive direction.

I was sad to leave Classic Stage Company. I'd helped lead it through a terrible pandemic, which I will discuss at more length in a later chapter. I did all I could to guide the company through the complex journey that followed the murder of George Floyd, again more on that to follow. I managed, with the help of many people, to take it from a financial deficit to one of a humble surplus, which is not an easy task in a fundamentally unsustainable funding system. I look forward to watching how the company moves forward and am excited to watch it grow stronger and stronger.

I feel hugely privileged to be one of the few directors to have helmed companies within both the UK subsidised system and the US not-for-profit one. Totally different ways of working with Boards, funding bodies and indeed different ways of programming. Those very differences are exciting and I wouldn't have missed it for the world. So, if you're a young theatremaker and you think you might like to be an Artistic Director – go for it. Look what happened to me after a chat at a party all those years ago!

"Mission" is in some ways an empty word. The truly living word is "Vision". Yes, without it, the people perish. Without it there is no excitement, no enchantment. Without it the empty words of that Mission Statement are not fulfilled. When I was leaving the University of Georgia in 1974, my friend Michael O'Brien gave me a gift. It's a wooden board and on it are carved out the words "*The Sole Purpose of an Artist is to increase the Treasure of Light in the Universe*". It leans against a wall in my study and I look at it every day.

5

Thinking Out of the Box

For some time I've been intending to write about the development of actor-musicianship as I experienced it. I am frequently asked how it all began as I'm so often credited as the person who invented the idea. I'm pleased to have this opportunity to make it clear that I'm not!

From the Greeks and of course William Shakespeare, we know that live music has long been part of making theatre. You only have to read Shakespeare's texts, particularly the comedies, to see that music and song featured large. From the eighteenth century *The Beggar's Opera* through to the twentieth century *The Threepenny Opera*, the musical theatre has been developing and changing. Opera, Operetta, Vaudeville, Music Hall and Minstrelsy all made early contributions to the growth of this highly popular art form. I think it's fair to call it a people's art form, almost always accessible to everybody. To me, actors playing their own instruments is a very natural next step in the development of today's musical theatre.

As technology has influenced theatremaking, music and certainly underscore have become more important in plays. A director choosing their music for a show, rather like the soundtrack in a movie, has always been a personal artistic gesture. As a young director I was always pleased with myself if the music I chose for a play was commented upon favourably. We started with simple reel-to-reel tape-recordings, spliced together with unsophisticated sticky tape, then we introduced some live playing with the occasional flute or cello in the corner of the stage, and now sophisticated sonic treatments mean that recorded sound and live sound can be merged together to create magical atmospheric soundscapes. In today's rehearsal rooms, budgetary considerations permitting, there is often a composer present, collaborating with the director and the cast. This makes for a unique musical contribution to modern theatre.

I was fascinated some years ago when I directed my only movie and it came to the process of identifying and creating the soundtrack. The great composer Patrick Doyle – no relation but we did go to the Royal Scottish Academy together – had agreed to write the score. Pat and I sat down and watched the edit of the movie, "spotting" where the music might go, always with the intention of enhancing the atmosphere and therefore the drama. Then Pat wrote the score and it was recorded, in this case by an orchestra in Eastern Europe, no doubt because that was economically prudent. Then the recorded music was inserted into the edit. The score made the tone of the movie a different experience. Without them knowing it, music had an effect upon the actors' performances. The script of that movie was written by the late Horton Foote, one of America's greatest playwrights and film writers of his generation. His writing is, in its Southern tonality, already rather lyrical. Yet the underscore still enhanced it. The power of harmonious sound is often more potent than the spoken word. Music is in itself seductive. When I'm sent a script and a recording of a new musical for consideration, I never start by listening to the music. I always read the script first and if I'm drawn to the content, I'll listen to the score. If I start with the score, the music can so often coax me into telling a story that really isn't for me!

I recall another example of how music and spoken text can work together. I was making a new adaptation of Henrik Ibsen's *Ghosts*, that claustrophobic disturbing drama about a mother, her broken son and their hidden past. Ibsen was a Norwegian playwright, but I relocated it to a contemporary Scottish setting, as the power of the church within the play reminded me so strongly of home. The production was commissioned as part of an Arts Festival to be held on Orkney, where Norse tradition is very strong. It was a co-production with a Norwegian Theatre Company, and it was arranged that a young Norse composer/singer would join us. She would sing a form of vocalese, best described as a jazz vocal orchestration. She gave live accompaniment to the actors' performances, changing her score to suit each and every moment. When the idea was presented to me, I was somewhat sceptical. Was this going to totally distract from Ibsen's great text? Somehow she managed to instead make the vocal accompaniment expose the subtext of the characters. She became the sound inside them, the sound they couldn't make. My mother, who saw less than half a dozen pieces of my work and didn't express unnecessary approval of any of them, saw and loved this *Ghosts*. All because of the young musician. Somehow, she touched my mother's soul. I wonder if she knew deep down that I'd based my interpretation of the play's complex mother on her? We certainly couldn't have talked about that at the time and now it's too late!

That's what music can do. It can take us to a place that the spoken word, particularly in contemporary text, may struggle to reach. Even more so when performed live, raw and free of a studio recording or a sound console. Music is associated with the great ceremonies of our lives, weddings, funerals, times when words aren't enough, when perhaps the act of speaking is too difficult. Music binds us together and puts us in communion with each other, without our necessarily being able to intellectually articulate why. We enjoy watching live musical performance, whether it be in the Cathedral where I worship on a Sunday, at a classical concert, or of course at a contemporary Music Festival.

So let's take a moment to analyse the power of the actor making their own music. The actors in my movie couldn't do that. Their music was a storytelling support but not present in the action. Then of course it would have looked bizarre had that mother in *Ghosts* suddenly started playing the trumpet. That movie, that play, were naturalistic and the music was there to enhance. Enhance but always in the background, and almost always unseen. When actors make their own music in a performance it is indeed that – performative. It isn't behind the actor, but rather seen right there in front of them, the instrument being almost always on their person. The presence of those beautiful instruments means that as an audience you have to suspend disbelief. You have to simultaneously hold your belief in the characters in front of you, whilst watching in wonder as the actors support themselves with their musical talent. Or, better still, when they support the other actors around them. They are becoming an actor/orchestral performer, solely there to serve the story. Actor-musicianship gives us the opportunity to experience live music-making blended with regular musical theatre performance. I've been much quoted as saying that I developed it for economic reasons. That's absolutely true! I couldn't afford to do musicals any other way. Mrs Thatcher had almost won the day. However, what grew from those financial constraints was our own form of "Poor Theatre". As the Greek philosopher Plato said, *"Necessity is the Mother of Invention"*.

Let's go back to Liverpool, back to the Everyman, and back to that Board asking me to put on a musical! That *"I'll show 'em"* production of *Candide*. For any of you who know *Candide*, you'll know it's written by the great American orchestral composer, Leonard Bernstein, and is musically large in scale. It's also notoriously problematic and has been contributed to by many writers including Lillian Hellman, Dorothy Parker and even a young Stephen Sondheim, all of whom were trying to save it. Bernstein was seeking to write what he thought could be the "great" American musical. Its subject matter concerns how we all seek to experience the wonders of life's adventure, but at the end of the day the secret to our happiness is to stay home and make our garden grow. Pangloss, the philosopher in the story, tells his young students that *"all's for the best in this best of all possible worlds"*. Was America that *"best of all possible worlds"*? They believed they were creating the ultimate American musical – until *West Side Story* came along. Interestingly there are musical themes in *West Side* that were originally intended for *Candide* and vice versa. *Candide* premiered on 1 December 1956 and *West Side Story* on 6 September 1957. The former played seventy-three performances on Broadway and was deemed a disaster. The latter played 732 performances in its first Broadway run and is arguably the greatest musical of all time.

I've always been interested in re-examining musicals that were deemed not to work in their first incarnation. Always fascinated by the challenge of how to see what's there beneath all the criticism. *Candide* was the perfect opportunity. It requires a large cast and an even larger orchestra. The overture is one of the highlights of the popular orchestral repertoire. Heaven knows how I thought I could pull this off. It wasn't mere audacity, it was actually madness! Perhaps even career suicide! Economically it was obvious that I couldn't achieve the original huge scale of the musical in our converted church on Hope Street – no matter how much hope was involved. Maybe I could do it in a semi-concert version with a smaller cast and two pianos? Yet that seemed inadequate, not only for the score but also for Voltaire's original picaresque source material. Wait – maybe I could do it with the actors making their own music?

The early building blocks of this method of making theatre grew primarily out of work being made at London's Bubble Theatre Company. The "Bubble" is a highly successful company which at that time was working in parks and public spaces all around the capital. Directors Bob Carlton, Bob Eaton and my Liverpool predecessor Glen Walford had all been working with the company and there did seem to be a creative and spiritual connection between the Bubble and the Everyman. These directors had been using actors to make their own music, often in plays, sometimes in musicals and even in reinventions of Opera. Outdoor theatre provides the opportunity for the playing of instruments to be more obvious, more present in the storytelling. After all, outdoor theatre follows the traditions of the original troubadours who set up their wagon, beat their drums and stood you in a circle to watch their stories. Very performative, rather like the circus. The music was almost always rock and roll in derivation. It was joyous work and audiences loved it. In fact, one of the Bubble shows was the acclaimed *Return to the Forbidden Planet*, a whacky musical version of *The Tempest*, which transferred to London's West End and won the coveted Laurence Olivier Award for Best Musical.

I don't come from those rock and roll, Jerry Lee Lewis influences. I'm much more traditional in my musical tastes, probably rather old-fashioned. As I've already indicated, music had always been a part of my life, primarily Scottish music. The family made music together. I grew up in the ceilidh tradition. If you were in the room then you contributed, often with the support of a glass of whiskey. At Hogmanay, the Scottish celebration of the New Year, my family would gather around the sitting room and each do a "turn". My mother with a song at the piano, Dad with a mandolin, me with my school cello and my granny Doyle with her annual dance. Nothing made me happier than seeing this diminutive shy lady give her familiar rendition of *Knees Up Mother Brown*. Music brought us together. The sheet music in the piano stool was either from the movies of Judy Garland, who my mother worshipped, or from the musicals of Broadway's Golden Age – *Oklahoma!*, *Carousel*, maybe even *Showboat*. The vinyl records in the house were either famed Scottish singers, or inexpensive show recordings. *The Sound of Music*, *Guys and Dolls* and of course *West Side Story*. I now realise that these recordings were being purchased not so very long after those now classic musicals were being performed for the first time.

Music for me was in our home, not in the concert hall. Still somewhat rough and ready, humble maybe. That informal ceilidh tradition has heavily influenced my somewhat informal style of theatremaking, acknowledging the presence of the audience in the experience. Let me share a brief story about the power of "sheet music". These were piano scores of individual songs from shows and were much valued by those who sang and played them. I recall my secretary at the Liverpool Everyman telling me how as teenagers they would run down to the ships as they entered the Mersey docks in order to be the first to get the sheet music that had arrived from America. What a wonderful idea. Running to catch music. It's a long way from YouTube!

Back to *Candide*. I managed to put together a group of actors almost all of whom could play instruments. They probably weren't playing to the standard expected of actor-musicians today, but they could all contribute, even if it were only three notes on a clarinet. Catherine Jayes agreed to orchestrate the piece. We had two pianos, which were played by two fine orchestral piano players who weren't actors, though they were costumed like everybody else in the cast. They formed a musical root that meant even if everything else fell apart, we could keep going. Then there was a company of ten actors, most of whom could play something. The orchestration incorporated violin, cello, trumpet, flute and many more. Any non-instrumentalist actors would provide the percussion section and indeed that has continued to be part of actor-musician practice to this day. In the case of *Candide* the giant cymbals were rigorously banged together by our leading lady Elena Ferrari.

Allow me to take a moment here to write about the orchestrator and the process of creating musical lines for actors playing their own instruments. Don't forget that in those early days they often played in a somewhat rudimentary manner. Catherine sat for long hours working out how to reduce that great orchestral score to suit a few instruments, to be played by actors who might be able to deliver a few notes on a school saxophone! Orchestration, particularly on the revival of a musical, is sometimes a reduction of the original as that's hard to avoid. However it's often a totally fresh reinterpretation, as the different available instruments demand. Put something on an accordion and it's going to sound very different to a string section. I have been very fortunate in having had a series of orchestrators who are all real artists in their own right.

The orchestrator has to do a great deal of preparation before the rehearsal period begins. They can never "wing" it! They are providing the musical text for the actor, in the same way the writer is providing the spoken text. After all, in many cases the actors have to learn those notes and interweave them into their delivery of learned text. Catherine is wonderful at it. We had done a lot of work together, reaching all the way back to Worcester. She orchestrated all the musicals I had done there and at Cheltenham. Those of course were for "proper" musicians in an orchestra pit, who didn't have to learn the score and aimed to make music with a relative degree of excellence. *Candide* was going to be a big risky experiment, and thank goodness we knew each other so well, meaning we had a common understanding of taste and style. It also meant there was a lot of trust. In the early days the first whole week of rehearsal was spent learning the score, though not necessarily memorising it. I'm often asked why actor-musician shows take longer to rehearse. My usual response is "*You try it!*"

Other orchestrators with whom I have worked closely in the actor-musician world include Sarah Travis, who so deservedly won her Tony Award for our production of *Sweeney Todd* on Broadway. A marvellous musician, she could really get inside the heads of the characters. Kate Edgar, who had been involved in those Bubble Shows, fearlessly never took no for an answer and was totally enabling of the actors. Mary-Mitchell Campbell orchestrated *Company* for me on Broadway. It was her first venture into the form and she created the sound in the rehearsal room in a very organic and theatrical way. More recently Greg Jarrett orchestrated the Sondheim/Weidman *Assassins*, which was a band/actor-musician hybrid. It was exciting to see an orchestrator of a new generation, who probably wasn't even born when we made that *Candide*, join the team of people who understand this form in all its complexity.

We gathered together and started on *Candide*. I will forever remember that Saturday morning of the first week of rehearsals, when the company came together to play that famous overture. I listened, thought "*Oh God!*", went home and drank a bottle of something strong to dull the pain. As I said, the casts didn't have to memorise the entire score in those days. They almost always got up from their music, acted and then sat down again and played. They were forming a musical accompaniment, which only occasionally required them to play within their own song or within a scene. The instrument really wasn't an emotional part of the actor's story, but rather it was there to support. They were being actors who made music rather than actor-musicians. This is not to belittle their extraordinary skill, but simply to record what was expected of an actor-musician at that time. The form hadn't been fully developed.

Let's go back to that overture. The wonderful Olivier Award Winner Jenny Galloway was playing a character called "The Lady with One Buttock". Jenny is a huge talent, funny to her core, however she isn't an orchestral musician and the timpani part in the overture of *Candide* is hard for anybody! She would constantly go out of rhythm, putting herself and her fellow players on the edge of rehearsal room hysteria! I sat with her and asked if she could knit whilst at her timpani – perhaps hitting the drum at the necessary moment between stitches. After all, I could remember my mother knitting a complicated pattern, doing the daily crossword, watching television and holding a conversation all at the same time! Jenny was nothing if not game. She gave it a try. *"Knit one, pearl one, bang. Knit one, pearl one, bang."* It worked! She was no longer under pressure to play perfectly, so of course she played perfectly. Her timpani playing came from a character who knitted. She was approaching her music-making as an actor. I have so often said, actors who make music may be skilled enough to play in an orchestra pit, but very few orchestral musicians can get up and act. So in Liverpool in 1992 we were just beginning the creation of a new form of performer, the "actor-musician".

Candide was quite a hit. My aforementioned colleague Kate Edgar saw it and said *"The Actor-Musician Show has come of age!"* In fact I'm not sure we had even started calling it actor-musicianship at that point, but her quote gives you a sense of how things were changing. The Arts Council funded the production to go on a National Tour and so began the journey of taking this very theatrical form to new audiences who had never seen anything quite like it! Allow me to continue to focus on *Candide* and to share one memory out of many. The old church pews at the Everyman now formed the seats on each side of the thrust stage. I fought to keep those as inexpensive seats so that people who otherwise may not have been able to afford to attend could experience the stories we were telling. You could sit there for £1. So, as you might expect, we attracted young, excited audiences. The Overture has some really jaunty sections and at one particular performance, banks of kids in the pews started bouncing up and down to the rhythm of the music. They weren't at a stuffy musical written by a great American composer which was influenced by an eighteenth-century Frenchman. They were at "The Ev", a place they knew well, and they were having a ball. They were at their very own ceilidh. Typical of Liverpool, the word got out and we had bouncing for countless performances thereafter.

As I said, the Greek chorus played instruments, Shakespeare's actors made music, and indeed music-making has been intrinsic to live theatre for as long as is on record. Somehow though, the modern "actor-musician" remains a relatively new, almost threatening concept. Does it create a language of theatremaking that belongs as part of a living theatre, in the same way as dance, song, circus, jazz? Most certainly. Why do those who question this new form think that a "dream ballet" in a musical is OK but an actor playing a fiddle isn't? I do think that the form was more quickly accepted in the United Kingdom than in the United States, perhaps because America is the home of the musical as we know it today and challenging the form seemed somehow disrespectful? It is important to note that there was a very successful US actor-musician show, long before my work. The guitar-based *Pump Boys and Dinettes* was a huge New York hit, perhaps acceptable because it was rooted in country music as opposed to a masterpiece by Stephen Sondheim!

Since those early days, courses have been set up in schools and universities to train future actor-musicians. I'm proud to have been made a Fellow of Rose Bruford College, delighted that my own Alma Mater has courses on the subject and I've loved teaching the skills of the form during my Professorship at Princeton. These initiatives, and many more, mean that actor-musicianship is becoming a recognisable and acceptable part of musical theatre as we know it today.

Auditioning actors for these shows is complex. You have to check the singing ability, the musical ability and of course, most importantly, the acting ability. You have to be sure you're finding performers who will be able to put the work before themselves. You really need to be able to leave your ego outside the door if you're going to work in this way, which is not easy for everybody.

The ensemble is what matters. Playing the lead one moment, accompanying somebody on the flute the next, moving the furniture the next. I believe though that they do need to be actors before everything else, always playing the instruments from the point of view of character, and exploring the playing as a manifestation of their inner emotional journey.

A perhaps overused phrase in modern theatre is "thinking-out-of-the box". There's nothing new in it! Great practitioners have challenged the methods of their predecessors for decades if not centuries. I believe good directors find new ways all the time. Thinking afresh, they find ways of telling the stories they want to tell, regardless of challenges. Has actor-musicianship encouraged me to think out of that box? It's certainly been a major contributive factor. I get frustrated when people refer to it as a concept. It isn't a concept, but rather I would define it as a means to an end. Tap dancing isn't a concept in *42nd Street*. It isn't dancing that roots *A Chorus Line* but rather the story of dancers. The concept is the bigger picture, and it encapsulates the how and the why of the story you're telling, not the technique you are using as your storytelling method. I admit I've had to think away from traditional norms when staging actor-musician shows, as it encourages one to push against realism. After all, how many times do you see a Spanish Gypsy play a mean trumpet? You would have in my production of *Carmen*. How often do you see a Doctor play fantastic violin? Try my production of *Allegro*. Most importantly though, as a director the task is to create a world where these events take on their own normality, find their natural place. If you live in New York City, you constantly see people play their instruments in the street and on the subway, yet audiences find it challenging to see it happen onstage. Time will tell! Can you learn to think "out-of-the-box"? I think so. I think it goes back to "*What are you trying to say?*" And what does your situation allow you in order that you can convincingly say what you're trying to say. Instead of fighting the constricts of restrictions, try to see those restrictions as positive. Find a way! If you believe in it, you will do it! I think the answer lies once again in the imagination. As Alice Walker says, "*If you fall in love with the imagination, you understand that it is a free spirit. It will go anywhere, and it can do anything.*"[1]

York was the next home for developing the work I was to make with actor-musicians. My first foray there was a musical adaptation of the eighteenth-century *Moll Flanders*, written by George Stiles and Paul Leigh, a very witty script with music based on English Folk songs. What fun we had and in the fun lay the creativity! Through the fun we thought out-of-the-box. After all, most children have the desire to play, to have fun playing and so they are always out of that box. We need to listen to the child within ourselves. Eight actor-musicians made up the cast of this picaresque tale of a young woman's journey through life! It was set in a prison, the actors playing a group of period inmates who could make their own music. I can picture it now, Jeremy Harrison riding his double-bass as if it were his horse, playing it at the same time of course! That was only one bit of childish nonsense in a production that thrived on such nonsense – more child-like than childish! Our fearless sense of invention brought its rewards. I didn't go into the rehearsal room thinking I could solve all the problems. These marvellous multi-skilled performers could help me do that. *Moll Flanders* won the Best Production of a Musical in the Barclay's UK Theatre Awards.

It's worth noting that there were no sound designers on those early shows. We didn't need one as they were all performed with no microphones. This made for a raw approach to the music. It also meant that the players were totally in control of the dynamic of the sound they were making. We did many of those early shows acoustically and something in me liked it that way. It was less sophisticated, less refined, somehow more honest. I will admit though that when a great sound designer comes along, like my New York colleague Dan Moses Schreier, then something new happens that can be very exciting. He can treat the sound to give it more theatricality, placing the mics on parts of the body that pick up the best orchestral quality. As an example, a clarinet mic being on a wrist whilst the same actor's vocal mic is on the forehead, meaning that voice and instrument can be separated and balanced accordingly, not something that's possible when it's acoustic. The fight for and against perfection is an ongoing tension in all of my work, in an effort to keep it as alive as is possible.

Moll Flanders heralded a series of actor-musician shows at York, always under the happiest of circumstances. Perhaps the relaxation of being in that beautiful city, and not having the pressure of going home to balance the budgets, meant that a freedom of energy could flow in the rehearsal room. *Cabaret*, set within the confines of a Nazi Concentration Camp, was heavily influenced by the Orchestras that played whilst people went to their death in the gas chambers. *Pal Joey* was perhaps a less successful attempt at trying to find a way of doing a very problematic musical, less successful because I made a crucial mistake. I had the instruments being played in silhouettes behind windows on the set, which looked like rather beautiful jazz prints, but the lack of connection between instrument and audience was in fact detrimental. For my York finale, I directed *Into the Woods*. In many senses this wonderful Stephen Sondheim/James Lapine musical is the perfect playground for the actor-musician. It's already full of fairy tales, already whacky and out-of-the-box, already has the childlike at its core, and is certainly more Chagall than Rembrandt. The piece really felt like it worked with the actors playing, and I saw the potential for the abstract in how the instruments could be utilised. The first act was all done on a revolving stage, with cartoon backings. In the second act, the revolving stage had broken down and the instruments became the visual language that formed the glue of the storytelling, as if they were what the actors were left holding on to out of the chaos around them. *Into the Woods* was a very happy conclusion to my body of work in York. Talking about Chagall, I often find myself referring to his work and using it as a stimulus in my work with actor-musicians. His fiddler flying through the air was a major influence on Peter and Wendy flying whilst playing their cellos in my production of *Peter Pan*.

Leaving York felt freeing. My private life was happy. My husband Robert and I had a nice home in Hastings on the south coast of England, "*By the Sea*" as Mrs Lovett sings to Sweeney. It felt like time to start slowing down a little. And then one fateful day I had a call from a colleague I'd worked with once before, at her lovely Watermill Theatre in Berkshire. The Watermill is just as it says it is. An old mill, converted into a theatre space, with the stream still running under the building. There are ducks in the garden and swans in the river. An English idyll, recorded in the Doomsday Book. Jill Fraser was the Artistic Director who made that call. Boy did she open a door! She had, unbeknownst to me, been following my work with actor-musicians. Ever alert and ever inventive, perhaps even opportunistic, she wanted some of that work in her lovely theatre. I was only too happy to join her on the journey. Now in fact I did have a relationship with Jill's theatre that went back even before her tenure. I worked there, directing a series of plays, in the summers of 1981/82 whilst being the Associate at Worcester. My memories of that time include a performance of an Alan Ayckbourn comedy. The audience members were very close and even sitting above the stage on the side. A lady had her shoe dangling from her foot in a very relaxed summery manner. The actors were playing a little tea scene just below. You guessed it! The shoe fell into the middle of the tea table. Typical actors, they simply carried on as if nothing had happened. You live on site at the Mill, a little bit of a summer camp vibe. I remember long balmy evenings out by the Mill Pond after the show, brave colleagues diving into the water! I remember puppies being born in one actress' bedroom. I could go on and on. Suffice it to say, I was happy to be back.

Our first venture was a new production of *Cabaret*, that masterpiece by the great John Kander and Fred Ebb. Little did I know that years later I would direct their last Broadway show. Jill was interested in changing the seating layout of her space, so we made the production in-the-round. An unconventional and challenging way of presenting a musical, but one which created another opportunity for reinvention and theatrical freedom. The music was all around the audience, who were in very close proximity to these wonderful performers in this remarkable piece. People talk about Immersive Theatre as if it's something new. It really isn't. The audience being within the story has been there forever.

Being believed in, and being given the freedom and support to do one's work, is invaluable for any artist. Everybody needs a Jill Fraser. Sadly she's no longer with us, but her legacy lives on. She was one of those rare producers who truly knew how to produce, supportive whilst being challenging, giving you freedom, whilst creating safe boundaries. Had she not come into my life, it is quite likely that I would have ceased making actor-musician shows. Without our mutual body of work, Broadway may never have seen this multi-skilled form of theatremaking. Who will ever know? Anyway, there was still a lot of work to be done before Broadway.

We rehearsed our shows in a small barn at the back of the theatre, even smaller than the minuscule stage where we breathed new life into so many big shows. Somehow there was nothing to lose. Feeling supported and with an audience that wanted to see our work, we felt free. It would be wrong to say that I didn't care, but I certainly felt care-free. We usually rehearsed for four weeks, bearing in mind that the performers were having to learn the entire score, apart that is from the piano players who were, at that time, always afforded the security of having the score in front of them. Let me give you an example of how complex the techniques are for an actor-musician. You could be playing a violin or a cello. You are playing a melodic line. However we also need somebody to sing the harmony part in the same song. So, you have to learn to sing that musical line whilst you are playing another, maybe even in a different rhythm. It's incredibly difficult to do. A good actor-musician will start by learning one task and then add in the other. I always think of making this kind of work as a means of fulfilling a number of tasks. As another example, let's look at the brass or woodwind players. Obviously it's a little harder for them to sing and play at the same time, however they could be asked to play a certain number of notes, remove the instruments to sing or even say a line, and then quickly get the instrument back to the mouth to rejoin the music. Beware the broken teeth that can occur! Then an example of how the instrument can be worked into the action, sometimes to disastrous effect. I was making that production of *Peter Pan* for Oxford Playhouse. All of the performers were actor-musicians. I had carefully worked out the Pirate Fight, involving the instruments as if they were weapons. It took hours to figure out and we built it up in slow motion until it became really quite impressive. We were doing a final rehearsal room run-through of the show before we moved into the theatre for tech. One of the pirates got a little over-enthusiastic and his cello was swept up in unrehearsed energy. I can still hear the sound of that beautiful instrument falling to the floor in three pieces. I share these stories to show how difficult it is, even though at its best it looks really easy!

A challenging area for me personally is the role of the choreographer in the process. I've worked with some extraordinary choreographers on non-actor-musician productions, but in the case of actor-musician shows I've almost always staged the movement myself. I've discovered as the rehearsal process has developed where the performers can or cannot move and built up the physical shapes accordingly. For me the music itself is the dance of the piece and I have no interest in infusing the complicated puzzle with "steps". That's not to belittle the skill of the choreographer, and not to say that there aren't directors who can perfectly work with more integrated dance.

I started to use the opportunity Jill offered me to create adaptations of known musical pieces. It helps if you adapt pieces that are out of copyright, and so along came Gilbert and Sullivan's *The Gondoliers*. Sarah Travis and I rewrote it considerably, Sarah giving it a wonderful jazz quality. I reconfigured the text into a modern vernacular, rewrote many of the lyrics and set it in the contemporary world of a North London Pizzeria. The eight performers each played two or three characters, so the evening was all about costume quick-changes and instrument swaps. It was a riot! So much so that it transferred to the Apollo Theatre on Shaftesbury Avenue, where we enjoyed a happy summer.

Then there were the attempts to reimagine more classic musical theatre pieces. Note I say reimagine not reinvent. These were great pieces and all I was aiming to do was take a fresh look. *Fiddler on the Roof* seemed like a perfect piece for this kind of theatremaking, a musical about a community where music would have been at the core of their very existence. The daughters sing whilst they clean house – remember my grandmother's sheets? The whole family sing on the Eve of the Sabbath – just like my own churchgoing, or even those ceilidhs. Art for a director is all about how you connect with the story you are telling and I had no trouble with this one. However, there was danger ahead.

A first hurdle had to be crossed when I was handed a large blue book, which contained the notation for all the Jerome Robbins choreography from the original Broadway production. You were legally obligated to recreate all his dance moves. I can still see that dreaded book and its blue cover! Well, we might have to turn a blind eye to that then, we're in the Berkshire countryside, who's going to know? In the same way that our brave Jill turned a blind eye to all the authorial contracts that asked her to guarantee we would have a certain number of musicians in the orchestra pit. There *was* no orchestra pit! We always hoped that when our work was actually seen, even by the powers that be, they would understand what we were trying to do. If we had abided by all those rules, so much would never have happened. Now, I'm not encouraging the breaking of those legalities, but perhaps there is a way nowadays in which they can be challenged? After all, this form of theatre is now much more understood. Open conversations can happen with the original creators to make sure that everybody is happy with what the process will be.

Sarah created a klezmer band orchestration for *Fiddler*, and I came up with a concept that happened around the Sabbath table. It started with a young woman, dressed in the style of the kibbutz, sitting at the table by herself. She had a lit candle on each side and a white shoe-box in front of her. From the box she took out photographs of her long-lost family. She picked up her violin and started to play that famous tune that the Fiddler on the Roof usually plays. This was Chava, the youngest of Tevye's daughters. As she played, her family joined her. The cloth on the table was the flag of Israel and each of the characters was dressed as they would have been at the end of their journeys. Yente the Matchmaker, now a rich Chicago lady, was in fur coat and 1940s hat. Motel the tailor dressed in the Auschwitz stipe – heartbreaking as we watched him sing his *"Wonder of Wonders, Miracle of Miracles"*. They were wearing their future. Again we performed it in the round, audiences loved it, and the critics went wild. Producers wanted to take it into the West End, and then the lawyers showed up. I was summoned to an office in London, told that the production would not be seen beyond the Watermill and it was only out of their generosity that they weren't banning it altogether! Where was the orchestra? Where was the Robbins??? The "Americans" must not know about this!!!

Fast forward to Broadway, 2005. *Sweeney Todd*. I had a call at the end of the show to go to Patti LuPone's dressing room. She wanted me to meet Joseph Stein. He had loved the show, and as he started to shower compliments it struck me that this was the book-writer of *Fiddler on the Roof*!!! Oh God! He said *"Have you ever thought of doing Fiddler this way?"* I swallowed hard and told him I indeed had, but that his "people" said that he, as one of the "Americans", must never know anything about it! He charmingly asked *"Can you come to my apartment early tomorrow morning?"* I did. On Park Avenue! I told him what we had made and shared the ideas behind the production with him. His eyes filled with tears and he said that what I was describing was his own family. His heart was broken. If we'd obeyed the rules I would never have had the privilege of sitting with Joe Stein on that autumn morning in New York City.

Other Watermill shows included *Piaf* – music is appropriate on the streets of Paris, particularly a haunting accordion. *Irma La Douce* fell into the same category. *Carmen*, after all it's about gypsies. *Pinafore Swing* was a swing-band

1940s adaptation of *HMS Pinafore*, as a follow-up to the madness of *The Gondoliers*. Then there was *A Star Danced*, a new musical Sarah and I wrote based around the story and characters of *Much Ado About Nothing*. Mentioning *Irma La Deuce* reminds me of a moment that occurred many years after the Newbury production. I was in a New York rehearsal room working with a lovely woman who was advising on the translation of a text. We got chatting on a coffee-break and she asked me if I knew the Watermill Theatre? She had visited it and saw a production of *Irma*. In fact she clearly remembered a particular moment when an accordion was used to represent the sound of the sea whilst the other actors sat on tables and pretended to use their instruments as oars of a slave ship. That very simple piece of nonsense had a memorable effect on her. She had no idea I'd directed the production.

Doing actor-musician musicals can most certainly create new opportunities for those shows deemed not to have worked originally. Letting go of any preconceptions of "how it should be done" is vital, stopping listening to the cast recordings and finding your own way in! To reinvent as well as reimagine. One such example was *Mack and Mabel*. I wanted to do a very stripped-down version of what is in fact a tough American story about human disappointment. A chair, a theatrical basket, a rough screen or curtain – these were the few elements used to tell the story. TV star David Soul played Mack and the wonderful Janie Dee was Mabel. I took a very "dark" approach, one that somewhat unsettled the show's composer Jerry Herman. It's one of the greatest scores ever written for a Broadway musical but is certainly the one that got away. Maybe its original audiences weren't ready for it? Nobody had ever solved the notoriously problematic ending. Maybe our performative music-theatre approach could remedy the situation? Well, again the audiences celebrated it and we had requests to take it into London's West End. Jerry Herman came over from the States, and whilst a little disturbed, loved what I had done, except perhaps the bleak ending. Jerry was a delight. He was joyous and always had a twinkle. However, it seems to me that he lovingly wanted the world to be an unrealistically better place. Quite why he wrote a musical about a broken early-movie director and a silent movie actress who died of a drug-induced overdose, I will never know! He asked me to make some adjustments to my interpretation of the notorious ending. Could I make it happier than the one I'd made at the

Watermill, after all the final song was called "*I Promised You a Happy Ending*"? Somehow Jerry didn't see that he had written something that had the potential to be extremely ironic, sadder and more devastating if that irony is allowed to shine through. I think he was haunted by the critical reaction to the original Broadway run, which starred Bernadette Peters. Well, of course I made the adjustments that Jerry asked for, after all it was his musical. We went to London. It did well, but not well enough. Years later I worked with Bernadette and she and I occasionally have tea together in New York City. We laugh about show business, we commiserate about life and we call it "Tea and Sympathy". I asked her about the ending of that original *Mack and Mabel*. Her response: "*They weren't brave enough.*" Perhaps neither was I. I should have kicked back but, after all, he was Jerry Herman!!! When I was little I was always told that pride was a curse, but I'm certainly very proud to be the only director to ever have worked closely with Jerry Herman, John Kander and Stephen Sondheim.

The show that I most need to write about in detail is *Sweeney Todd*, the actor-musician show that I believe had the most profound effect on audiences and critics, and the one that truly established this as an art-form. Forgive me if I save writing about it until I write about the genius who created it, Stephen Sondheim. My two Broadway actor-musician shows, *Sweeney* and *Company*, both by Steve, established, perhaps even legitimised this new form on both sides of the Atlantic. For now, let me quickly share with you a few projects that followed those two productions.

The first was *Amadeus*, Peter Shaffer's wonderful play that centres on Mozart but is really about his rival Salieri. I was invited to make a new production of it at the now famous Wilton's Music Hall in London. Wilton's is the oldest music hall in the world, full of atmosphere including the cracks in the walls. I wanted as much as possible to integrate Mozart's music into the telling of the story. I chose to do it with sixteen actor-musicians, the set being the gold chairs they might have sat on at an orchestral concert. I wanted us to see what Mozart might have imagined. Once again Catherine Jayes orchestrated it. To hear that text suddenly erupt into a living version of the great C Minor Mass, in this extraordinary space that was built in Mozart's time, really was a thing to behold. How thrilling that Peter Shaffer was with us during the process. Even more thrilling that he loved it!

Ten Cents A Dance was a revue I created around the work of the great Rodgers and Hart. It started with a man at a grand piano, the brilliant Malcolm Gets. Out of the darkness of his past, the rest of the company joined him. Five women, all actor-musicians, playing the same woman at five ages of her life. The older woman singing to her young self and vice versa, somewhat thematic in my work, as was proved some years later with *The Visit* on Broadway. *Ten Cents* had originally enjoyed a UK production at the Watermill, being commissioned by the Cardiff Festival of Musical Theatre. I made a new US production, which played at Williamstown Theatre Festival and then at the McCarter Theatre, Princeton. It starred the great Donna McKechnie, one of the finest Broadway dancers of her generation. To hear Donna sing "Ten Cents A Dance", with younger versions of herself playing her music, was indeed a thrill. The *New York Times* Critic Ben Brantley wrote in his review "*a precise yet ineffable evocation of how we recognise music that was important in our lives*".[2] Ben always saw through the critical tendency to call it a gimmick or the need to see me as a one-trick pony, and was able to look deeply into my soul, for right or for wrong. An almost unique example of an artist and a critic figuratively dancing together.

Then there was my final show at the Watermill. Jill Fraser had asked if, after the Broadway success, I would come back to do the last show at the Watermill before she retired. She asked me well in advance and I promised her that I would do one more. Sadly she died before retirement came along. However, I kept my promise. *Merrily We Roll Along* felt like the perfect choice. A show about looking back. A show about people who seek a Tony Award. Ending with them as much younger people gathering on the rooftop "*where it began*".

Does every musical suit actor-musicianship? No. Please don't try *West Side Story*! If you are a director who is attracted to working this way, find pieces that either centre on a musical community, or that have music-making at their core. Find pieces that are in themselves challenging realism and even naturalism. This is a form that truly belongs in the theatre. It has been thrilling to watch other directors work this way. I was pleased and indeed relieved when John Tiffany so successfully directed the musical *Once*, as it freed actor-musicianship from being solely that "*John Doyle thing*"! It has been an honour to be central to the development of this challenging performative art-form and I'm excited to see where it goes next.

I was delighted when, quite recently, I was travelling on the New York subway. There were two young women sitting opposite. One had a violin case. Her friend asked her where she was going and what she was doing with her violin? She said *"I'm going to an audition. For an actor-musician show"*. I smiled. She had no idea who I was. Actor-musicianship belonged to her now! Looking back, I certainly had no idea that we were developing something that would have such a profound effect on modern theatremaking. I hate to say it, but – thank you Mrs Thatcher!

6

Why God Was a Woman!

On various occasions during my career I've found myself being drawn back to the Church, both in terms of my personal journey and also my professional one, though I suppose it isn't surprising that they intermingle. While I wasn't necessarily seeking to be a traditional churchgoer, I was being drawn toward telling the stories of Faith through theatre, and particularly in community settings where the casts are not professional actors. I myself have learned so much through these experiences, and have never failed to be surprised by the power of human engagement in storytelling.

It's important to say that I never sought the opportunities I am going to share with you. In many ways, they came to me, perhaps when I was ready to face the questions they forced me to address. It would be pretentious to say that these opportunities were in themselves a ministry. No, rather they were a chance to revisit my own faith through the interactive nature of my work. It's interesting to note that most of the events I'm going to highlight presented themselves once I decided I was no longer going to lead theatre companies.

On going to drama school I gradually broke my childhood pattern of regular church attendance. Going to church on a Sunday wasn't cool! Not that I ceased to believe, or at least I don't think I did, but rather I started to question the established institution of the Church itself. Did I want to be part of something where women were excluded, where sexuality was at question, where the basic message of "love one another" was so often interpreted in ways that suited the powers that be? In those student days I explored all sorts of avenues. I even recall one scary night in a Glasgow tenement when I joined a dozen women sitting round a candle in a darkened room invoking the spirits! Theatrical perhaps, but certainly not for me!

Now, as I write this, I do need to acknowledge that I once again go to church with regularity. I haven't found a better way of finding some understanding of our mortality and, perhaps more importantly, of our humanity. Interestingly as I've got older I've gone to the theatre less and to church more, and so it doesn't take much analysis to see that I need professional satisfaction less and spiritual exploration more! I'm not drawn to the sort of churchgoing that focusses on community spirit. I have no interest in the camaraderie of coffee club after the main event on a Sunday. I prefer a more solitary, quiet way of practising my belief through the power of prayer, and of good church music. I actually prefer word-based religious practices, enjoying the seventeenth-century language of the King James Bible. I have no interest in evangelising my Faith. Indeed I'm not sure I even understand what my Faith is. Perhaps that lack of understanding is the whole point? In a world where we need answers for everything, and as instantly as possible please, it's challenging to keep believing in the unbelievable, indeed in the inexplicable.

The Faith projects I've been involved in during my professional life have all been "By the people for the people". Theatre as a visible and personal means of exploring the religious story. Now, I have to be transparent and acknowledge that for me this means the Christian story. Not that I question or reject the other Faiths, far from it, but it's simply that the story of Jesus Christ is the one I know, the one I sometimes understand, and certainly the one I have looked at since my earliest childhood. I can't remember not knowing about the Feeding of the Five Thousand or about Mary on a donkey. So let's take a look at some of the theatrical opportunities that have presented themselves during my career.

During my Worcester tenure, 1984 to be exact, the Dean of Worcester Cathedral approached me to ask if I would put together a theatrical event to mark the 800th anniversary of the consecration of that beautiful place. By this point I had been in Worcester long enough to know a lot of people in the wider community. So I brought many participants together and we told the story of the Cathedral, in the central nave of the cruciform space. A Pageant is the best way of describing it. I don't remember all that much about it, can't recall anything about the rehearsals, and have no memorabilia pertaining to it.

Though I do remember being in the Pulpit, narrating the event! Nothing is more thrilling to me than theatre presentations that involve ordinary people – however one may define ordinary. Such events certainly bring out the extraordinary in the ordinary, a theme that has always interested me in the stories I like to tell. Let's assume that by ordinary I mean people who live and work in the community, teachers, factory workers, nurses, cleaners, all of whom want to come together to tell a story. Theatrically non-professional, but almost always fully committed.

The "community play" was becoming quite a national trend in the UK during the 1980s. As our government was trying, in so many ways, to fragment our communities, the theatre was doing all it could to strengthen community voices. In the United Kingdom, these plays tended to be about those communities, by those communities, for those communities, in order to better understand the history and contemporary issues of those communities. They were often researched and rehearsed over quite long periods of time, with the professional leaders of the project settling in the community. Frequently these were outdoor events, involving hundreds of people and having only one performance, making them unique and memorable to audience and participant alike. So, the Worcester Cathedral project was a very modest version of a community play.

Then there was religious drama in a professional setting. I mentioned that the Liverpool Everyman was situated between two magnificent cathedrals of totally differing architectural styles, one Catholic, one Protestant, in a religiously divided city. I was interested in making theatre that built bridges between those two places. So, at the Everyman, I directed a production of *The Nativity*, a modern adaptation by poet Tony Harrison of the *Wakefield Cycle*, one of the Medieval religious dramas first performed centuries ago. This new adaptation had been presented in 1977 at the Royal National Theatre in a thrilling production directed by Bill Bryden. It very much involved the audience, who were free to roam within the action, creating outdoor behaviour in an indoor setting.

These pre-Reformation cycles of plays told stories from the Old and the New Testament for people who didn't understand the Latin that was read in their churches. The plays were performed in the streets of a city, traditionally on the Feast of Corpus Christi. There were up to twelve hours of short plays usually presented by the trades groups of the city. The bakers would present one play, the carpenters another, performing them on wooden carts which acted as stages. They were called the *Cycles of Mystery Plays*, the Mystery being the Mystery of Faith, not the Agatha Christie form of mystery. Some of the original texts of the *Coventry Cycle*, the *Wakefield Cycle*, the *Chester Cycle* and the famous *York Cycle* still survive. Having been preserved in church libraries, these are amongst the oldest theatrical texts in the English language.

The Nativity was Part One of Harrison's *Mysteries*, and I came up with the idea of doing some performances of it in one Liverpool cathedral and then some in the other, finishing with a number of shows back in the theatre itself. A recognition of the fact that much of our existing theatrical symbolism comes from the Church. The altar, the pulpit, even the monetary collection, are all central images that have been inherited by our theatrical structures. The actors in our production were dressed in contemporary clothing. The plays were performed in regional dialects, in this case Northern, allowing the audience to listen to itself. God was a caretaker. Mary a nurse. And so on. We performed it in the round, circling a big factory-like structure, the top of which represented the caretaker's office, where God acted as a human CCTV upon the mortals below. The Catholic Cathedral in Liverpool, affectionately known as Paddy's Wigwam because of its teepee-like shape, had its challenges because of an inherent echo, wonderful for sung praise, but tough on words. The Anglican Cathedral is a huge quasi-Medieval structure, again causing audibility challenges. Yet both were spectacular visually and the juxtaposition of their magnificence and our humble staging was very effective. It was thrilling in all its incarnations and I'm hopeful that it helped in some way to bring communities, and maybe even churches, together.

As I said, the *York Cycle of Mystery Plays* was preserved and although the plays lay dormant for many centuries, they have, since the early 1950s, been performed every three or four years. I believe the tradition was restarted as part of the celebrations for the 1951 Festival of Britain. Interestingly, whilst still at school, the great Judi Dench participated in the plays, first in 1951 as the Forgetful Angel, then in 1954 as The Young Man in White Clothing, and ultimately three years later in the starring role of the Virgin Mary. It very much follows the pattern of the great German *Oberammergau Passion Play*, which is presented every ten years and which people travel to from all over the world. That version tells the story of the last days of Jesus Christ. The York plays, which exist almost in totality, were performed by up to forty-eight Guilds of workers, who each annually did their own same section of the plays. For example, the Shipwrights always did the Story of the Building of the Ark, the Goldsmiths did the Adoration of the Three Kings, and so the connections went on. From 1951 it had usually been performed outdoors, much as it had been in Medieval times. However in 1996 the governing body of the plays approached the York Theatre Royal, asking if they could mount the plays indoors in the theatre itself. It therefore fell to me, as Artistic Director of the theatre, to direct the project. The plays had been given a wonderful new translation by Scottish poet Liz Lochhead and the aim was to gather 300 people to be involved onstage, backstage et cetera.

The first task was to collect a cast large enough to perform in the event and so I set about auditioning. I always knew that, in the spirit of the story we were telling, nobody was going to be turned away. So the core of each audition was not to ask them to do an "audition piece" but rather to ask each individual the question "*Why do you want to do this?*" Checking their commitment was vital to the success of the project. There were going to be lots of rehearsals. There would be a three-week run of performances. It was going to be exhausting! We would audition some of their other skills, for example singing, dancing, but in fact standard was not our priority. Rather we were looking for enthusiasm, for what they could individually contribute to the collective whole. Should you ever be involved in staging a big event of this nature, allow for the fact that excellence is not quantifiable in the usual way. It helps if they can be heard, it helps if they can be understood, skills that with suitable support can be developed to an acceptable standard during the rehearsal period. More important is to assess their joy, the spirit they bring to the storytelling, and to bear in mind that they may know more about the story than you do.

I clearly remember one audition session when a diminutive lady dressed in black came into the room. She was gentle but strong, thoughtful but very much alive. Her name was Ruth Ford and she was owner of a local antique shop. I asked her our usual "*Why?*" question. Her response – "*I need to do it. My husband of fifty years died only a few weeks ago. I'm alone for the first time in a very long time. I need to be with people. I need to contribute."* No self-pity. No tears. Quite simply a joyous spirit. She left the room and I said to my associate director: *"If there's a God, then He's in that Woman!"* Oh, what a simple thought can lead to! I cast the role of God to be played by a lovely Yorkshire woman called Ruth Ford, and all hell broke loose! If you had met my maternal grandmother, you would have had no problem with the concept of God being represented by a Woman! Anyway, in no time at all the word got out. I was publicly deemed a heretic on national radio by no less than the Venerable Archdeacon of York. I received sacks of hate mail. I endured months of having a stalker, with no help from the local police department or from the mental hospital from which she had discharged herself. I was accused of being cynical and of casting it in this way in order to sell tickets. All because I met a lovely woman who I felt carried God inside her. I was invited to speak about it on International Television. Coincidentally a Georgia teacher of mine, Dr Jackson Kesler, with whom I had lost contact, woke late one night in his home in Kentucky, USA. He couldn't sleep so he turned on the television and there I was, on the roof garden of my London apartment, talking about God! He reached out by contacting the theatre in York, and we remained friends for the rest of his life.

The Venerable George Austin was forever on the radio. A contributor to BBC Radio Four's "Thought For The Day" programme, he was a prominent opponent to the ordination of women within the Anglican Communion. He found any way he could to voice that opposition and I was his new target. Bear in mind somebody actually asked me *"How could God be a woman?"* When I responded with *"What do you think God is?"* The response was – *"An old man with a long white beard!"* Really? 1996? Did this, I wonder, have anything to do with the Church of England struggling with the notion of a female priesthood? Only four years before, in 1992, the Church of England's parliament the General Synod voted, after nineteen years of debate, on the issue of whether women could be ordained. The motion passed by a margin of only two votes! The first group of women were ordained priest in 1994. In this context, the concept that the Godhead could be Female was simply too much for many people to bear! Dealing with the Rt Reverend Austin was one thing, but dealing with the general public was something else. The sacks of hate mail were amusing to begin with. However, some of the personal threats were really disturbing and so to stop reading them felt like a safer place to live! The obsessed stalker is best forgotten, other than to say that I hope such a thing never happens to you.

I do need to say though that, in one important personal way, I am very grateful to George Austin. A few weeks after he accused me of heresy on national radio, I was due to have a quick lunch with my old school friend Harry, the tenor from the Inverness Royal Academy. He said he knew a gentleman he thought I would enjoy meeting. They came to my apartment, I opened the door and Robert, the new gentleman, recognised my voice from the radio. Himself a committed Christian, he'd thought "*I'd like to meet that man.*" So, thanks George! You'd probably be appalled that you brought together two middle-aged men who would go on to marry and share their lives. There really is a God!

I asked the talented Mark Bailey, designer of the project, if he would base his set on the Salvador Dali painting *Christ of St John on the Cross*, and he did a wonderful job. The cross was set into a beautiful wooden floor and at the key moment, it raised up out of that floor and leaned out toward the audience, just like the cross in the painting. The extremely brave actor playing Christ was suspended above their heads, and that audience was pretty stunned. Looking back, I now realise that hugely inspiring painting was the first piece of visual art to have an impact upon me. For years it was housed in the wonderful Kelvingrove Art Gallery in Glasgow. I visited it with regularity on lonesome student Sunday afternoons. Much of my work has been influenced by art. Chagall influencing the actor-musician work, the paintings of Paulo Uccello influencing *The Wars of the Roses*, the list goes on. I almost always start from the visual, so give me a gallery over a library any day. Above the floor of Mark's set was suspended a giant fluorescent halo, and many of the scenes happened within that beautiful circle. The *York Cycle* covers the Old and the New Testaments, making some scenes quite complicated to reenact. Adam and Eve, Abraham and Isaac, these are just two of the challenges of Part One of the evening. Part Two has many of the more familiar stories, focussing on the crucifixion and the resurrection. I particularly remember one beautiful scene between Mary Magdalene and a gardener she meets outside the empty tomb. Of course that gardener is the risen Jesus. It's human, very moving and full of majestic language. Another wonderful moment is the Last Supper, an image familiar to so many, particularly from the great Renaissance painters.

Theatre, particularly theatre in the community, really can change lives. Directing large numbers of people toward a common goal is exhausting, overwhelming and, ultimately, thoroughly inspiring. A simple, perhaps spiritual, idea can go worldwide, without you even seeking for it to do so. However, more important is what it can do for the individual. Let me share with you the story of one young man, probably in his late teens, who bravely came along to those auditions. I asked him the "*Why?*" question. He responded with great honesty and vulnerability. "*I need to do it. I find it so difficult to make friends.*" I looked at his hands. They were covered in psoriasis. I cast him as a disciple. I believe he played St Peter. After all, those twelve ordinary men were all a little broken, searching for a new way, a new life. How that young man flourished. I will forever remember him at the closing night party. There he was, dancing with his cast-mates. I looked at his hands and they were totally clear! Maybe theatre can perform miracles? Whatever happened to that young disciple, I hope that now, almost thirty years later, he remembers that evening as much as I do.

If you ever want to direct a big community project, you have to be super-organised, you have to surround yourself with the support of terrific collaborators, and you need to befriend a lot of people. Only recently, I had an email from a cast member telling me how much the experience had meant to him. We hadn't connected for all these years, yet there will always be the spiritual connection of having told a great story together.

I was leading an audience/actor talk-back after one of the York performances and when it finished, an elegant lady came up to speak with me. I'm usually the first out the door after those events, but luckily she got to me in time. Her name was Sue White. She was in fact the mother of two very talented actor-musicians, Jeremy Harrison and Rebecca Jackson. Jeremy, who had ridden that double-bass horse, was in many shows at York and Newbury and went on to direct the actor-musician programme at Rose Bruford College. Rebecca and I have worked together many times. She played Yente the Matchmaker in *Fiddler on the Roof*, the Beggar Woman in *Sweeney Todd*, and she was in that final

Merrily We Roll Along at the Watermill. Somehow though I hadn't met Sue until this moment. She was a lecturer at the drama school in Coventry and here she was inviting me to direct the *Coventry Cycle* in the ruins of Coventry Cathedral. Was I really ready to do another big event so soon, especially after the impactful nature of the York plays? Anyway, I liked Sue, who is sadly no longer with us. She was a fine teacher, great fun, very driven and became a really good friend. I said yes!

Coventry is a city in the Midlands. As home to the British Motor Industry, it had been badly bombed during World War Two. On the night of 14 November 1940, much of the historic centre of the city was destroyed, including its beautiful Cathedral. A new cathedral was built in 1962 and behind the altar is one of the world's largest tapestries, designed by artist Graham Sutherland. It magnificently represents *Christ Rising in Glory* and was woven on a 500-year-old loom. Benjamin Britten wrote his glorious *War Requiem* to be played at the consecration of the new cathedral. The bombed remains of the old church sit just outside the door of the new one, as an eternal reminder of the horrors of war but also as a site of reconciliation and the need for all of us to forgive. It was in this ruined sanctuary that we performed our plays.

This presentation was more modest than the York plays, but no less thrilling. The stories told were only from the New Testament and the ancient language of the *Coventry Cycle* felt oddly familiar. It sounded like Shakespeare! Of course it did, Stratford-Upon-Avon is only a few miles from Coventry. I have no doubt that he saw the plays and may even have stolen a line or two! The cast again involved young and old, pupil and teacher, with the students from the drama school forming the basis of the cast. Their presence made scheduling easier as I could work on their scenes during class time. A few of the older participants had even survived the bombing of that terrible November night in 1940. I remember one elderly lady in the cast telling the younger members how, when she was their age, she remembered the morning after the bombing raid. She opened what remained of her front door and everything around her was flattened. Sadly the 1945 bombing of the beautiful city of Dresden, a joint British and American attack, was partly in retribution for Coventry. Two beautiful cities destroyed because of man's inhumanity to man. A past that could be very present in our telling of the Christian story.

Taking the event of the plays outdoors was interesting, and of course it had to be short because of the lack of evening light. Voices had to be bigger, with no amplification, which perfectly suited the strong virile nature of the language. In fact we started the plays inside the modern Cathedral and processed into the Medieval one with the whole audience following, which was really rather moving. I also remember one very special moment near the end of the evening. There's a large cross mounted on the stone altar of the ruined Cathedral. The cross was created from two fallen charred roof timbers, bound together and placed on an altar built from the rubble of that destruction. They have been there ever since. On the wall behind the altar are movingly carved the two words *Father Forgive*. Our young actor who was playing Jesus Christ climbed onto that stone plinth in the penultimate scenes of the plays and was theatrically crucified on that charred cross. Unforgettably, that terrible wartime event was informing the reenactment of another terrible event, an event that, in many senses, changed the Western world.

In tandem with the Cathedral version, I also directed a truncated presentation of the plays, the cast of which were inmates in a nearby prison. The prisoners in the facility had helped the Coventry project. In their well-equipped workshops they made huge banners which we used in the outdoor production, banners based on religious art painted by my husband. Now it's probably obvious to state that the prisoners couldn't come out to see their work in action, though it did make me sad that it wasn't in some way possible. So I suggested that I would go into the prison, with a few of our student cast members, and we would rehearse their own version of the plays. We rehearsed in the chapel of the prison. Me, the young students and a group of twenty inmates. We put together a shortened and very accessible staging of some of the story. No costumes! No props! Nothing was allowed to be brought in. Being locked into a room to make theatre is fascinating. I never enjoyed that metal door banging shut behind me, nor did I like the sound of the key, but working with the prisoners was a remarkable experience. I know that I certainly got more from being with them than they ever got from being with me. Their knowledge of the Bible was intense, after all each cell had its own *Gideon Bible*. Like so many people who have little opportunity for outside stimulus, their imaginations were rich. There is one moment which has stayed with me and influenced everything I have done since. I asked the question *"We have no props, no pieces of wood, how are were going to indicate a cross?"* Without hesitation, a prisoner said, *"That's easy."* He quickly went to another prisoner and told him to turn around so that they could stand back to back. He then put his arms out like a cross and asked his fellow prisoner to do the same. Next he entwined his arms into the other's arms and dragged his partner along as if he were a living cross. The imagination conjuring a human representation of what is the core of the Christian story. You see, with a rich imagination, you don't need "stuff" to help you communicate a theatrical truth. We only did one performance in the prison, with 300 fellow inmates making the audience. I thought – *"What's going to happen here?"* Suddenly the big Black guy playing God walked forward. He pointed at his fellow inmates and said: *"This is our play. I'm going to be playing God – so shut up and enjoy the show! Or else!"* Much more potent than *"Turn off your cellphones!"*

It was around this time that I was invited by the International Salvation Army to become an arts consultant to their work in the United Kingdom. This included advising on various projects, but primarily it involved creating and directing their annual carol concert in London. I did this for the next ten years. I had no previous experience of the Army – and an Army they certainly are, with a deep commitment to Faith within the community. They have always used song and brass band music to convey the Christian story, originally in outdoor settings. So much love for the Salvation Army meant that actors, broadcasters, politicians would seldom turn down an opportunity to be involved in these high-profile concerts. Each year I would try to find a fresh way of bringing the familiar Christmas story to life, working with choirs, young music groups, celebrities, the International Staff Songsters and the International Staff Band in venues such as Wembley, The Royal Festival Hall, Methodist Central Hall and for a number of years the majestic Royal Albert Hall. I would travel to each group in their own venue to rehearse. Together we would find ways of making that story and the music that celebrated it come alive. A good time was had by all, including the audiences of up to 5,000 people who attended on any one occasion.

In 1999 I was commissioned to write and direct a 1,000-person version of the Mystery Plays to be performed in London's Greenwich Park on Good

Friday of the year 2000. It was to be a key component in the city's Millennium celebrations, with many South London churches and religious groups working together. Greenwich Park is a beautiful public space, famous for the Greenwich Prime Meridian International Time Line running through it. The event was to be for one performance starting at noon on Good Friday and finishing at 3.00pm, the apocryphal time of Christ's death. A cast of 1,000 with only one professional actor, Ben Thomas, who played Christ. Ben was an actor of colour who had been in that *Antony and Cleopatra* at the Liverpool Everyman, as well as playing Orlando for me in *As You Like It* – the one with the beards!

It goes without saying that it would not be possible to direct all those people in one space at one time, at least not with any degree of humanity. Nobody wants to direct using a loudhailer! So I split the cast into sections, each section fulfilling a different part of the story and only coming together for large communal moments, which we would rehearse on the morning of the performance. Scary! For the first part of the event, there was a series of stages encircling a central platform. A different story or parable was told on each stage by a pre-rehearsed group. The plays were all timed to perfection, seven minutes, with each group reenacting one of the Miracles in different theatrical forms. After the seven minutes, a bell rang and the audience moved on to the next stage until each audience member had seen all the plays. These different stages meant that each group didn't have an overwhelming rehearsal commitment and allowed for already existing groups to be involved. As an example, the Jewish Dance Group, whose contribution was to tell the story of the *Wedding at Cana of Galilee* in dance.

Once all the Miracles had been reenacted the audience turned toward the central platform, where some of the company acted out the story of the Crucifixion. In a very festive atmosphere, with ice cream vendors and food stalls available to keep everybody going, the audience were encouraged to join in, that encouragement being supported by the actors from the earlier plays, who had by now joined the audience. Placards were held high with the audience's text on, and to hear all those people yell "*Crucify Him!*" was pretty chilling.

Eventually Ben bravely climbed the enormous ladder sculpture, which had been present all the way through our celebrations. It was really tall, and was a slow climb for a man who had been beaten and tortured. Ben hung there, simulating Christ on the cross. The weather, always a feature of any British outdoor event, had been fine. However, gradually during the Crucifixion scenes it clouded over and truly, at 3.00pm, as Christ died on the cross, the skies opened and there was thunder. Nature, being much more powerful than any planned stage effect. There was Ben up there with all the vulnerability of the original character in the story, soaked by the rain and very much alone. A band struck up and the crowd started to sing "*Were You There When They Crucified My Lord?*" During their singing they were encouraged to leave the park by various exits, led by all the cast members. All that is except Ben Thomas. They were leaving Christ alone in the rain. I will remember it as long as I live.

Next I was invited by my college friend Charlotte Headrick to join her in Corvallis, Oregon. There I did another version of the Crucifixion story, the role of Jesus played this time by a woman. Diverse reactions to the staging of a Faith story will never end and that's exactly how it should be. For those of you interested in participating in community events, I highly recommend it. To the actor, the shared experience can be life-changing, perhaps in a genuinely authentic way. For those interested in directing for the community, my best advice is to figure out what you want to get across, don't worry about it being perfect, gather together as many age groups as you can and relish them making theatre together. Of course your success lies in your schedule, which will give you the structure that will mean everybody knowing what they are doing and what is expected of them at any point in time. It will also provide the reassurance that you will need in terms of getting through it. If you think you can get through it with no panic, then you bring a smile to my face.

Most recently I directed a musical version of a particular moment in the lives of the Twelve Disciples. *The 12* rehearsed at the 42nd Street Studios in New York and was performed at the delightful Goodspeed Opera House in Connecticut, with professional actors. The musical had a beautifully crafted book written by Robert Schenkkan and a contemporary score by Neil Berg. I designed it to be set in a modern homeless encampment, and it had a musical score that felt both angry and very beautiful, just as the story requires. Our cast was totally integrated racially, Mary the Mother being played by the wonderful

Rema Webb, who had appeared for me in *The Color Purple* on Broadway. I aimed to turn that homeless shelter into a series of Renaissance images, which I'm hopeful we achieved. When audience members entered the theatre they were dismayed by the broken mess of a set they saw waiting for them, but the power of the story always captivated and they were straight on their feet at the end. It was another profound and humbling experience. The story eventually allows that Mary Magdalene is the Twelfth Disciple. A few years before, we had women being ordained – and now one of them was being honoured as a Disciple! Thank God for the theatre!

I sought none of these projects. They all found me. Was this what I was meant to do? At one career crossroads in my mid-forties, I decided I'd had enough of this play-acting nonsense and seriously contemplated becoming a social worker, or even finally going to that university to read Divinity. It was a dark time in my life, a time when my vulnerability could certainly have taken me on a quite different trajectory. One day a colleague invited me out for a coffee and, out of the blue, she said "*You wanted to be a Minister didn't you? You think maybe you should still do that? Don't! You can do it through the way you make theatre and through the kind of theatre you make!*"

7

Then Along Came Steve

I hope it doesn't appear sacrilegious to take you from a spiritual God to the God of the American Musical Theatre, but here goes.

It was that night in early November 2005. That moment of sitting beside Stephen Sondheim on that old Broadway radiator. That night which, in many senses, changed the course of my theatrical journey. Here I was with the guy who had been my hero, as he was for so many artists of my generation. Here I was beside arguably the "Shakespeare of our Times". The man who created the musical personalities of Dot and Desiree and Fosca and of course Mrs Lovett. It was the night that would give New York a new Nellie Lovett and a new Sweeney Todd. One described by Terry Teachout in the *Wall Street Journal* as *"an event that theatregoers will be talking about for years to come"*.[1] First, though, let's go back a couple of beats.

To 2003. Gosh, more than twenty years ago. Jill Fraser at the Watermill asked me if I would do a musical in the early Winter of 2004. Well, nobody wanted to go down to the Watermill in the Winter! The beauty of the English Country Garden is somehow diminished by the bleakness of January and February. Worse still, Jill wanted me to do an actor-musician production of *Sweeney Todd*. I thought she'd finally lost her mind. Bear in mind this was one of the last musicals I'd done in a "traditional" fashion. It's a masterpiece, sublimely complex in every way, and perhaps shouldn't be done by actors playing the score. I came up with every excuse in the book, but when Jill said that it would help get the theatre out of a challenging financial situation, and bearing in mind that I knew by this point that my dear friend was battling the terrible cancer that would eventually take her from us, I said *"Yes"*. After all, it was a very limited run, at a tricky time of the year, and it would soon be over and no harm would have been done.

As I anticipated, the casting process was challenging. Sarah Travis was going to need skilled performers to provide a wide range of orchestral instruments. The theatre could only afford a cast of nine performers, so at least two of them would have to be terrific piano players. We would need a double-bass, as one almost always needs the musical root that particular instrument can provide, and then representatives of each family of the orchestra. I was going to need wonderful actors who were also able to sing that extraordinary score. At one casting session, a young woman came in to play her cello. The cello is the perfect instrument for an actor-musician show. It's beautiful to listen to, beautiful to look at, and relatively portable. She could play Joanna, Sweeney's long-lost daughter. There was the slight problem in that Rebecca Jenkins had long dark hair, yet the script demanded her to be blonde, and of course we weren't going to be able to afford wigs! It interested me that, in post-show talk-backs after performances, audience members were challenged by her sitting atop a coffin playing her cello, yet they had no problem with a dark-haired Joanna, even though everybody sings about her having blonde, even yellow, hair. Immediately after her audition, a young man, David Ricardo-Pearce, was next in. He had a lovely tenor voice and another beautiful cello. He could play Anthony, the young romantic sailor in the piece. Two lovers with two cellos was going to give lots of opportunity for wonderful theatrical imagery. This style of work requires that you cast against "type" so our Beadle, usually characterised in a rotund "Mr Bumble" manner, was played by Michael Howcroft, a slim young man who played a fine double-bass and could look a little scary in the right light.

A challenge arose in finding a Pirelli, the fellow barber who challenges Sweeney to a competition, the character being an Italian operatic tenor in style. We needed a male singer with a very high voice who could play the accordion. The accordion is one of the most versatile instruments for this way of working, it being after all a walking keyboard. Now, it was, as I said, the winter. The time of year when the TV shows did their casting, known in the profession as "pilot season". Many male actors, for whom there was more television work at that time, didn't take theatre jobs during those months. And anyway, none of them wanted a freezing cold season at the Watermill for not much money. I ran out of male possibilities and so decided I would cast the role of Pirelli as a woman, after all I'd set some pretty lofty precedents! I knew a terrific performer, Stephanie Jacob, who could sing it, act it and play the accordion – and as I said, it would all be over in the blink of an eye. So the casting was gradually achieved. Paul Hegarty, who I had worked with in Worcester days, would make a wonderful Sweeney and indeed he went on to receive an Olivier Award nomination for his excellent work. Karen Mann was an hilarious trumpet-wielding Mrs Lovett, Sam Kenyon a flute-playing Tobias, Rebecca Jackson a clarinetist Beggar Woman, and Colin Wakefield a stylish but scary Judge Turpin. Our band of nine actor-musicians was going to "Tell the Tale of Sweeney Todd".

As I indicated, money was tight at the Watermill during that season, so I volunteered to design the show myself. Set and costumes. I based the set on the UK's first Operating Theatre at Guy's Hospital in London. Do visit it one day – it's open to the public, situated high in a building that looks somewhat like a church. It has elevated standing levels all around the central surgery area, intended as places for students, and even the public, to view the work of the surgeons. It reminded me of that childhood cattle market in Inverness, having the same bleacher seating on steep steps. Now remember surgery was in its very early stages when that Operating Room was built. I do love that it's called an Operating "Theatre" in the UK. There was an audience, so a theatre it was. There was no anaesthetic. Patients were made ready in a small adjoining dressing room, and brought in blindfold. Amputations were performed by the barbers of Fleet Street, who were known to be the most efficient "cutters". There was a table in the centre of the room, and an enamel bucket at each corner of the table, ready to catch the blood. There were shelves in a dresser against the wooden wall at the back, containing the necessary tools of the gory trade. White coats, spattered with blood, hung on wooden pegs. There was even a sign asking viewers for silence. That room became the inspiration for the design. To me, the interesting fact is that I didn't plan to go there. Robert and I were driving by one Saturday morning. We had time on our hands and I suggested we take a look for the fun of it. We climbed the stairs, walked in and there it was. That chance visit would lead to a Drama Desk Award nomination for Outstanding Set Design.

I had approximately £500 to spend on the costumes. I wanted them to be contemporary, as I've always been interested in finding ways of taking classic stories and bringing them into our time and place. I came up with a series of visual archetypes parallel to the original characters. I found all the clothing for these characters in a Salvation Army centre for the distribution of used clothes. For some reason that clothing centre was in the middle of a field on a farm quite near the theatre! Mrs Lovett wore a short leather mini-skirt and knee-high stockings, somewhat typical of an East End market stall holder today. Judge Turpin wore an Armani suit that I found for very little money, a suit a judge at London's Old Bailey might wear today. In fact I'd only recently seen a High Court judge on television, very smartly and stylishly dressed. It turned out he himself was a child-abuser, just like the character in the musical, and was convicted accordingly! Toby, the innocent boy who helps Mrs Lovett, eventually goes mad in the piece. Once again I clothed him in his future, old hospital pyjamas, with bandages at his wrist and head, as if he had escaped from a Victorian lunatic asylum. What we built was a strange world that in itself could have been described as a house for the insane. The performers were theatrically locked in at the beginning of the evening. The room smelled of the carbolic smell associated with old hospitals. The dark table of the Operating Theatre became a black wooden coffin, the type that Victorians used to bury paupers. At the beginning of every performance, the lid was removed and the Sweeney stood up out of the coffin. A truly scary moment, though it had meant that our actor needed to be in that closed box for up to fifteen minutes, as the audience was coming in. There was no front curtain at the Watermill! He never complained, maybe because he could feel the effect it had when he stood up from the box. It's worth noting that when we transferred to Broadway the Union rules wouldn't allow for this, as the actor would have had to be in the coffin for much longer while we waited for the larger audience to take their seats. Also New York shows are notorious for starting irritatingly late. I designed a front curtain for Broadway, so he could get into the coffin just before the lights went down and come out not long after that curtain went up. Never quite so effective but certainly much more humane. One of the challenges in Sweeney is how do you cut the throats? In Hal Prince's brilliant original production they used prop blood knives, which, when squeezed, released blood. I couldn't do this, after all you couldn't get blood on a cello! So, that's where those buckets came in. At the moment of throat-cutting, which is progressively frequent in *Sweeney Todd*, blood was poured from one bucket to another. The sound of the liquid on that enamel was indeed a scary thing. Brecht meets musical theatre head-on. The actor was carrying out a simple action. Pouring liquid into a bucket. Something you might do any day in your kitchen or your garden. The rest was in the eye of the beholder. I clearly recall one performance at the Watermill. An audience member was sitting with her coat over her knees. As the blood ritual repeated itself that coat started to become a comfort blanket, and then eventually as she saw an actor walk once again toward a bucket, she put the coat over her head so that she didn't have to behold. Pure theatre. Yet she was actually doing all the work. Needing to solve the blood spattering problem had given me a way forward. Again necessity fired the imagination and the outcome became somewhat iconic. The fun fact is that I had been at a meeting in London about another project. Somebody at the meeting knew I was about to embark on *Sweeney Todd*. He casually said "*I'd like my Sweeney to have buckets of blood!*" His casual remark sealed the deal!

The rehearsal room at the Watermill was out of commission, so Jill had to find somewhere else for us to work and, of course, it had to be inexpensive! Newbury has a rather famous race-course, which doesn't function in the dead of winter, and where there is a typical British fish-and-chip shop selling food and beverages for the racegoers. It had an upper storage room and that's where we rehearsed *Sweeney Todd*. The one drawback? No heating! So I spent a hopefully creative month wrapped in blankets.

I'd like to share a couple of rehearsal moments that may interest you. The actors sat on black Victorian chairs lined around the "room". It came to the moment in the story when a new barber's chair was to be delivered. I'd omitted to solve this problem in advance. If I'm honest I prefer not to solve too many of the problems in advance but rather stay open to any inspiration that may come in the moment. It can be scary but I know of no better way, though I don't necessarily recommend this approach to new young directors. I'm unafraid of saying to the actors that I'll come up with an answer to the problem tomorrow, but that could lose their confidence if you're less tried and tested.

We couldn't use one of the black chairs as this special chair, as they were by now too familiar to the audience. I looked around the room – for some reason I remember that it was a Thursday evening – and there, in a corner, was a small white box. I think a white shoe-box. Was this the Sweeney equivalent of Grusha's pillow? I picked it up and asked our Sweeney to carry it as if it were a gift he had been given. Then, because of the way he was moving, I was suddenly reminded of television news images I had from my earlier life of seeing fathers, during the Troubles in Northern Ireland, carrying the coffin of their dead child. A child killed in those terrible bombings. Those coffins were always carried on the father's shoulders, the casket always an innocent white. So, our white box became a little white baby coffin. A metaphor for Sweeney's lost daughter Joanna. Sweeney would sit his next victim on that white coffin and cut their throat as the blood poured from bucket to bucket.

And so for another very different equally practical problem. The keyboard was placed on a shelf upstage. The piano players, a task taken by many members of the company, therefore had their backs to the singers. Of course, there were musical moments they had to see. Bear in mind actor-musician shows never have a conductor. The performers *feel* their way in and out of the music. They get used to one player giving a loud "sniff" to bring everybody in together musically. They have to listen in a very acute manner, but for a show as complicated as *Sweeney*, they needed a little extra help. I had found all the "props" that were on shelves on our back wall, all from my local junk shops in Hastings. I came up with the idea of using a Victorian "butler's mirror", one of those circular convex mirrors often mounted in the corner of sophisticated dining rooms, mirrors that aided the butler to see if the guests had finished a course and were ready for the next one. The same principle as the little mirror the organist used in my childhood church to help see if the bride was ready to come down the aisle. That mirror again became part of the iconography of the production. Some years later a university student sent me a copy of his final dissertation, which he had written about that mirror. Fifty thousand excellent words about how it reflected our lives, reflected our humanity or lack of it. Indeed the audience could see itself in the mirror, but the real function was practical. I wrote to that student and congratulated him on his excellent presentation. My problem-solving wasn't what mattered, rather it was what he saw that mattered. Theatre is an art form rooted in how we interpret, both artist and audience. Our mechanisms for interpretation are already within us and may indeed go all the way back to early childhood.

We were in our second of only two previews at the Watermill when a young theatre producer and entrepreneur, Adam Kenwright, came to see it. Quite what he was doing in Newbury in February I don't know! As he was leaving the tiny auditorium he said to me *"John, I'm going to take this to London."* Very nice Adam, but I'd heard it all before. Well – he did! After its run at the Watermill, the production went on a quite brief UK tour and then, following a short break, we reconvened to get ready for our London run. As I've already said, this wasn't the first actor-musician show to reach the West End, but it was the first time that the skills were used to revive a major musical theatre classic. On 22 July 2004, we settled down in the Trafalgar Studios, originally the Whitehall Theatre and now a delightful refurbished space run by the Ambassador Theatre Group and led by the inestimable Howard Panter, who has been a major force in British theatre. The critics generally approved, audiences poured in, and that theatre where my granny had taken me to see my first West End show was buzzing. Eventually we transferred from the Trafalgar to the New Ambassadors Theatre on St Martin's Lane, a beautiful intimate Victorian theatre that was perfect for the production. By now more than a year had passed and the company had been together all that time doing this dark, somewhat malevolent musical. Being together for too long can be a challenge for a company and whilst it remained joyous on the surface, in fact it was becoming less so underneath. We had started as an "ensemble" but the divisive moments of some being nominated for awards and some being overlooked complicated the situation. A theatre company can become a dysfunctional family and one can so easily feel responsible for it, just as I did for my own dysfunctional one. I now believe that no actor should tell any story every night for any more than six months. I know that would be financially challenging for producers and actors alike, but I do think it would be better for both the work and for the mental health of the participants.

It was at the New Ambassadors Theatre that Stephen Sondheim first saw the production. However I need to share the tricky phone call that preceded his visit. Steve loved to tell people that he and I didn't get off to a good start, and he was certainly correct! It was in my house in Hastings on a Saturday evening. Gin and tonic hour. The phone rang. "*Hi, this is Stephen Sondheim.*" I thought it was a joke and that one of my friends was winding me up. After a few minutes of nervous banter, all coming from me, I realised it was indeed Stephen Sondheim. Unbeknownst to me, our producers had sent him a one-camera video recording of a live performance the show – and, worst of all, they'd given him my telephone number. They were obviously seeking his approval in order to take the show beyond London. He'd watched this back-of-the-auditorium video and he wasn't happy! As the late Elaine Stritch would have told you, you didn't want the Steve that wasn't happy. He proceeded to tear me apart. Why did I cut this, why did I change that? All perfectly fair but very upsetting to receive. I tried to give him the context of where it had started and how little time we had to rehearse it, with almost no financial resource. His anger continued and, believe it or not, I started to cry. I was devastated. None of us want to upset our heroes. This was a once-in-a-lifetime moment and it was going horribly wrong. Then, quite suddenly, his tone changed and I heard the caring voice I came to know so well. He said "*You've been put in an unfair situation. I'm going to fly over to see the show!*" Indeed he saw it a couple of weeks later. I was sworn to secrecy by the producers, who didn't want any of the creative team or the cast to know. Not an easy situation for me, made more tricky by a chance meeting on the day he was to appear. I was walking through the foyer of the Royal National Theatre and there he was! I went up to him and somewhat tentatively introduced myself. He was perfectly cordial, but I think the "phone call" was a little too present for us both! Anyway he saw the show that evening, and his words to me were "*I had no idea! This is something that can only be seen in the theatre.*" And so, after a few twists and turns, that little production, which I hadn't originally wanted to do, was going to Broadway! Steve Sondheim brought me to the attention of the New York critics and gave me the opportunity to collaborate with artists who were at the very peak of their profession. Patti LuPone, Michael Cerveris, Bernadette Peters and many more are my friends because of Steve.

First though, there was work to do. I was flown to New York and a new group of producers took me on a tour of a number of possible venues both on and off Broadway. Was this real? We all agreed on the delightful Eugene O'Neill

Theatre. Next, I had to alter the design to meet the scale of its new home. No longer could we use the simple scale model that my husband, my daughter and I had built on my kitchen table one Saturday afternoon! This time I was being taken to visit highly resourced scenic shops, where the show was going to be built to last. Just as well, as that set was on Broadway for a year and then toured America for two years! Then I had to take the costume designs to one of New York's premier costume shops, where they would build the costumes. We'd come a long way from that Salvation Army store, even though the recreated costumes looked almost exactly the same as they did at the Watermill, just a great deal more costly! We had a terrific wardrobe supervisor who took great care of the costumes, but was used to Broadway clothes being custom-built to withstand the rigorous repetition of all those shows. The shirts I had originally used were from a cheap clothing store in London. This sent her into a state of shock. I was equally shocked by the proposed cost of getting each shirt specially made. I gently insisted she bought the shirts from a similar New York inexpensive store, which is what we did. A lot of money was saved and everybody was very happy. The complicated established rules of how theatre is made are a contributive factor in the prohibitive nature of ticket prices. Why are some Broadway producers being allowed to charge over $1,000 for a seat and who are they excluding in the process? At what point does the expensive business of theatremaking simply become an excuse for greed? Let's not kill the theatre. Let's find every possible way to make it accessible, with all its participants, writers, creative collaborators, actors, producers and, most importantly, audiences being given a fair chance.

I had to re-source many of the props for the show and have them shipped to New York. So it was back to my junk shops in Hastings. I can remember our excellent New York General Manager giving me a financial cash float of $15,000 to cover the cost of purchasing a new set of props. I told her this was far too much and she looked at me in bewilderment. This was Broadway, it was inevitably expensive. I dispatched the props from the UK and returned seventy five percent of the dollars. Eventually the props arrived and I went out to a warehouse in Queens with the Prop Supervisor to see that everything was OK. He laid them out on tables, we labelled them to check the inventory and then, because of the Union rules, I was never allowed to touch them again! The system is very structured, maybe even restrictive, even though it does quite rightly protect the individual skills of the Union members. Only the crew move the set pieces, only the prop guy touches the props. Because there was no prop person on the shows at the Watermill, I'd worked out a way for the actors to gradually replace them to their initial settings during the course of the action. This ritual became part of how we made the production – and it saved a salary. Well, saving the salary wasn't going to be allowed in New York, after all this was the business of show, so our excellent props guy had a rather easy year. Mixing blood and mopping up!

And then, of course, I had to find a cast. I had been so used to having a pool of known and experienced actor-musicians to choose from, performers who not only had the skills, but who also understood the methods used to make the eventual product. It was only when in auditions in New York City that I remembered going to the football game at the University of Georgia and seeing the marching band, a tradition that had probably come to the States from the streets of Italy. Of course we were going to find a cast. Mark Jacoby unpacked his trumpet, which he hadn't played since high school. This highly lauded Broadway performer nervously auditioned his musical skills. He went on to make a wonderful Judge. Alexander Gemignani is a true all-round musical star and played the perfect Beadle, more as a mobster than an as an elderly Victorian church officer. Interesting to note that Alex's father is Paul Gemignani, Sondheim's go-to musical director and conductor. Manoel Felciano, a terrific violinist who I later worked with in San Francisco, made a wonderful Tobias. Toby sings the famous "*Not While I'm Around*" and Mano went on to be Tony-nominated for the role. And so we assembled a wonderful musically accomplished company, all of whom were also wonderful actors. Orchestrator and Director were both delighted. There had been talk about letting me bring over two of the London cast for a limited part of the run, to help facilitate communicating the style of the work. The drawback was that we couldn't bring the Lovett or the Sweeney. The producers needed stars. It really would have been Sophie's choice to decide who to bring so I thought it best to start afresh. Now I had to find those two central characters.

Before telling you about that process, I'd like to share one auditioning anecdote. I was in New York in the early stages of the audition process. I was by myself, probably at lunchtime. Other shows were auditioning in adjoining rooms and an elderly gentleman came in. I asked him if I could help him? He looked at my list of who was expected that afternoon. I asked him if he was auditioning? He said yes. I thought him a little too old for our production but you never know! I asked him what instrument he played. He looked at me with a twinkle in his eye and I realised I was speaking to the late great Neil Simon – another of my heroes! He was indeed auditioning – auditioning actors for his next play, in the room next door to ours. I never met him again, but that moment was quite wonderful.

I should also say that for the first time the production was to have understudies from the very beginning of the process. Broadway understudies are a remarkable breed. All excellent dedicated performers with fine careers in their own rights. We found the four we needed, they memorised multiple musical versions of the score in order to cover every instrument required, they stayed with us for a year, and some of them went on to play the roles on tour, which made them, and me, very happy.

So. I was asked by the casting directors if I would like to meet the Tony Award winning performer Michael Cerveris. Michael and I met for the first time in the lobby of the Royalton Hotel on 44th Street. A short way into a very pleasant breakfast, I knew this was the man who should play Sweeney Todd. Charismatic, gentle and somewhat extraordinary, he had a "downtown" vibe. He had of course done the Broadway thing, playing the title role in *Tommy* and more recently winning the Tony Award for playing John Wilkes Booth in *Assassins*, but he was also a bit of a "rocker" and I just knew from speaking with him that he was a great actor. Star actors don't have to endure auditions as they've earned the right for their body of work to speak for itself. I didn't hear Michael sing. I just went to Steve and told him I'd met the actor who I wanted to play the role. In fact I told him during that drinking date at that bar in Joe Allens. He said *"Michael can do anything!"* That sealed it. Nobody, producers included, was going to argue with Stephen Sondheim.

Then Mrs Lovett. So many names were suggested because musical theatre actresses recognise Nelly Lovett as being amongst the cream of casting opportunities. I felt like I was meeting most of my CD collection! Our producers wanted me to meet Patti LuPone. Now bear in mind I didn't know any Broadway stars but I had certainly heard of Ms LuPone. She had originated the role of Fantine in the Royal Shakespeare Company cast of *Les Miserables*. She'd won the Tony for playing Evita on Broadway. She was a high-calibre Broadway star. What on earth would she be doing in this little production of *Sweeney Todd*? Especially in that leather mini-skirt! I was flown from London to Portland Oregon, which was a stop on her concert tour. I was to meet her at 10.00pm after her concert and had to get on the 6.00am flight back to NYC the following morning. I can remember the first moment of our first meeting. She was wearing a light raincoat, and didn't seem to project the temperamental star at all! She suggested we go to a local pub for a drink – or two! She told me of her years with the Acting Company, which followed her study at the famous Juilliard School. This was a lady who would get her hands dirty. I liked her – a lot. We walked arm-in-arm back to the hotel and stopped to look at a store to "window-shop" shirts for our husbands. Not only had I found my Mrs Lovett, I'd found a life-long friend. I called to check in with Mr Sondheim, who described Patti as "*a force of nature*". How right he was. She needed no follow spot. She fitted in so perfectly to that production. She is indeed a Broadway star! I'd like to share a couple of memories of Patti that happened even before rehearsals began. I went to a small studio in Midtown Manhattan to hear she and Michael sing through the score, to check musical keys et cetera, in case adjustments had to be made. The session was led at the piano by David Loud, who I would work with on many subsequent occasions. After the session Patti and I were walking out together. For some reason I remember it was a very hot day. I plucked up courage and said "*Patti, would you like to see your costume designs?*" I was terrified! How the heck was she going to react to that mini-skirt? Well, I needn't have worried. She saw it and shrieked out "*I love it!*" Then on another occasion we went together to Paul Huntley's Manhattan studio to have a fitting for her wig. And what a wig designer Paul Huntley was! Patti had the sense to always have him in her contract. He was a Londoner, a legend, a genius and we did many more shows together. He created a wonderful quirky wig, closely following what he saw on my costume designs. Here was one of the world's most famous wig designers trying to create what he hoped I wanted. After the wig fitting, he asked if I'd like to see round the studio. There were walls covered in photographs of famous actresses he had made wigs for, and one day I'm sure our iconic Mrs Lovett joined them on the wall. Paul was a unique and very amusing human being who sadly is no longer with us. I was so fortunate to get the chance to collaborate with the greatest.

And so we began an absolutely terrific rehearsal period, one I will remember always. Everybody worked so hard. Patti and Michael really joined in. Sarah did a wonderful job of adjusting the orchestrations to suit the players she had available to her. I recall one day Patti said *"Johnny – this could never have started over here."* I was a little surprised at the time. I certainly could see that the collaborative way of working, the need to all "muck in", the need for the actor to take full responsibility for every moment, to be an accompanist one moment and a star the next, were perhaps new experiences for these performers. They weren't being told what to do. It didn't have to be the same twice. It didn't even have to be good – it just had to *be*. A musician starts their journey from a place of excellence. They immediately aim to provide the perfectly tuned harmony. An actor starts from a place of chaos – at least a good one does – and eventually finds order and perhaps even excellence. Being an actor-musician means aiming to work with both those parts of the mind and to gradually allow them to meet in the middle. If you haven't done it before, it can be scary.

At the end of each rehearsal day, I did what I always do. I sat down with the actors and asked them how they felt about the work we'd been making that day, about their observations, their impulses, their concerns. I always ask if they have anything they want to say and usually go round the room accordingly. On this one occasion, Mark Jacoby, our aforementioned Judge, looked straight at me and said *"Do you mean you want us to forget everything we ever learned about the American Musical Theatre?"* Mark is the most delightful man, but in those early days he scared me a little! My response, *"Well, yes Mark. And – no!"* You could only do what we were doing if you discarded your preconceptions, whilst drawing upon all of your previous experience.

Then there were the technical rehearsals. Richard G. Jones was our lighting designer, who came over from the UK. Richard had designed lights for many of the actor-musician productions. Dan Moses Schreier was the aforementioned sound designer recommended by, in fact insisted upon, by Steve. Adam Hunter was our Production Stage Manager, who really took on the mantle of Associate

Director. We've done many shows together now, and I was even the lodger in his house for almost ten years. A perfectly balanced working relationship. We had a week of tech, for a show that only had a day at the Watermill. As I said the Watermill budget was tiny. Not so tiny on Broadway, even though it looked exactly the same! I must say though, for the record, the quality of work, discipline and craftsmanship that you experience on a Broadway musical is unlike anything you will ever find anywhere else. It really is the American art form, and they certainly know how to execute it. But there was fun too. During one long evening of rigorous technical rehearsal, when one marries the lights and sound with the work we had made in the rehearsal room, Patti was suddenly seen coming off the stage and making her way to my desk in the auditorium. She was carrying a mug – I assumed a very welcome cup of tea. It was only when I took a sip in the darkened auditorium that I realised it was a very strong gin and tonic! They broke the mould after they made that lady! She, her husband Matt and son Josh have become dear friends of Rob and I, and we have enjoyed many Thanksgivings and other family occasions together. She never forgets my birthday and is one of the most loyal friends a person could have.

Then we commenced the long Preview period. I was raised in the theatre at a time when previews didn't exist. You had to be ready at the first performance and of course the critics were there too! The two previews at the Watermill were considered a luxury. Forty was a whole other story. I must say I now rather enjoy the preview period. You gather as a company every afternoon and rehearse or make changes to the production. If these are big changes they may not go into the show that night, so actors often have to carry two versions in their heads until the new version goes in. It can be very productive and always leaves me totally admiring of what actors can tolerate during the building of a commercial production. It gives you time to test things out with an audience, and gives time for a build-up of word-of-mouth.

During the *Sweeney* previews, audiences were rather accepting of our modest production. They were loving seeing Patti back on Broadway. Now, I'll be honest and say that I prefer not to listen to an audience. There is much talk today about being "in conversation" with your audience. I'm not sure. By no means do I think one should ignore or be disrespectful of the audience.

However, as an artist, it would be fatal if I tried to listen too much, as I might then aim to "please". My job is to tell a story as honestly as I can, not to seek approval. Talking about hearing the audience, I was outside the theatre on 49th Street, under the marquee, on a balmy Fall evening. It was Intermission. Two gentlemen were standing there, having no idea who I was. One, with an ashen face and an appalled expression, said to his friend, "*Do you think Stephen Sondheim knows this is happening?*" I thought to myself "*Steve Sondheim lives on 49th Street. He knows!*" They were angry. They felt cheated. This wasn't the show they wanted to see. It wasn't a copy of the original production. There and then I thought we might close before we got to the end of the Preview Period. How wrong I was.

Every morning I called Mr Sondheim and asked him for any notes from the previous night's performance. His observations were always succinct and extremely helpful. However, I do remember one morning, maybe I was a little tired, and he said "*One of my friends thought that . . . . .*" Well, how I had the courage I will never know, but out came "*Steve, I don't know your friends so I'm not taking notes from them.*" In fairness to him he quite simply said "*Fair enough!*" Regarding "notes", everybody always has an opinion to offer and, as a director, you can start to feel like you're losing your mind. I had the good sense to say to our wonderful producer Richard Frankel that I was very open to hearing notes, but only from him. The deal was that he would listen to the comments from the other producers, decide what was useful, and only give me those. It worked, and I have taken that approach ever since. I advise anybody in the same situation to do likewise. Otherwise you really can be in the position of a producer or investor saying "*You need to change that costume – my wife doesn't like red!*" It's true!

What a surprise the journey through a life in the theatre can be. I'm not sure one can ever really plan it, but one can certainly be open to the extraordinary opportunities it may bring your way. As Sondheim wrote in *Merrily We Roll Along*, "*Success is like failure. It's how you perceive it. It's what you do with it, not how you achieve it.*"[2] Well, there we were, behind that curtain, waiting for that familiar comforting darkness of an auditorium in performance. Steve understandably always preferred to quietly slip into the theatre once the lights had gone down, as he would otherwise be stared at. Protecting your anonymity and being allowed to simply do your job is harder now, particularly with the chatter of the Internet. Almost everybody has become a critic. I actually prefer not to be in a theatre when the ladies and gentlemen of the press are there, as I have a habit of foreseeing what might go wrong! Not good for me or for those around me. I'm always in the building but not necessarily in the auditorium. Anyway, we seemed to be starting to do well. The show was receiving standing ovations, though Steve wasn't slow in telling me that I needn't get excited because "*They do it all the time in New York.*" However, as one of our producers said after a performance with a particularly enthusiastic response, "*They can smell a hit!*"

Opening Night, 3 November 2005. It was an ecstatic audience of friends, family and stars, with flowers onstage at the end. There were gift tables for each of us, all piled high with presents from cast and producers, much of which I treasure to this day. I'd been part of exciting West End Openings, but this was something I'd never experienced before. I declined going onto the stage at the end of the show to take applause or make a speech, and Mr Sondheim happily supported my decision. He didn't want to go up there either. In fact I met him for a quick drink before the performance began and he was much more nervous than I was. I recall him saying he felt sure they would like the production but thought the audience and the critics might think the show itself was simply old-fashioned. His lack of certainty was one of the most wonderful things about him. Well the audience was thrilled with the show, and of course thrilled that Patti was back. Her first Broadway musical in, I believe, seventeen years. She was home!

I remember being under the stage after the show, with Robert and my then London agent and dear friend, Clare Vidal-Hall. I was handed a copy of the *New York Times*, open at the page with the review. It really is like you see in the movies. If the reviews they read at the party are good, you have a great night. If not, the party venue empties rather swiftly. Nowadays everybody secretly reads them on their mobile phones – maybe even during the course of the performance! Anyway, what Ben Brantley had written was what I believe is called a love letter. "*This thrilling revival. . . . burrows into your thoughts with the poisoned seductiveness of a campfire storyteller who knows what really scares you.*"[3]

Then I heard over the tannoy *"Would Mr Doyle please come to the stage door."* There, leaning against the backstage water fountain, was Elaine Stritch. A legend, dressed in a short cream mini-dress and a rain-hat! She pointed at me. *"Are you Mr Doyle?" "Yes, Ms Stritch, I am." "Well, that* (pointing toward the stage) *just goes to prove that they can't kill the theatre!"* I was so taken aback I said *"Are you coming to the party?"* Her response *"I either see the show or go to the party, I can't do both!"* Elaine was famous for never paying for her theatre tickets. Every box-office employee knew her, so the moment she showed up they simply handed her a ticket. Now, that's class! I was fortunate enough to get to know her quite well. We planned to work on a project that in fact didn't materialise. I didn't care about that. I just recall with joy those afternoon get-togethers at the Carlyle Hotel, which was in fact her home. Complex, hysterically funny, dark and infinitely human, she was one of the most honest people I've ever met.

For me, the most meaningful thing was that Jill Fraser and her husband James were able be in New York to attend the Opening Night of *Sweeney Todd* on Broadway. If it hadn't been for her, it would never have happened. Thank you Jill for forcing me into it. That evening was the last time I saw her, as she died only a few months later. I miss her as much now as I did when she first left us. She believed in theatre with great passion and gave opportunities to so many people in her relatively short life. Our world needs more people like Jill Fraser.

The Opening Night party was a lot of fun. The second night party at Steve's house was even better. Just the cast, the collaborators and the writer. He always held such a party in case the critics had decimated the show and everybody needed cheering up. He'd had that decimation many times! No worries this time. We were a Hit! I have two letters in my small collection that I truly treasure. One was a handwritten note from Hal Prince when he saw the production in London. He delivered it to the stage door. It said how pleased he was that at long last a director had done a *Sweeney* that wasn't a copy of his. For me, better than any prize. The other? It's framed above my desk. I can see it as I write this. It says: *"Thank you for revivifying my musical. Love Steve."* That moment when Steve saw *Sweeney* at the New Ambassadors started a journey, indeed a collaboration, that I'm proud to say would leave its mark on musical theatre. I found out what it feels like to work with your hero. I got to know that complicated, loving, genius. The best times were the one-on-one get-togethers. No audience. Simply friends.

In the next chapter I will be sharing more of the times with Steve, but I'd like to take this opportunity to write about *Merrily We Roll Along*. It was in Cincinnati, Ohio. Scott Pask had designed a wonderful set, all based around notes of Steve's scores. I was interested in it being a "blue" world and having a magical, almost unreal quality. After all it was looking at "time", and how time takes us through life. Even writing this book feels like an exploration of time, perhaps that's why the great Arthur Miller called his autobiography *Timebends*. Anyway, for *Merrily*, I asked Steve if we could use copies of sheet music of his score of *Merrily* in the set. He was quite happy to let me do what I needed to do. He said to come to his house and he would have some of the manuscripts ready to show me. There on a table were boxes of his original scores for *Merrily*, most of which had been cut at various times in the process. It felt like opening a treasure trove. He gave me copies of the sheets of music to give to Scott and those became the wallpaper of the set, it was printed into the paper lamps that hung above, and bundles of it were used to create chairs and seating areas. All copies I hasten to add! The show travels backwards in time. I cast three seasoned performers, Malcolm Gets, Becky Ann Baker and Daniel Jenkins, who were all older than the age of the characters at the beginning of the story. The show is usually played by young actors who "act" being older at the beginning and get nearer their real age as the show goes on. I believe there is a difference between asking an actor to play an age they haven't experienced, that is asking a young actor to play their older self, than there is asking an older actor to play their younger self. Confused? So, usually, are the actors. We also did this show with actor-musicians, which certainly added to the complexity. Steve flew down to Cincinnati. He'd had some trouble with his flights and I was hopeful that wouldn't get in the way of his enjoyment of the show. I needn't have worried – he loved it. I can still picture him after the show having drinks with the cast and sharing stories. He loved to tell a story. He loved to talk about Oscar, and Lenny, and Hal, and Arthur and Angie. The list goes on. How we all loved those stories. I didn't mind if I was hearing the re-runs, as it put one in touch with a remarkable era in American Musical Theatre.

Some years later I created a production that I named *A Bed and a Chair*. It was performed at the New York City Center, as a collaboration between Steve, Wynton Marsalis, and the Jazz at Lincoln Center Orchestra. Well, I had the gift of working with Bernadette Peters and nothing could possibly make any director happier. Before we got to the rehearsal room though, it was my task to take a selection of Steve's songs that might be able to have a jazz treatment. I can see Steve lying back on his daybed in his studio in the townhouse, and as I read a potential list he would give a yay or nay. I then took the songs and worked through them with musical director David Loud. Having therefore established a potential score, we took our choices to Wynton Marsalis, one of the finest jazz practitioners of his generation, who then distributed the material amongst his musicians and they each orchestrated a song for the evening. I then found a way of weaving the songs together with an unspoken narrative, using four singers and four dancers. It was about love affairs in New York City and was also a love letter to the city itself. It came to the sitz probe, the rehearsal where singers and orchestra come together for the first time. It just happened to be my birthday and Steve joyously found out about it. He asked Wynton and the band to play "*Happy Birthday*". Typical Steve. While Bernadette sang it! He seemed happier with that than with all the listening to his own music. Talking about birthdays, I was fortunate in that Steve asked me to put together a celebration for his eightieth birthday, again at City Center. I gathered together singers who had originally created roles in his shows and those who had done distinguished revivals. For example Michael Cerveris was singing "*These Are My Friends*" and was about to cut Mark Jacoby's throat, when on walked the original Sweeney, Len Cariou, who took the razor from Michael's hand and finished the song. There were so many more equally glorious moments. The evening was compered by myself and Steve's dear friend Mia Farrow. Certainly one for the Ages!

On 26 November 2021 I had an early-morning call from Steve's lawyer and friend Rick Pappas. Rick was making two such calls, one to me and one to Marianne Elliott, the directors of the two Sondheim productions currently running in NYC. Marianne was directing *Company* on Broadway and I was directing *Assassins* Off-Broadway. Stephen Sondheim had passed away and Rick wanted us to be able to share this news with our respective companies before it was released to the press. I was of course very sad, but I also had a sense of wanting to celebrate my friend. He had a wonderful long life. He didn't suffer an extended illness. He had left us with so much. It was some months later that I was struck by what had happened. I was doing an interview for a New York TV company, and the interviewer introduced me as the late Stephen Sondheim's go-to director. I was overwhelmed by the thought that I could be perceived in this way. Tears came into my eyes, the same tears as that very first phone call.

We had so much in common, yet came from such different places. We shared stories of tricky mothers and he always came out on top. He could compliment me and then put me in my place in one fell swoop. We came full circle when he saw *Assassins* at Classic Stage Company, that theatre he thought I should get to know. The next day he sent me a note. "*As A-rab says to Anybodys near the end of West Side Story, 'you done good buddy Boy'.*"

I miss you Steve.

Plate 1 *A BOY OF NO IMPORTANCE: Looks like first day at school! Private Collection.*

Plate 2 *GEORGIA ON MY MIND: Alice Walker at* The Color Purple *Opening Night, The Jacobs Theatre, December 10, 2015. Photo by Mark Sagliocco/Getty Images.*

Plate 3 *THESE ARE MY FRIENDS: With Patti LuPone (right) and Jill Fraser (left) at the* Sweeney Todd *Opening Night, November 3, 2005. Photo by Bruce Glikas/FilmMagic.*

Plate 4 *ATTEND THE TALE:* Sweeney Todd, *the 2005 Broadway Revival at the O'Neill Theatre. Photo by Bruce Glikas/FilmMagic.*

STEPHEN SONDHEIM

November 7, 2005

Dear John —

Thanks for the opening night gift, and even more for revivifying the show. It's been a deserved triumph for you — savour it.

Steve

Plate 5 ONE OF THOSE LETTERS!: *A letter from Stephen Sondheim. Private Collection.*

Plate 6 *FINISHING "THE BOX SET": With Stephen Sondheim (centre) and John Weidman, working on* Road Show *at the Menier Chocolate Factory, 2011. Photo credit: Adam Lenson.*

Plate 7 *I WAS YOUNGER THEN!:* Pacific Overtures, *Classic Stage Company, 2017.* Photo credit: © Joan Marcus.

Plate 8 "SIDE BY SIDE": The company of Company, *Cincinnati Playhouse in the Park, 2006. Photo by Buzz Ward.*

Plate 9 *HANGING IN SARDI'S – WHO KNEW!: With my dear husband, May 24, 2016. Photo by Walter McBride/WireImage.*

Plate 10 *HAPPY DAYS ON THE VISIT!: With Graciela Daniele (top-right), Terrence McNally (bottom-left) and John Kander (bottom-right), at the Williamstown Theatre Festival, 2014. Private Collection.*

Plate 11 *A PERSONAL FAVORITE: Anika Noni Rose as Carmen Jones, Classic Stage Company, 2018. Photo credit: © Joan Marcus.*

Plate 12 *MY DARLING CHITA: Opening Night of her Cabaret, Café Carlyle, 2016. Photo by Brent N. Clarke/Getty Images.*

Plate 13 RECOGNISE THE ARTIST?: The cast of The 12, Goodspeed Musicals, 2023. Photo credit © 2023 Diane Sobolewski, Goodspeed Musicals.

Plate 14 HAPPY BIRTHDAY STEVE: 80th Birthday Concert, at the New York City Center, April 26, 2010. Photo by Al Pereira/Michael Ochs Archives/Getty Images.

Plate 15 *"THE COLOR PURPLE....LOOK WHAT GOD HAS DONE": with Danielle Brooks and Cynthia Erivo at the 2016 Tony Awards Meet The Nominees Press Reception. Photo by Jenny Anderson/Getty Images for Tony Awards Productions.*

Plate 16 *KEEP KNOCKING ON THOSE DOORS!: Tony Night, June 11, 2006. Photo by Evan Agostini/Getty Images.*

8

Building The Box Set

Increasingly I'm asked by producers to help put together the writing team and to take the creative lead in the often protracted process of developing a musical. It takes many artists to make a musical – sometimes too many! Every musical of course needs a composer, and also a lyricist, though now the work of the latter is often done by the composer or as a collaboration between composer and book-writer. Terrence McNally, who wrote many wonderful books of musicals, always said that the book-writer provides the "architecture" of the piece. The shape, the structure within which the songs sit. So, I'd like to dedicate this chapter to the great unsung hero of the musical theatre – so often the person who comes up with the idea in the first place – the book-writer.

Steve Sondheim learned his craft from the brilliant Oscar Hammerstein II. Hammerstein created the template for great book-writing, starting with *Showboat* and then progressing through all of his work with Richard Rodgers. He knew Steve from the earliest days, after all they were neighbours at their country houses in Doylestown, Pennsylvania. As a boy, Steve was great friends with both of Oscar's sons, and Oscar Hammerstein gave Steve Sondheim an apprenticeship in how to write a musical. I'm sure it was because of Oscar that Steve so valued his own book-writers. James Goldman wrote a poignant book for *Follies*, whilst the very funny Bert Shevelove and Larry Gelbart did *A Funny Thing Happened on the Way to the Forum*. Hugh Wheeler did magnificent work on *A Little Night Music* and *Sweeney Todd*, both of which are exemplary examples of great book-writing. It's interesting to note how much of *Sweeney* is actually sung, leaving a very sparse book, but with wonderful structure. There had also been the work with Arthur Laurents, *West Side Story, Gypsy* and *Anyone Can Whistle*, which I sense was a complicated but hugely successful partnership.

Through my work with Sondheim I was fortunate to work closely with all his then living collaborators. First the late George Furth on *Company*. George was a wonderful character, full of quick wit and intelligent naughtiness. I remember having drinks with Steve and George and experiencing first-hand where it all came from! They communicated, or indeed performed, with the same humour that runs through *Company* and *Merrily we Roll Along*. Well of course it was the same humour! Isn't that the job? To put one's whole self into the work? To allow oneself to be heard through the characters one creates in such a way as to then be able to hide behind those characters? To hear one's own voice in the text? George and Steve that night were just like characters from their ground-breaking musical. More on *Company* later.

I was next fortunate enough to get to know James Lapine because of that production of *Passion* at Classic Stage Company. Directing a revival of a musical with the book-writer in the room is not without complexity, especially if you have my tendency to take a fine scalpel to their original work. Never re-writing a word, simply getting rid of a few! It's even more complex if the original director is there. I don't believe it happens very often. James successfully directed all three of the productions he and Steve wrote together, *Sunday in the Park with George*, *Into the Woods* and *Passion*, each a masterpiece in its own right. I've directed *Into the Woods* and *Passion* but I have no desire to direct *Sunday*. Not that I don't like it – in fact I absolutely love it. No, rather I think there is only one way to do it and that totally comes from James' extraordinary vision. He very much let me "do my thing" with *Passion*, professionally and respectfully distancing himself from my rehearsal process, which was the most liberating thing he could possibly have done. And then there was the other very-much-alive Sondheim book-writer, John Weidman.

Out of the blue I received a call from Oskar Eustis, the Artistic Director of the New York Public Theatre. The Public is one of the city's most exciting companies, with a number of venues and an adventurous reputation that began with its founding director, the legendary Joe Papp. Oskar was calling to ask if I would be interested in looking at the materials for a little-known musical written by Steve and John. Would I be interested? I should think so!

The show had already experienced a challenging journey. It went through some workshops directed by Sam Mendes. Then it had an arguably unsuccessful out-of-town production directed by Hal Prince. The show began its journey under the title *Wise Guys*. Hal's production was called *Bounce*, and that was still the title of the script that was sent to me.

The first step was to meet John Weidman. I had seen him in the distance at the Opening Night party for *Company* but I was too nervous to go over and make myself known. So, you can imagine how I felt when asked to go to Steve's townhouse on East 49th Street to meet John. I now know there was nothing to be nervous about. Within minutes I could tell that what everybody said about John Weidman was true. He is a "mensch". That Yiddish word translates to "a person of integrity, morality, dignity, with a sense of what is right". Not only that, but he's also one of the smartest people I've ever met. He has Degrees from Harvard and from Yale. His father was the great Pulitzer Prize winning novelist and playwright, Jerome Weidman. This man was pedigree! Not only that but, as I was later to discover, he's a lot of fun.

I sat with them doing all I could to appear calm. We started to discuss what had and hadn't worked in the different versions of the musical to date. Both men were self-critical and thoughtful about the content of the piece. After much fascinating discussion I somehow gathered the courage to ask *"What do you think it's about?"* Steve proceeded to say it was about Willy and Addison Mizner, two wise guys who both had a big influence on the era they lived in, although in very different ways. I summoned even more courage and said *"Yes, but what's it about? What are you trying to say?"* Silence. I then said *"Isn't it about America?"* A musical about complicated brotherly love, about tricksters, about people who are, at heart, opportunists. Yet people who are alive, vital and capable of extraordinary vision. John then said – quietly and somewhat joyously – *"That's it! That's what it's about!"* Over a long period of writing and rewriting, these great creative geniuses had perhaps lost their way a little. Any artist, no matter how experienced, can lose sight of what they're trying to say. I think that's when a director can usefully come into the picture, bringing a fresh, objective perspective.

Now, after plucking up the courage to say what I thought it was about, I progressed to the audacious. This meeting was on a Friday. I asked John if he could send me an electronic version of the text. I said I would like to spend the weekend editing, restructuring, getting rid of old stage directions, building in a "concept". I believe the concept is the overarching primarily visual metaphor around which one frames a production, sometimes in terms of time and place, sometimes in terms of how it reflects upon our contemporary world. These were all things that, if I'm honest, I wouldn't have been able to express right there in front of them. I needed the privacy of just me and my computer to be able to do what I needed to do. I used the word audacious because that is unquestionably what it was. These weren't inexperienced young writers! Their mutual body of work was impressive, to say the least. Goodness knows what John thought, but he simply said "*OK.*" Off I went. As I said, I'd told them I would need the weekend and would send the rework to them on Monday. If they didn't like it, that would be okay and I'd still love to do the piece, should they still want me? So, I undertook the proposed work, submitting it on the Monday as promised. We quite quickly met again and John said he approved. In my experience Steve was always wonderfully respectful and supportive over how his book-writer wanted to proceed. After that privileged weekend of delving into their material, the text I presented to them on that nervous Monday was pretty nearly the text that is published today. It went from a full traditional musical with intermission to a one- act musical. The editing simply accentuated what was already there. A love story between Addison Mizner and a younger man, Hollis Bessemer. "*You Are the Best Thing That Ever Has Happened to Me*", a song that had belonged to Willy and a girlfriend who was no longer in the script, arguably one of the first love songs between two men in musical theatre history. The real beauty, though, lies in the love story between the two brothers themselves. As Steve's lyric says of them, "*We were stuck from hello*". Like so much of his work, so utterly simple and yet so humanly complex.

The next step was casting. The excellent folks at the Public helped to create an absolutely wonderful ensemble. It was led by Michael Cerveris and Alexander Gemignani, both from *Sweeney* of course. Other major roles were played by Claybourne Elder, who has gone on to have a terrific Broadway career, and then there was Alma Cuervo. She played MaMa in *Road Show* and we had further fruitful collaborations with *The Three Sisters* in Cincinnati, and *Allegro* and *A Man of No Importance* at Classic Stage.

Road Show at the Public. I can't quite recall when the title changed, but this is what stuck and it became the third in a trilogy by Sondheim and Weidman, the predecessors being *Pacific Overtures* and *Assassins*. I was to be surrounded and supported by wonderful collaborators, who you closely work with being the key to your success. Jonathan Tunick created the orchestrations. Jonathan was one of Sondheim's long-time collaborators and it may be an overused word, but I assure you Jonathan is, without any question, a genius. He once explained to me his theory that the orchestrator is the lighting designer of the orchestra pit. He illuminates the sounds of the music. We have worked together many times, even though he did ask me never to invite him to orchestrate "*one of those actors-musician shows!*" Unlike many contemporary orchestrators, Jonathan doesn't work on a computer. He writes out every note of the score by hand. He can hear and hold on to the whole thing in his head. One of the few EGOT (Emmy, Grammy, Oscar and Tony Award) recipients, he's a remarkable artist.

Jane Cox, the lighting designer, was new to me. We were introduced by the Public Theatre and I will be forever grateful to them. Jane and I have gone on to work together on numerous occasions, including *The Color Purple* on Broadway. When you work with as little actual stage set as I lean toward, the lighting designer becomes a primary element in the storytelling. In fact I often say to young directors that if your budget is very limited and you can't have a big team of collaborators, hire a lighting designer! Jane has also been my boss, a wonderfully freeing role-reversal as she very successfully leads the theatre department at Princeton University.

Mary-Mitchell Campbell, who orchestrated the production of *Company* I did on Broadway, was the musical director. We hit it off from the get-go, and have done many projects together since. A terrific orchestrator and a fine musical director, she is probably the finest accompanist I've ever heard. She has gone on to become one of the most sought-after Broadway musicians.

Ann Hould-Ward was the costume designer for *Road Show*. She has had a remarkably distinguished career, designing the original *Sunday* and the original *Into The Woods*, as well as winning her Tony Award for *Beauty and the Beast*. We have done almost all my American work together and have a great friendship as well as a rich working relationship.

Dan Moses Schreier was once again designing sound, which is a vital area in Sondheim's challenging material. Giving support to all that complicated word-play is imperative. Bringing out the minutia of each note and word with clarity and with excellent taste is a remarkable art in itself. It's no wonder that Steve always wanted Dan.

As well as directing, I also designed the set and discovered my answer as to how to do this one in a somewhat extraordinary fashion. I'd been struggling a little with how to set and visualise a story that happened in many locations. In a movie you can flow from scene to scene, location to location. On stage, particularly in a musical, you have to find a way of containing those locations in a much more manageable and indeed theatrical way. I knew it should be something to do with people who can't stop travelling, always on the move both physically and emotionally. Always "on the road". It was also a story told from the point of view of a dying man. It needed a deathbed. It needed useful pieces of furniture to help to indicate different locations. So, here's how I found the answer. Robert and I were out for a Sunday stroll in Brooklyn. We were walking down Atlantic Avenue when I saw a small antique store and, never being able to resist the opportunity to rummage around, I suggested to Robert that we take a look inside. There it was. Piles of furniture, like an abstract New York skyline. Not only that but, and I promise you this is true, the proprietor's music system was playing the cast recording of *Bounce*. Just like that Operating Theatre in London – it was a sign. I encourage all you director/designers out there to simply keep your eyes open! The "answer" is likely to be right there in front of you. I asked Oskar if it would be okay for me to have the rehearsal room piled high with furniture? Being the excellent Artistic Director that he is, he wanted to do everything possible to facilitate the process and really never said "*no*". The Props Master rented a truck and we went searching. A mountain of furniture evolved. Eventually Jane would light from within and behind the furnishings and it did indeed end up looking like an installation representative of the Manhattan skyline. Most of my design work does end up looking like an installation. As I've indicated before, I'm not drawn toward realism or naturalism. I don't want to see a working kitchen sink on stage – I have one at home.

The linking of direction and design is an interesting one. For young directors, I recommend always working with a designer, just as I did for many years and indeed I still do. However on some pieces, where I have a clear picture of what I want to see in the onstage storytelling, I now design myself. I've been very fortunate in being blessed with a visual imagination, and it all goes back to that childhood bedroom! The struggle for me lies in inhibiting my natural instinct to change everything, and not simply to allow things to settle. I always need to create a safe and secure physical environment for myself and for the actors to play on without getting stuck, so it works for me to design a world that facilitates a degree of change during the rehearsal period. I always show up for rehearsal early. Sometimes more than an hour early. I like to start working with the actors immediately once the official call begins, take a short lunch break and finish early. Ideally I wouldn't work past that 4.00pm – out-of-school time. For me it can be counter-productive to do too many hours in any one stretch. We all get tired and then danger can occur. On *Road Show* I showed up early every day and by the time the actors had arrived, the stage management team and I had moved the furniture pieces to try a different picture. It certainly kept everybody on their toes and the changing meant they had to keep thinking, keep inventing.

We had a thrilling rehearsal period, entered into previews and eventually realised there was a song missing. We needed something that showed the brothers as young, fun-loving boys, before their deep psychological conflicts began. If I remember correctly, Frank Rich, a highly respected former theatre critic for the *New York Times*, offered some thoughts on the potential song, John and Steve worked out what it should "say", and then the writing process began. Time was running out and I said to Steve that if the song was going to go in, it needed to go in on that Saturday evening, a couple of days before we froze the show for the critics. This meant Steve had forty-eight hours to write it and so he disappeared into his studio. On the Saturday morning, John and I went to 49th Street to hear what had been written. We met outside the house and I said "*What do we say if it's wrong?*" I will forever remember a nervous Stephen Sondheim going to his piano to play and sing the song, which is called "*Brotherly Love*". It wasn't wrong of course, rather it was short, concise and perfect. I went to the theatre, sheet music in hand. The boys learned and rehearsed it that afternoon, whilst Jonathan was doing an orchestration. It went into the show that night and transformed the audience's reaction to the piece. I still have a treasured copy of that sheet music. Just as I still have some of the sheet music from that childhood piano stool.

When at the Public, we were invited to remake the production with a British cast at London's prestigious Menier Chocolate Factory. So many exiting productions have originated at that small theatrical crucible, which is led by the tenacious Artistic Director, David Babani. The space was such that I decided to stage it with the audience on two sides of the action. It's always interesting rehearsing over with an entirely different cast, especially with something one has done so recently. The theatre couldn't afford to bring all of the "team", so we had a new Sound Designer, new Music Director and new Costume Designer. The company was very different from the New York company, but equally talented and equally hard-working. Everybody was just thrilled to be doing a Sondheim show, especially one that London audiences had never seen. John was there for much of the rehearsal period, refining and reworking moments in the text. We entered into previews and there was a noticeable difference between the London audience and the audience at the Public. This one laughed more! Much more! I think it's fair to say that the British audience has always approved of Sondheim. Perhaps it is the mutual love of irony? In this case, it was easier for a British audience to laugh at the American story. We all find it hard to have a sense of humour about ourselves.

One interesting anecdote remains firmly in my mind. It was the final dress rehearsal in London and Steve was seeing this version for the first time. Now, the show being set with audience on two sides certainly created differences, making you more aware of movement and of different dynamics between the characters. Also the audience was much closer to the action than the configuration had allowed in New York. Mr Sondheim wasn't happy! Not seeing what he had seen before somehow unsettled him. It was decided that he, John and I would meet for breakfast the next day to try to "*sort this out!*" Steve had a number of observations, all of which were going to be very helpful, but I could tell he remained unsettled. John and I left the hotel and I said that I was worried about making lots of changes before a first preview, and anyway neither he nor I shared Steve's anxieties. John's sage advice was to do nothing! He wasn't being disrespectful of his beloved working partner, but rather helping me steer a steady ship at a very crucial moment in its journey. The preview was a real success. I saw Steve immediately afterward. He had tears in his eyes and was thrilled. I hadn't changed a thing. I don't share this story for any sort of *"told you so"* reason. I share it because it points out that even the very greatest amongst us have anxiety. Even the greatest are scared. He had been scared that day when he played that song for the first time. He was scared that this audience wasn't going to approve of what we had made. It is that very fear that makes a truly great artist.

My working relationship with John Weidman has been very special to me. The three of us worked closely to make *Road Show* a success in New York and later in London. *"I was in the room when"* that work was being created and heard some of those songs with the composer/lyricist at the piano playing and singing them for the very first time. As Sondheim said, *"John Weidman is a political writer."* John and I come from an age when we believed that the world could be changed. It could be changed through the making of theatre. We still share this unstinting belief at our regular breakfast get-togethers. As I said before, all three of their musicals have been a big part of my desire to work on projects that question our human behaviour, that hold a very large mirror up to our complicated nature. However it's also important to say that this can all be achieved in an entertaining and uplifting manner. I have little interest in agitprop theatre, the theatre of agitation and propaganda. You can make a point and yet still give the audience the opportunity to leave the theatre with a degree of joy, a sense of hope. So many songs in *Road Show*, *Pacific Overtures* and *Assassins* are joyous and full of ironic fun. I don't want a reputation that sees me as an activist of any kind. However, I do want to feel that I made people sit up and take note.

Some time after *Road Show* we next worked at Classic Stage Company on a revival of *Pacific Overtures*. Or should I say a *"revivify"*? After all, Mr Sondheim invented the word! Revivifying. Reinventing. Reinvesting in the story. Exploring it as if it has never been done before. That's what any good piece of interpretative art deserves.

John's three shows with Steve are arguably the most politically driven of the Sondheim body of work, challenging familiar musical theatre structures, whilst at the same time exploring humanity through song and text. Most theatre lovers will try to choose their favourite Sondheim show in the same way they would their favourite Shakespeare, although usually that "favourite" changes depending upon where you are in your own life. I would certainly say that *Pacific Overtures* is my "desert-island musical" from Steve's canon, and there's no question that it is an incredibly challenging musical to work on. It's set in nineteenth-century Japan and tells the story of that country's Westernisation, starting in 1853, when American ships forcibly opened the country to the rest of the world. John originally wrote it as a play, when just out of university, and he shared it with Hal Prince. Hal thought it should be turned into a musical and asked Sondheim to take a look at it. It played on Broadway in 1976 at the Winter Garden Theatre, in kabuki style, with men playing the female roles. Because of the casting challenges, the whole cast being Asian, and because of the scale of that original production, it's one of the lesser-performed Sondheim shows.

As already described, Classic Stage is intimate. The space determines the scale of the set, and I designed an image that represented a great sheet of white parchment with the audience again on two sides of the action. There was only one piece of furniture. A rather beautiful wooden stool. It was all we needed. Probably as close to "essentialism" as I've ever achieved. I find that the greater the theatrical material, the less you need. This was the first production of the musical to cast women in leading roles and the group was led by the iconic Asian-American actor, George Takei. It was powerful to see an actor such as George in a piece that so represented Japan, especially as he had spent much of his childhood in an American internment camp. George illuminated what I always felt about *Pacific Overtures*, that it's just as much about the Americans as it is about the Japanese. It's also interesting to note that much of our cast wasn't Japanese but rather Chinese Americans. These casting conundrums are so complicated. What I do know is that they were all thrilled to be doing it, not only because of the Sondheim connection, but because they had grown up connecting with a piece of theatre that was one of the very few musicals that in any way represented them. One of the few opportunities to see people onstage who looked like them.

John and I got together to discuss the piece, casting, et cetera. I voiced my concern about a few scenes, after all even though it was about Japan it was, in fact, written by two Jewish Americans. Indeed there was one scene where one of the female characters seemed more like an Upper East Side Jewish Matron than she did a Japanese lady. This scene had always been of particular concern to John and he was glad to have the opportunity to cut it. The unfortunate thing was that it contained one of the most beloved songs from the score, "*Chrysanthemum Tea*". John discussed it with Steve and the scene and the song were cut. It's interesting to note that I've been blamed for it ever since!

I cut it down to an intermission-less ninety minutes from the two-and-a-half-hour original, and performed it with our cast of ten performers in modern dress. It had beautiful new orchestrations by Jonathan Tunick, who, of course, had also done the original. It received critical acclaim and many prize-giving plaudits. That version, which caused much unrest from the aficionados, is now performed internationally and is informally called, I'm embarrassed to say, the "John Doyle Version".

If I may, I want to share a couple of moments from that time. "*Someone in a Tree*" is one of Sondheim's greatest pieces of writing. Complex and difficult, its majestic storytelling is rooted totally in character. Not only is it an intellectual example of great music theatre writing, being in itself almost a one-act play, but it was also said to be Steve's own favourite of all the songs he had written. I told it as simply as I could, with very large scrolls, a few leaves and the singers themselves. I remember him attending the dress rehearsal of our production, something so different from any production he had ever previously seen. John, Steve and I were sitting together. It came to one moment in "*Someone in a Tree*" and Steve gasped loudly. He turned and looked at me in childlike wonder. Nothing further needed to be said.

There is a song near the beginning of the story called "*There Is No Other Way*", which is sung when the young lovers are parting. It had traditionally been sung about them by two male onlookers. I changed it to their singing it to each other, with a woman's voice being heard singing this beautiful material for the first time. This turned it into a love song, which of course really made you care about them. Also there was the lovely but terrifying trio "*Pretty Lady*". Three American sailors are singing to a geisha. Typical of Sondheim, the melody is beautiful but the ideas not so much. This was the first time the geisha had ever been played by a woman and so the tone of the song felt quite different. I'm proud that I opened the door to women in *Pacific Overtures*.

And then there was *Assassins*, the third of what we affectionately called "the box set", just like the box sets you can buy of books or even, in olden days, of videos. *Assassins* was first performed at Playwright's Horizons in New York City in 1990, opening to a mixed to negative critical response. Fourteen years later it played on Broadway, a major hit, winning five Tony Awards. The first production was hampered by the Gulf War. The Broadway production was delayed by 9/11. Our CSC production was hit by another devastating series of events.

I entered the rehearsal room to direct *Assassins* in early 2020. I'd gathered a terrific cast including Steven Pasquale, Judy Kuhn, Will Swenson and many more. *Assassins* is about exactly what it suggests – the disturbed characters who had successfully or unsuccessfully attempted to assassinate Presidents of the United States of America. An obvious subject for a musical? John and I had met many times to discuss the show and its characters. His main message to me was "*Don't mess with it!*" Both he and Steve felt that it was the closest to what they had aimed for – if you pardon the pun! Indeed, tears always came to Steve's eyes when he talked about his first reading of John's book for *Assassins*. Characters like John Wilkes Booth and Sarah Jane Moore join with cohorts from across the centuries. They do that wonderful thing that only a musical can do – abandon a sense of time and place. After all, these killers didn't sing in real life, and they certainly never met!

So, we happily gathered for our first rehearsal. Always an exciting day, but for me a terrifying one. "Starting" is always difficult. Your initial choices are those you tussle with for the entire rehearsal period. Their immediacy always seems questionable, even though your initial instinct is so often the one to which you finally return. John and Steve were with us for the morning, both disappearing when the work began. John would come back when I wanted to show him something. Steve would probably return for the final run-through, or perhaps the Dress Rehearsal. I always felt that he didn't enjoy the actors seeing him watch them, at least not until we were in a darkened auditorium. He knew it inhibited the process and was always sensitive to their feelings and experiences.

We started. No read-through. I should explain why. Unless it's a new play, when it's useful for the writer to hear the play read aloud, I find the traditional "read-through" to be counter-productive. Some actors demonstrate the performances they want to give, others mumble in a non-committal fashion. Anyway, surely everybody has read the script before accepting the job?! Also, contrary to most American processes, I don't do what's called "table work". I believe this involves sitting at a table, sometimes for more than a week, analysing and fragmenting the text. No. I like to get straight "on the floor", straight into the sand-box!

During our early weeks of rehearsal, one could sense a growing national anxiety. We were becoming more and more aware of a lethal virus that appeared to be spreading at a somewhat alarming rate. I scheduled plans for us to work in smaller groups, so that we could contain the number of people who were in contact with each other, staying home if you had a sniffle. It was the end of the second of four rehearsal weeks, and we all went away as usual for the weekend. I joined Rob in our house in the country, which was our usual New York routine. I didn't return to that rehearsal room for almost one and a half years. Lockdown had been announced. Testing protocols began. There were so many unknowns. The one thing I did know was that we would all stay home. Perhaps for a month until things calmed down? In fact, I didn't see John or Steve in person for a very long time.

Leading the theatre company through that difficult period was, to say the least, challenging. The indomitable Toni Davis and I led all meetings from our respective homes, on the Internet site that would become part of our everyday vocabulary, Zoom. The office closed down. The set, which was built, painted and finished, stood there in that dark and empty auditorium. Waiting! The irony was that it was a solid re-construction of the American flag. It still moves me to see images of that flag, in that gloomy room, with a ghost light on (the light that's left on overnight in a theatre, following the centuries-old tradition of not letting the ghosts in!). That gloomy, yet hopeful, light on that painted flag says it all!

I didn't return to New York City but instead I had a challenging but personally very pleasant year. We were lucky as we could sit in our large garden and didn't have to see other people. We could communicate with our UK families over the Internet. I had always thought that you could cut my arm off rather than stop me being in a rehearsal room. That awful pandemic taught me that I could sit still. The world was going to keep turning anyway and I didn't lose an arm. When I did return to the rehearsal room, I had the new sensation that whilst I love what I do, I no longer *had* to do it. I still *wanted* to do it, but was a whole person without it. I wish I'd learned this a long time ago. That contentment provides a great deal of freedom, proving that it isn't necessary to have anxiety and stress in order to be an artist.

Good things happened. The United States government provided Classic Stage Company with financial support to help the organisation get through those difficult times. How ironic that it took a pandemic for them to understand that the Arts do need funding in a meaningful way in order to be able to survive. Generous patrons and supporters also helped us in a most moving fashion, with equally meaningful donations, large or small – this terrible pandemic brought out the best in the human condition. I created a fundraising effort that centred around an audience seeing a very special video that we made, and donating money accordingly. I gathered together, remotely of course, cast members from the original 1990 cast of *Assassins*, plus cast members from the Broadway production and members of our own cast. We filmed a series of conversations and musical moments, all around this great piece of theatre. Secretary of State Hillary Clinton kindly agreed to introduce the evening. Performers recorded from their bedrooms, I was filmed sitting in the empty theatre, and of course the climax of the event was a very touching conversation between Steve and John.

Conversation was what we could offer. Indeed there was a very big conversation happening in the US at that time. The murder of George Floyd and the flourishing of Black Lives Matter collided with our culture head-on. Perhaps if we had still been rushing from place to place acting out our daily lives, we wouldn't have stopped to reflect upon the enormous challenges that we were facing. I decided that one way CSC could contribute was to create an online series of our own, *Classic Conversations*. Over the course of almost a year I had virtual conversations with numerous individual artists. These involved the movers and shapers, as well as artists who were starting out on their journeys. A fascinating archive arose, all of which were watched from the computer in one's home. To stop, to talk, to share, to contemplate. To realise that theatre still had a role to play in the public discourse, indeed a meaningful one. We didn't yet have the communion of going back to the theatre, but that would, and indeed did, come.

Eventually, masked and tested daily, we returned to the rehearsal room. The whole cast had stayed together, which was wonderful. In making a post-pandemic, post-George Floyd *Assassins* we realised we held a grave responsibility. However, there were two more important ingredients. When we started the initial rehearsal process, there was a Republican President in the White House. When we reconvened, there was a Democrat! Not only that, but a terrifying moment had happened. On 6 January 2021 democracy had been threatened by an attack on the United States Capitol. It would have been irresponsible to tell our story without an acknowledgement of that terrible event. I was asked at the time why I hadn't cast actors of colour in the roles of the assassins, especially as we had been building a reputation for integrated casting at CSC. After considerable discussion with John Weidman, we both thought it important to highlight that no person of colour has ever tried to assassinate a President. However, in a final image of the production, it was a Black actor who held the real folded American flag, just as would be held at a military funeral. You need guns onstage to assassinate Presidents, so many of the lyrics are about weapons, and how chilling this was against the dark shadows of America's gun culture and the terrible shootings that are happening with terrifying regularity. Much of the musical centres on the shooting range at a funfair. I'd created a big "bullseye" above the set and projected images into the centre of the circle. Informative images of the Presidents who were being shot, in the realisation that a good percentage of our audience hadn't been alive when President Kennedy was assassinated.

One of the great scenes in *Assassins* takes place in the Dallas Book Depository on 23 November 1963. It's a scene between John Wilkes Booth, who had assassinated Abraham Lincoln, and Lee Harvey Oswald, who is about to assassinate John Kennedy. It's an absolutely brilliant piece of writing, very much a one-act play and certainly much longer than a scene is supposed to be in a musical. In it, Booth encourages Oswald to follow in his footsteps and to allow himself the immortality that comes with assassinating a President. It's John Weidman at his best and I recommend having a read. Those who had been alive could, like me, remember where they were on that terrible November day. They could remember their personal equivalents of my black piano. For those who may not have been fully aware of the awfulness of what happened in Dallas, Texas, we projected a portion of that disturbing Zapruder film footage of Jackie Kennedy climbing over the back of the limousine.

Our very final image though was of that mob riot on January 6. It was chilling. I hope that image will always chill. World truth really can effect storytelling. Sometimes an audience needs it "on the nose", especially in these days of visual media bombardment. Tragically, our world had changed during our pause! We cannot and must not forget. We must keep reminding our audiences of what matters.

A frail but determined Stephen Sondheim attended our opening night. It was to be his final New York opening. He was devastated at the end of the show. The whole audience could see him in this tiny theatre, the tears running down his cheeks. He didn't care. What mattered to him was that *Assassins* is as important now as it ever was. Like Shakespeare, it lives for the time and the audience to which it is being told. I spoke to Steve on the telephone a few days later. Still his scary, challenging, loving self. We'd travelled a long way since we leaned on that radiator behind those curtains at the O'Neill Theatre. Our relationship started with a phone call and ended with a phone call. Only a few days later, he died.

In *Anyone Can Whistle*, Steve wrote some of my favourite lines from a musical. They sum up what I feel about him: "*It was marvellous to know you, and it's never really through, crazy business this, this life we live in, can't complain about the time we're given, with so little to be sure of in this world, we had a moment, a marvellous moment. . . .*"[1]

And so we are left with the "box set". I am so fortunate to have directed important productions of all three shows. I do have a dream left though. The dream of doing them all in repertoire. The same company of actors, and programming that meant that you could see all three in one day. They represent, to me, all that is intelligent, entertaining, political and thrilling in the best of American Musical Theatre! What are they about? America.

9

Give My Regards to Broadway

I saw my first Broadway show in 1978. It was *Hello, Dolly!* starring Carol Channing as Mrs Dolly Gallagher Levi. It was in the Shubert Theatre on 44th Street and I was very excited. We sat down, the house lights went to half and there was an announcement. "*Ladies and Gentlemen . . .*" Oh No! She wasn't appearing! She was a legend and we weren't going to see her! "*Ladies and Gentlemen. . . . . this is Miss Carol Channing's two thousand one hundred and forty seventh performance as Dolly Gallagher Levi!*" The audience erupted, straight to its feet! She'd managed to receive a standing ovation before leaving her dressing room! That is Broadway! A manufactured piece of magic that made everybody very happy. That is show business – or certainly the business of show.

It was a glorious evening. A good old-fashioned musical comedy written by the one and only Jerry Herman. Ms Channing was nothing if not extraordinary. Could she sing? Well, it depends upon how you interpret the word. Could she dance? No longer. Could she act? Not to my taste. Could she perform? Yes, yes, yes! I know she was helped a little by the soft follow-spot that was pointed at her all evening, but I can assure you, I simply couldn't take my eyes off of her. She was the ultimate performer, totally charismatic and justifiably a star! Perhaps one of the last of the breed – and boy am I happy I saw her in person. Some years later I was dining in Sardi's, the famous Midtown theatre restaurant. The place where they hang your caricature when you've "*made it!*" Believe me,

I was beyond thrilled when they hung mine. Anyway, it was late in the evening. I looked over at the little old lady at a nearby table, sitting alone, coat on and woolly hat on her head. Yes, you got it, it was Carol Channing. The 'Broadway Baby' at the end of a long day. This was years later and she was back in town doing Dolly again!

As the great Ethel Merman reputedly said, *"Broadway ain't for sissies!"* Doing eight shows a week, the Broadway performer is an athlete of the highest order. Broadway is a well-oiled machine. It has so many great producers. When I started in the theatre the word "producer" was actually the name given to the director. These tenacious ladies and gentlemen are not directors, but rather they raise the money to make the work and then manage the work once it's made. They are truly the business of show, optimistically seeking the next "hit". Now bear in mind, when Broadway talks about a "hit" it doesn't mean critical acclaim, or award-winning performances. No, the Broadway definition of the word "hit" is that the show has made its money back and repaid its investors. A show that recoups its costs is a hit. It used to be that the money people behind the producers were called the "angels". I'm always amused by the heavenly connotation. Now the angels *are* the producers with a greater voice at the table. If they can get their names above the title on the poster by giving sizeable amounts of money, they become eligible for a Tony Award. That's why at that award show you see the stage flooded with people surrounding the winners podium. I should point out that only the Lead Producer receives an actual physical award. The others are given the opportunity to purchase theirs. It really is a business! Rather a long way from why I came into the theatre in the first place.

Well, the years passed and at last count I've directed five Broadway musicals. All very different and equally enriching experiences, they have brought with them a level of attention I never expected to have to negotiate. When you walk through Central Park and a stranger comes up to thank you for directing a particular Broadway show, it really is a very strange and somewhat uncomfortable feeling. I don't believe that would happen in London's Hyde Park. In fact I know it wouldn't. This is Broadway! Anyway, I'd like to share the journey of each of these five shows with you.

Number One: *SWEENEY TODD*, Eugene O'Neill Theatre, 03 November 2005 – 03 September 2006

I've already written a great deal about *Sweeney Todd*. It had a wonderful year on 49th Street and then started its national tour with a launch date in San Francisco, by this point starring the hugely talented Judy Kaye as Mrs Lovett. Indeed, there were two national tours, playing theatres all over America. It even played four weeks at the Fox Theatre in Atlanta, which seats 4,665 people. I saw it for the final time at a matinee at the Heinz Hall in Pittsburgh. Another huge hall, and I was so surprised that this little show that started in that tiny UK theatre was playing to full houses in all these iconic American venues. I had only opened out the stage space a little from the original design, and so the set wasn't all that much bigger than it had been when the journey began. *Sweeney* recouped on the road, meaning that it paid back all its investors whilst on tour. At that point I believe it was the first Sondheim show to go into profit. It was, officially, a hit! It won many prizes, including Drama Desk Awards, the Drama League Award, The NY Critics Special Award and many more. Sarah Travis and I both won Tony Awards in our respective categories.

The awards pale into insignificance when I think of the personal joy that came with the show on Broadway. Moments like when I would sit on the steps at the back of the auditorium to be able to write my notes when I was watching the show. Nobody could see me writing there and so I had no reason to feel self-conscious. The ushers on Broadway are extraordinarily dedicated people, who traditionally all lived in Hell's Kitchen, the area near the theatres. Whenever I was there, one particular usher would quietly come and sit beside me at the same point of the show. It was always when Patti was singing "By The Sea". It became a little ritual that she would join me at that moment. One night she said, "*I originally did this show with Angela and now I'm doing it with Patti.*" She believed in her work with such love that she spoke as if she was actually in the show! For me – she was!

One last brief anecdote. There is a terrific duet at the end of Act One sung by Sweeney and Mrs Lovett. It's called "*A Little Priest*" and is full of Steve's wonderful word-play about all the people they could murder and put into pies. In fact the dramatic reason for the song is to allow Mrs Lovett to have the terrible realisation that she could, with Mr Todd's help, become a financial success. The song is made up of a number of verses and choruses, in the form of an old-fashioned music hall number. In Newbury and in London I cut out one verse and chorus, because if I'm honest, I thought the song was too long. Mr Sondheim correctly insisted it be restored and of course that's what I did. Then it came to previews in New York. On one of our daily phone calls, Steve said, *"You know, there's something wrong with Little Priest. What is it?"* I said *"You really want me to tell you?"* He said *"Of course!"* I swallowed hard and replied *"It's a verse and chorus too long."* He immediately said *"Cut it!"* Before we went any further I said *"Over my dead body! There are people all over Manhattan who practise that song in the privacy of their own kitchens. I'm NOT taking the blame for it being cut."* The number remained intact, Patti and Michael made it a triumph, and I smiled.

Many years later, something wonderful happened for our little production of *Sweeney Todd*. In 2020, the *New York Times* identified the pieces of theatre, dance, music, visual arts that journalist Patricia Cohen believed had the most influence on the arts in the first two decades of our century. As the theatre representative, she chose our production, calling it a Frontrunner, and said of it *"Every now and then a piece of American performance is so memorable that it redefines its medium and reframes the culture at large."*[1] They gathered the Broadway cast together for a group photo of us now. In relation to the business of show, the article states: *"It helped persuade audiences and producers that artistic innovation was just as commanding as lavish sets and effects, and cleared the way for shows in the same vein, many of them new works developed off-Broadway, where scarcity regularly prompts invention."*[2] That article made it all worthwhile. Not a review but a true critical assessment. I'm still shocked when people tell me that it was their first Broadway show, certainly the antithesis of mine! Both equally valuable, as you can't have one without the other. You can only reinvent something if you understand what it is that you're reinventing.

I was with Sondheim one day, just the two of us. I felt he was due an apology. There was one particularly difficult section in the second act, around the chaos in London, called *"City On Fire"* that I felt I hadn't made clear and apologised accordingly. His response: *"I don't know what you're apologising for – we didn't get it right either!"* The message? Musicals are never finished, never perfect. You just stop working on them. No matter. He'd still written a masterpiece!

Number Two: *COMPANY*, Ethel Barrymore Theatre, 29 November 2006 – 01 July 2007

When *Sweeney Todd* was running in London, my agent received a call from a gentleman named Ed Stern. He was a theatre director from the US and he wondered if we could have lunch together. I can still picture the very nice restaurant on St Martin's Lane where we met. He was in fact the Artistic Director of the Cincinnati Playhouse in the Park. I want you to forgive me if I tell you that I didn't know where Cincinnati was! Anyway, we had a lovely lunch and I liked him very much. He'd seen *Sweeney* and invited me to bring the production to Ohio once it closed in London. There was by now talk of it going to New York and if that didn't happen, I was done with the Demon Barber of Fleet Street. However, because I liked him and because my gut told me we would get on well, I asked if he might want me to do another Sondheim show at his theatre. He himself was a Sondheim devotee and had previously done some of the repertoire, but he was certainly very keen for us to work together. I suggested, with no commitments, that I would ask Mr Sondheim if he felt there was another of his shows that might be done in what he was referring to as "*That John Doyle way*". Actors who have worked closely with me call themselves "*Doylies*"! Steve Sondheim proudly wore a black tee-shirt printed with "*I Am A Doylie*" in white lettering. Anyway, I did ask him and he immediately said that *A Little Night Music* was the obvious one, as it already had a boy playing a cello and a girl playing piano. However, he thought I should have a go at *Company*, as I might be able to give it the glue he felt it needed.

I'd loved *Company* since a friend gave me a cassette recording of it back in the early 70s. It's hard to believe that it opened on Broadway just a few months before I went to drama school. You may remember, or at least have heard of, the cassette recording? Well, I listened to it so much that eventually the tape ran thin and it became unplayable. I could sing almost every lyric. I hardly knew of Stephen Sondheim – in fact I don't think I knew him at all. Maybe because of *West Side Story*, but I doubt it. What I did think was that this guy had written this musical about me!!! As Bobby, the leading character, says, "*Always on the outside looking in*". So, *Company* it was. In Cincinnati, Ohio.

My recommendation to any young director is, if somebody offers you a job, and you really like them, then do it! That gut feeling is so vital. The challenge is when you experience the reverse. Being offered a nice job when your gut says no is the difficult one. I've ignored my instincts many times and was always mistaken for doing so. Saying "No" is hard though – I still think I'll never work again.

I put together a group of wonderful performers to come to Cincinnati with me, the cast led by Tony nominees Raul Esparza and Barbara Walsh. Mary-Mitchell Campbell was to orchestrate. Alex Gemignani recommended her to me and he was absolutely right. I can still picture our first day of rehearsal when Mary-Mitchell had roughly taught the opening number by lunchtime. If you know the show – that's hard stuff! I started staging that afternoon. Sheets of music all over the floor, actor-musicians on the verge of tears, and yet so much laughter. And that's exactly how it continued. Cincinnati Playhouse was an incredibly supportive place in which to work, all emanating from its Artistic Director, Ed Stern. I felt so well looked after and my work was so protected, that after *Company* I went on to do two more productions with Ed, *The Three Sisters* and *Merrily We Roll Along*. For now though, let me take you into the rehearsal room for *Company*.

I suppose it's fair to say that things were going really well for me at this time. *Sweeney Todd* was a big success on Broadway, and so I was able not only to attract a wonderful cast, but I also had a care-free approach to the rehearsal room that hadn't always been there. Now, by care-free I certainly don't mean that I didn't care. Far from it. I just didn't feel that I had to justify the way I worked and the kind of work I wanted to make. That rehearsal room, with those committed and trusting performers, was exactly where I wanted to live. The set design, by the prolific David Gallo, was sleek and simple, giving me an exciting playground on which to work. It was a metaphoric Tribeca apartment, with a shiny blonde wood floor, a beautiful black Steinway grand piano, a central Greek column of the sort that you would see below 14th Street, and a suspended bank of designer lamps hanging above the space, resembling a modern art gallery. Often described as "cool", even "cold", that is exactly what we were trying to achieve. There's nothing more gratifying than when a critic or an audience member says something derogatory about your work and you think, "*Hurrah! They got it!*" Anyway, the imagery was handsome, sleek and somewhat remote, just like our leading character. The shiny piano was simply a design feature, not played by its owner, Bobby. The periphery of the room was built up with perspex cubes, each having a high revolving stool set onto it. This allowed the characters who were not in the story to observe, and with the spin of a stool they could be in or out of the action.

Originally, in the actor-musician work, there were some simple reasons why the actors remained onstage. First of all, one needs everybody there to accompany the singer, so they become an omnipresent chamber orchestra. Then another even simpler and very pragmatic reason. At the Watermill the backstage toilet was on the next floor, directly above the stage. If an actor used the facility during a performance, you could hear them! It may sound ridiculous, but it's true. So in a sense, that's partly why everybody was locked into the lunatic asylum in *Sweeney*. It became a trademark and so they were always there for Bobby in *Company*, as if they were in his head. This element of orchestral Greek chorus means that the music itself is forever present. It isn't hidden in an orchestra pit below the audience, or as happens in so many contemporary musicals when the musicians are in a room backstage and the music is piped in. No, the music is right there, you see it physically played and this gives the director wonderful theatrical opportunities to visually interweave the music. The music no longer acts solely as a sonic support but rather it is totally part of the picture. The orchestration is seen as well as heard. As the actors are learning the music I sit in the room and listen to the themes that both composer and orchestrator have been exploring. I listen out for what they tell me about the story, particularly about its psychological aspect. Music makes you feel, and I then stage those feelings. In fact I stage the orchestration. The juxtaposition of musical notes tells me when people should move. So a solo is no longer a solo; it becomes, for want of a better description, a theatrical dance. In *Company* I would explore staging where in some songs only the men are seen playing for Bobby, in other songs, only the ladies. It starts to tell its own story.

In the musical it's Bobby's birthday and the action happens when his friends show up to celebrate. To be specific, it happens in his head in the moments between his doorbell ringing and his answering the door to them. His whole life flashing before him in an instant. It's interesting that the Furth scripts,

Company and *Merrily*, both focus on the use of time. In *Merrily* the musical goes backwards in time. In *Company*, time is condensed into an instant. Bobby is at the centre, even though he says he is looking in. So often critics and public alike have asked whether Bobby is gay. I chose to think not, as I wasn't at all comfortable with the implication that only gay men find committed relationships difficult to negotiate. I think Bobby is like so many people today. City life seems so busy and connected, but in reality a city full of strangers, often glued to their devices, can often be the loneliest of places. As Marta, one of Bobby's past girlfriends, sings, "*Another hundred people just got off of the train, and the plane and the bus . . . maybe yesterday?*"[3] I wonder if our modern age is creating an increasing number of Bobbys?

In order to accentuate the loneliness of Bobby's story I did one rehearsal exercise as an experiment in clarifying this. This exercise could only be done once everybody knew their material. I asked the whole company to sit around the rehearsal room, not together, and with no sense of upstage or downstage. They stayed in those positions and we ran the entire show with Bobby being the only person in the "space". I asked him to act out all the scenes as if the others were there, even though he was in fact by himself. It proved invaluable, accentuating his aloneness, the fact that he could be hearing, maybe even remembering his friends. It also elevated the feeling that this man was having some form of crisis. I always think of putting on a play or a musical as an exercise in storytelling, each rehearsal period being its own experiment. That very word suggests an exploration of the unknown, an action to which we do not yet have an answer. Why rehearse if you already know the answers? Indeed isn't it arrogance to think that you do? Another exercise, which I do with most shows, is to take a section and ask the actors to run it from the point of view of a particular character. Make that character, no matter how seemingly insignificant, the "lead". In fact no character is insignificant. They all matter or they wouldn't be there. No small characters, only small actors. Within this exercise, every actor has to "connect" with the new central character at some time in their journey. It can be a touch, or a glance, it doesn't matter. What is interesting is that many of those discovered moments will find their way into the staging. The richness that grows is fascinating and certainly invaluable in creating a living piece of storytelling.

In every rehearsal room there is a problem to solve. The new chair in *Sweeney*, the little boy in *Caucasian Chalk Circle*. In *Company*, it's the birthday cake. The theatre's props department made a beautiful, very realistic-looking cake, and in a totally naturalistic production it would have been perfect. However I soon realised that this degree of naturalism is a problem in an actor-musician show. You've spent all evening believing in the woman playing her flute at a cocktail party, and then on comes a real cake with candles et cetera. The actress who carried on the cake in our production played the French Horn, or Cor Anglais, which is visually a beautiful instrument and has a large bell front where the sound comes out. I suggested to her that she put the cake down and try turning the horn upside down, imagining it was a cake. Worth a try, but it looked absolutely ridiculous. So, I had to think quickly. What do you associate with a birthday cake? Candles. What comes from a candle? A light that you blow out. So, I asked the lighting designer to provide a small circle of light on the downstage point of the set. Bobby would walk toward it and blow hard and the light would flicker and go out. At the end of the musical he walked forward and this time stood in the non-flickering light, a metaphoric acceptance of who he was and how to face the rest of his life. He'd stepped into the light!

Company has a wonderful trio for Bobby's three girlfriends, "*You Could Drive A Person Crazy*". Michael Bennett, of *A Chorus Line* fame, had choreographed the number brilliantly in the original production, with one of the three, Kathy, being played by Donna McKechnie. Anyway, I certainly wasn't going to repeat his choreography, but like so much great work, there didn't immediately appear to be another way to do it. Until I came up with the idea of the three girls having saxophones, and playing in harmony in the little breaks that had once been danced. It went down a storm and I bet lots of actors started learning the sax after that! I should like to put on record that *Company* was the first actor-musician production where the entire piano part was memorised. The characters of Peter and his wife Susan, played by Matt Castle and Amy Justman, were our brilliant piano players and they successfully navigated this gargantuan task. All the actors played musical instruments, all that is except Bobby. Toward the beginning of Act Two, when the couples played short solos on their instruments to musically question and answer each other, he took a little childlike kazoo from his suit pocket. He played a toy fanfare, but there was nobody there to answer his musical question. Now remember that big beautiful piano was in Bobby's room. His friends played it, but never him. One afternoon, I will never know if I was just being naughty, I said to Raul – do you play the piano? He looked a little concerned but bravely said – "*Well, a little.*" I said – "*I think Bobby should play his own piano for 'Being Alive'*", his big anthem at the end of the show where he realises he has to join the dance of humanity. The slight fear I saw in Raul's eyes made me realise we were onto something. He was a little afraid, and Bobby is very afraid. The two could go hand in hand. I asked Mary-Mitchell if she could orchestrate the beginning of the song for piano only and then bring the company in much later. It made for one of the most potent and memorable moments in the production, maybe even of any production I've done. His fear, that piano playing, that great song, everything just came together. Without knowing it, we had created something iconic. People who saw the production always immediately recall how they felt during that moment. So many strangers have told me about that piano moment in *Company*.

We opened in Cincinnati. I felt very happy with what we had made. It was simple and complex at the same time. Perhaps understandably, everybody is always hopeful about whether their show will "transfer" to Broadway. I didn't care. I've never made work in order that it have some unknown future. Steve came to Ohio. The actors were nervous, and I recall saying to him that I would take him backstage after the show and that, even if he didn't like the show, he had to be nice to them. Though of course he loved actors and really always celebrated them. At the performance he saw, he came out at the intermission looking ashen. He was very quiet. Oh dear! Were we heading for another of those angry moments? I swallowed hard and said "*Are you all right?*" He said, "*I had no idea we'd written a tragedy!*" I said "*Well, a man is having a life crisis – a nervous breakdown really – what did you think it was?*" He said "*A good old-fashioned musical comedy!*" He did like it though, he was of course lovely to those actors and we all retired to the local pub. I can remember him calling George Furth, who lived in California, and saying "*George, you've got to get here to see this.*" Broadway beckoned. I recall chatting with a rather well-known producer on Opening Night, who probably would never normally have travelled to Ohio to see a show. Word was out! He said, "I'd like to take it to New York. We'll change some of the casting of course. We'll get stars for these roles, et cetera." I stopped him. I said *"These actors came to Cincinnati, Ohio, in the dead of winter to make this show with me. Either they all go to Broadway or it doesn't happen!"* Needless to say, it didn't happen with that producer, but it did happen with the Frankel Group, the same excellent producers who did *Sweeney*. It opened at the Barrymore Theatre on 48th Street on 29 November 2006. I'd had two shows on Broadway in two consecutive seasons.

One of the wonderful things about doing *Company* for a New York audience is that it's actually *about* a New York audience. It really is a mirror up to nature. This was my first show with the famous costume designer Ann Hould-Ward. We were introduced by Ed Stern. How grateful am I? I didn't want us to dress it with 1970s clothes, which by now look a little ridiculous. I wanted it to be about now. She created a striking visual world, with all the characters dressing in differing forms of modern New York Black. The look seen at almost any Manhattan party. It looked terrific and the audience indeed saw itself. Amy, our character with the horn, was dressed as a bride. She was to get married during one scene of the show. There she was, a bride in black, in mourning for her life. Hysterical and tragic in the same Chekhovian moment.

Well, it was certainly a critical and audience hit. Raul Esparza and that company helped me to make that production. You can't do my job without actors in front of you. I make the work on their uniqueness. That's why I can't plan it in advance. I was nominated for another Tony Award. I didn't care if I won as we'd recently become grandparents to lovely twin boys. That was prize enough! The show itself won for Best Revival of a Musical. Raul was nominated for his wonderful portrayal of Bobby. He was expected to win, but sadly, he didn't. We all gathered for our after-Tony party. I was standing beside Raul and Steve Sondheim. I said to Raul: *"You deserved to win it. I'm so sorry."* Raul bravely said *"Thanks John. It's OK. I'll get over it."* Steve Sondheim, seething with years of deep frustration, said *"You'll never get over it! I've never gotten over the fact that 'The Music Man' won over 'West Side Story'."* Brilliant! That, my friends, is Broadway!

Number Three: *A CATERED AFFAIR*, Walter Kerr Theatre, 17 April 2008 – 27 July 2008

I met the great Harvey Fierstein in Patti LuPone's dressing room, that small space being a microcosm of Broadway. She had a little area where she changed, did her hair and make-up et cetera. Before that though was a lounge, where she could rest between shows and received her guests after performances. There was comfy furniture, a small bar and a table with a visitors' book. Steve Sondheim used to sit in there before previews, doing his *New York Times* crossword puzzle. Much fun was had by all who visited. That's where I met the late great Barry Humphries, where I met the beautiful Jessica Lange, where I first met the original Mrs Lovett, Angela Lansbury, and of course, Harvey!

Harvey Fierstein is Broadway royalty, the renaissance man of the American Theatre. He came to everybody's attention when he won two Tonys for his play *Torch Song Trilogy*, one for writing the play and one as Leading Actor, and he's one of the few recipients to win awards for both plays and musicals. He came from Brooklyn and started work as a very young man at La MaMa Theatre down on East Fourth Street. He won a further Tony for writing the book of *La Cage Aux Folles* and was one of the first openly gay celebrities in the US, helping to make gay and lesbian life an acceptable subject for the contemporary theatre. Recently he was deservedly awarded the 2025 Tony Award for Lifetime Achievement. Harvey is fascinating, highly intelligent and a lot of fun to be around.

I think it was in that dressing room that he told me he had a musical he'd like me to take a look at. I was flattered. With *Company* about to open, my agents were encouraging me to seek projects that didn't involve actor-musicians. Looking back, I'm not sure it was the best advice. I think they should have been looking to find subjects that may or may not be done using those skills, not making decisions that denied the very work I had success with. They had a fear that I would be seen as a "one-trick-pony", known only for asking Patti LuPone to play a tuba. In my early-to-mid fifties, I was the new kid on the block. This British director who had supposedly led the transformation of the American musical. To be honest, I shouldn't have listened. I was then and am now happy to be known for that tuba!

I was flattered that Harvey wanted me to read his musical. Being sought out or requested by a writer is the most beautiful thing. After all, the writer is where the story begins! The score was written by a very talented songwriter named John Bucchino, and the musical was called *A Catered Affair*, based on a 1956 movie of the same name by the great Paddy Chayefsky. It's set in the Bronx, and centres on the Hurley family, dominated by their matriarch Agnes. The daughter of the household is getting married and the story is about this poor but proud mother's struggle to give her the best possible "send off", a "catered affair". I could totally relate to the material. I came from that 1950s poverty and knew about the importance of the family wedding. I understood the working-class pride that underpinned the story. With great excitement, I accepted the offer. Tony winner Faith Prince would play Aggie. Tom Wopat, a fine actor, would play her long-suffering husband. Harvey himself would play Aggie's brother, a closet gay middle-aged man who lived in the apartment with Aggie, Tom and their daughter Janie. We went off to the Old Globe Theatre in beautiful San Diego to do a pre-Broadway try-out of our show. It was bliss. Wonderful theatre, wonderful weather, a very relaxing environment in which to make theatre. My accommodation opened onto the beach on Coronado Island, a short stroll from the hotel where they filmed *Some Like It Hot*. It felt like one big working holiday. However, even by those early stages, I believe I may have made some bad decisions. Our set, again designed by David Gallo, was bigger and more "Broadway" than I was happy with, very beautiful but perhaps not quite right. However, it was a musical. Audiences had expectations – maybe? Ann did the costumes and beautiful they were too. There were just too many of them! Again, we were trying to meet Broadway expectations for a musical, with major stars above the title. To this day I think we should simply have had a dining table, four chairs and some lines of laundry.

We learned a lot in San Diego. The audiences liked it very much, it won awards, but there was still work to do. We were moving to the beautiful Walter Kerr Theatre on 48th Street. Script changes were made, performances altered in relation to what we had discovered, things were pared back – just not enough. I was concerned that the Old Globe orchestrations were too lush, and my friend Jonathan Tunick came in and rewrote for a more intimate sound. So what was the problem? I think it goes back to that word "expectation". Maybe it should have been bigger, brighter, louder – but that just wasn't my taste. Looking back on it, I perhaps just wasn't the right person for the job. I was seeking something a little bleaker, a little sadder, a little poorer. Maybe we should have started the journey in a small downtown theatre that had no money. Maybe then we would have got nearer the truth of the source material.

It received ten Drama Desk nominations and a number of Tony Award nominations. To this day, people who saw it speak of it with deep fondness. It was very well produced by Jordan Roth, had a lovely score, and the book was very touching and honest. An honesty that I personally feel we didn't deliver to its fullest. It had a short but happy run at the Walter Kerr, and I don't regret a moment of it. Nobody died. Maybe I should have said it wasn't for me? I think the reality is, I wasn't for it!

Number Four: *THE VISIT*, Lyceum Theatre, 23 April 2015 – 14 June 2015

Now here's one I can confidently say was right for me and I was right for it. I was on a flight between New York and London. As I walked down the aisle to go to the toilet, I bumped into Broadway producer Tom Kirdahy. Tom and his husband, playwright Terrence McNally, had been very kind when I first came to New York. Tom said, in the moments we had before getting scowls for blocking the passageway, "*I have a musical that I'd like you to take a look at. It's called The Visit.*" Well, talk about being in the right place at the right time! Tom sent me a copy of the material. A musical based on a play of the same name by the European playwright Friedrich Dürrenmatt, it had been turned into a musical by Terrence, with music by John Kander and lyrics by the late Fred Ebb. Terrence had been involved in so many plays and musicals, and was one of the most prolific American playwrights of all time. Kander and Ebb had written some of the most popular Broadway shows including, of course, *Cabaret*, *Chicago* and *Kiss of the Spiderwoman*. All three of these great gentlemen had been writing serious and important musicals, always challenging and yet always accessible.

The piece is about a dying community and indeed a dying woman. She has come back with vengeance to the town that had persecuted her so many years before. Now an extremely wealthy woman, she particularly wants to meet with the man who, as a young woman, she had been in love with. It was the last musical that John and Fred wrote together, Fred having died some years before, and it had received a couple of productions previously, in Chicago and then in Washington. I had in fact been approached to direct a Benefit performance of it some time before I met Tom on that plane. I declined as I thought there would not be time to work on the piece, and that could be dangerous for it and for me.

I met with Terrence, who I obviously knew, and John Kander, who I hadn't met. John is simply the loveliest and youngest nonagenarian you could ever know. You have to meet with a lot of people before they sign you to do a musical, so the next was lunch with the star attached to the project, Chita Rivera. One is always nervous before meeting with a legend. This is the woman who Jerome Robbins built Anita on in *West Side Story*, the woman for whom Bob Fosse created *Chicago*. She had won Tonys for her performances in *The Rink* and *Kiss of the Spiderwoman*, and she had a total of ten Tony nominations. Chita was the Queen of Broadway, at that time a remarkably fit octogenarian, and proved herself to be one of the finest people I have ever met. We had a couple of delightful lunches and proceeded to become dear friends.

So, next we had to find a leading man to play opposite Chita. We were booked to do a try-out at the Williamstown Theatre Festival, a terrific summer festival theatre in Massachusetts. If things went well there, we would be going to Broadway and we needed a really good actor to play opposite Chita. Somebody who had a proven record of being a good company member, and ideally an actor who had done classical work as well as musical theatre. And so I met with Roger Rees in his apartment overlooking Central Park. I could hardly believe it! First of all, Roger was British. He had a remarkable theatre career behind him, on Broadway of course, but also at the Royal Shakespeare Company. I first saw him playing Malcolm in the acclaimed Judi Dench/Ian McKellen *Macbeth*. His game-changing role though was *Nicholas Nickleby*, that remarkable two-part event by the RSC, which of course transferred to the West End and later to Broadway.

I'd like to share a happy memory of *Nickleby*. I'd seen it, both parts, and found it both inspiring and remarkable. To this day it's one of the greatest theatre events I've ever experienced. I was passing the Aldwych Theatre one Saturday morning in 1980 and took the off-chance that they might have a single ticket so that I could see it again. They had one ticket, in the Dress Circle! *Nickleby* was long, and we'd been in there for hours. It was approaching 10.30pm and we were in those last great scenes from the play. All of a sudden the middle-aged lady next to me reached over and held my hand. She could sense that we were both experiencing the same love of storytelling at the same time. We didn't look at each other. There was nothing threatening about it. (Though I don't recommend trying it! You never know!) There was lean, handsome, thrilling Roger Rees, carrying a broken boy on his back. This was Trevor Nunn's work at its very best, one of the world's finest theatremakers. She held my hand, and indeed I held hers, until the applause at the end. We had a connection that would forever remain unspoken. We smiled and went our separate ways. I assure you there was nothing inappropriate about the gesture. I hope she still loves going to the theatre. I had a great meeting with Roger and he was exactly the man to play Anton in *The Visit*. How blessed we were to have him on board.

Next was the piece itself. I was enjoying a brief period as "Artist in Residence" at Pace University in New York. I was offered a number of sessions during which I could workshop any project I wanted to work on, the students helping facilitate the process. It was a perfect opportunity to explore this musical. I knew I wanted to cut the piece, I knew I wanted to do it in one act. I knew I wanted it to be darker and bleaker than it had probably been in other productions. So, we did our workshop, the roles being played by those young students. I invited Terrence and John to the presentation of our work. Once again I'd made some sweeping choices, choices that I would have found difficult to articulate to them. Anyway, they loved it and that was the template for the show we eventually did on Broadway.

Our run in Williamstown was everything one could have hoped for. I admit I was a little concerned that my somewhat unconventional approach might not be comfortable for Chita. How wrong I was. She loved to rehearse. She loved anything that was new to her. She really was an extraordinary artist. I usually told my mother what I was doing. She predictably asked who was in it, and habitually said, probably just to irritate me, *"Never heard of him/her!"* Didn't matter how famous they were. Anyway, I told her I was about to work with Chita Rivera. Her response: *"What? You???"* She certainly knew this lady. I'd love to have seen what would have happened had they met!

There was another great artist in the mix. Graciela Daniele had been a famous Broadway dancer, and was a Fosse favourite. When her dance career ended, she went on to choreograph and direct many iconic Broadway musicals. I couldn't believe it when she agreed to choreograph this production. She was an old friend of Chita – they were almost surrogate sisters – and she wanted to be there to support her. Grazie is a true artist, the oldest of old souls. Terrence was as wonderful as always. Very hands-off, very supportive. John was a dream. I remember the day when I was working on a particular scene and though there was some musical underscore written, it didn't seem quite right for what we were doing. John could sense this and went to the piano, listening to what I was saying to the actors. Then as we did the scene, he started playing a completely new underscore, which was quite perfect. That's skill. That's an art you don't see any more. That indeed is art! I remember looking around at one rehearsal and thinking, *"That's John Kander, Terrence McNally and Graciela Daniele sitting there beside me. That's Nicholas Nickleby and Anita standing in front of me. Good God, how did this happen?"*

Chita's attention to detail was staggering. I remember one day we worked for an hour on a tiny exit she had to make. It didn't seem right and we both knew it. She was, after all, a great dancer, so she knew how to listen to what her body was telling her. I eventually suggested she exit taking the turn to the left not the right, almost creating a circle as she went. She tried it. It was perfect. Many performers would have gone on with the imperfect move. Not Chita Rivera.

Our show was very successful at Williamstown and it was decided that we would go to Broadway's Lyceum Theatre, which is one of New York's oldest theatres and had the perfect atmosphere for our show. My brilliant collaborator Scott Pask had designed a wonderful set, a decayed railway station. In the centre was a coffin that Claire, Chita's character, rode back into town on. Death was an intrinsic part of our production, both creatively and personally. Just before we were due to re-rehearse for Broadway, I myself faced death, having gone into cardiac arrest on coming in off a flight to JFK Airport. A very different landing to that first one Georgia-bound! After some crucial days in intensive care, I came through and went into the New York rehearsals supported by two sticks and my trusty friend and colleague Adam Hunter. Then after one early rehearsal Roger, and his husband writer Rick Elice, asked if they could have a chat with me. Roger had been diagnosed with a brain tumour. Should he leave the production? I rejected the idea, saying that we were in this together, and asked that he stay with us for as long as he felt able. That's what he did and he gave this world his final touching complex characterisation, remaining with us almost to the end. One of the finest actors of his generation.

That show had a wonderful cast. It gave me great delight to have Donna McKechnie being the "standby" or understudy for Chita Rivera. Two of the greatest Broadway dancers in the room at the same time both working with equal intensity and unmatched humility.

We didn't run very long at The Lyric. Sadly the piece may not have been right for the Broadway of today. It earned a Tony nomination for Best Musical and provided Chita Rivera with what was in fact her Broadway farewell. During the rehearsal period, I suggested to Grazie that Chita should dance with the actress who was playing her younger self. John loved the idea and immediately created music for it. It was a thing of beauty and it was the last time Chita danced on Broadway. Not long after we closed, Chita and her assistant Rosie joined Robert and I at our house in Italy and we enjoyed a most wonderful week together. Gossiping, laughing, eating good food and visiting churches, all the things Chita loved to do. Chita always called me "*Father*". She thought I was some sort of theatre priest! I hope that was a good thing! I miss you Ms Rivera and I am so blessed to have been able to call you my friend.

Number Five: *THE COLOR PURPLE*, 10 December 2015 – 08 January 2017

I'm going to leave this one until the following chapter.

The inimitable Elaine Stritch left a message on my voice mail on the morning after I won my Tony Award. "*John, I'm really pleased for you! Now put it on the mantle and forget all about it!"* Typical. No nonsense. She knew about the ups and downs of award shows. I was almost in the autumn of my career when it happened and I'm very happy it didn't come along earlier. I disliked myself for the voice in my head in the weeks between nomination day and the awards ceremony. One half of me didn't care about it, the other half really wanted it! As Tony night at Radio City Music Hall approached, I was becoming the odds-on favourite. Ghastly! I just decided that I had to enjoy myself. Robert and I were walking the red carpet that warm Manhattan evening and I said to him *"Don't look now, but we're being followed by Mary Poppins!"* Of course he looked! There she was – Julie Andrews. And so it continued. It came to my category and they called out my name. Rob and I had been together ten years at this point and I was happy to be able to thank him from the microphone in that great hall. Remember, even then people weren't as open as you might think. I would be fooling myself and indeed you if I said it was anything other than a thrill to win.

The following day, I was crossing 8th Avenue with the Tony in a carrier bag, taking it back to our Producers office in order that it could go to be engraved. I decided I ought to call my mother in Scotland to tell her what had happened. So, I nervously announced to her that I'd won the Tony Award as Best Director of a Musical on Broadway. Her response? *"Well. . . . it only goes to prove it's all luck!"* There you see – *"Who do you think you are?"* Never able to express the sinful sense of pride – even though, on her death, I found many scrapbooks with cuttings from many of my shows. All part of life's rich tapestry.

Further nomination certificates for *Company* and *The Color Purple* sit in my metaphoric awards cabinet, the centrepieces of numerous nominations and awards. It may not *"all be luck"* but it certainly was lucky! Our cultures have become very prize-orientated. It's sad, in that for everybody who wins, somebody else has disappointment. Also, you really can't expect an art-form to be a competitive sport. If you are starting your career and dreaming of the awards show, stop! Enjoy what you do and do it because it matters, not because of what it can give you. There's nothing wrong with the prizes, but keep them in proportion. As Patti LuPone sagely said about the Tony Award, *"Johnny, never forget, the base is plastic!"*

10

Now I Was Driving the Bus!

I'd like to use this chapter to take a personal look at who should or shouldn't helm the telling of a story. Is it important to be Black in order to direct a Black story? Can only someone who's gay tell a story that focusses upon a gay character? I don't doubt there will be more questions than answers in this particular analysis. Too many definitive answers would give the impression that there is a formula and that one has it all figured out. I don't believe there is a formula, or even definitive answers. Inevitably some of what I write may read as defensive, which is not my intention, but again please bear in mind I'm viewing this through the lens of a personal journey. So let's start by examining a production of mine that some readers may be familiar with – the Broadway Revival of *The Color Purple*.

Let me take you back to the Opening Night of *Road Show* at the Menier Chocolate Factory. David Babani was chatting with me at the after-show party and suddenly he said *"I have a project I'd like to talk to you about."* This is always music to a freelance artist's ears, particularly if it's to return to a theatre where you had a good experience. I asked him what the project was and he rather quietly said *The Color Purple*. My initial somewhat stunned response was *"You've got to be joking!"* After all, I'm a very white, very middle-aged, man! Let's investigate these words in reverse order. "Man." The question is, should a man have directed a piece where the source material is written by a woman? Where the central character is a woman and indeed almost all of the key characters in the story are women. Three of the four-person book, music and lyrics team were women. Can I, as a man, understand? "Middle-aged." Indeed that is certainly what I was when I was invited to direct the musical. The characters in the story are generally young, though the central character does have a wide-ranging life journey. However, the music had an energy that may not have been totally that which you would associate with me. Can I, as a middle-aged man, understand? "White." We can certainly argue that this is the big one. The show is entirely about Black people. Alice Walker is of course a Black woman. Two of those four writers are Black. So the repeated question is, *"Can I as a white man truly understand the story?"* I will only ever be able to answer that question subjectively.

I did all I could to get out of doing *The Color Purple* at the Chocolate Factory. I tried simply saying *"No"*, which made the tenacious David Babani even more determined. Broadway producer, Scott Sanders, was also involved and remained hopeful that I would accept, so I tried being too expensive. They offered what I asked for. So, I took a look into myself because there was a strong part of me that was attracted to doing it. I had been through Liverpool and all that it entailed. I had helped set up new methods of recruitment, and made inroads into changing the racial profile of the audience there. I had helped drive that co-production with Talawa Theatre Company, and changed our casting processes to ensure that actors of colour started playing leading roles, not just the diminutive ones. The Arts Council of Great Britain asked me to advise other companies on similar processes. I had cast the role of Jesus Christ as a Black man, certainly nearer authenticity than the white pastel-clad figure with the long fair hair that dominated my childhood Bible. I did attend the University of Georgia in the 1970s, not so very long after desegregation.

Athens was only a very short distance from Putnam County, Georgia, where Alice Walker was raised and where Celie's story is told. I had been, after all, the only white guy on the bus! So, after a lot of thought, I took the plunge and, rightly or wrongly, I said *"Yes"* to directing a revival of *The Color Purple*.

The original Broadway run of the musical opened in the same season as our revival of *Sweeney Todd*. It was a big show, the antithesis of our modest, intimate offering. So many Broadway shows start big, often a knee-jerk reaction to audience expectation as I indicated in a previous chapter. Gary

Griffin, who directed that first production, is a very fine director and we later worked alongside each other up at the beautiful Stratford Theatre Festival in Stratford, Ontario. I can only imagine the pressure he was under to put as many bells and whistles as possible into that original production. It was highly successful and had a respectable Broadway run, followed by national tours. Scott Sanders had been its original producer, along with the legendary Oprah Winfrey. I sense that one of the reasons they were taking an interest in my doing it in London is because they would have been familiar with my reputation for stripping away the bells and whistles. If they were going to bring the show back to Broadway, particularly so soon, it really needed to be artistically contrasting and of a different scale. Perhaps even less expensive? I was also to design the set, and working in the Chocolate Factory space certainly determines the scale of your production. The theatre is small, and I believe most effective when not overwhelmed by large set pieces. I hope this gives me a moment to write about my predilection toward telling stories using very little.

My work is often called minimalist, though I myself have never used that word. I like to visually support the story whilst getting out of the audience's way. I wonder if there is any connection between my childhood and my adult need for simplicity? My parents, like so many people of their generation, filled their tiny home with a lot of "stuff". The glass and china ornaments were all very lovely, but even as a child I remember thinking that if I ever had my own home it wouldn't have all that clutter. So, that need to declutter goes into my work. I go through a number of mechanisms to simplify things in the rehearsal room. Going all the way back to Liverpool days I've often had a large cardboard box in the corner of the room where all the "cut" props and costumes go. I invite actors to discard things into the box if they feel they no longer need them, whether it be a prop or a costume piece. Actors have been known to climb into the box! It's a fun method of focussing on what is really necessary, what, indeed, is "essential". Alex Gemignani made a wonderful visual collage of all the elements I cut from *Sweeney Todd*. It hung backstage at the O'Neill Theatre. Anyway, I was determined this production of *The Color Purple* would be visually simple, and of course in typical British fashion, the budget didn't allow for anything more!

There was a bleached wooden floor, again with the audience seated on three sides. As you would see if you followed through my work, I like a wooden floor, the less sophisticated and the rougher the better! When I redesigned the space at Classic Stage, I had the entire floor of the acting space clad in reclaimed wood from an old Brooklyn building. *Sweeney* had a grey wooden floor, with a light box under it so that light, sometimes white, sometimes red, could seep through the boards. I like my homes to have wooden floors, most Scottish churches have naked floorboards, and the floor upon which the black piano sat was black wooden floorboards, until they were covered up by the inevitable 1960s fixation with wall-to-wall carpeting. The set of *The Color Purple* had a wooden back wall, in the same planking as the floor, and hanging on the wall were twelve plain chairs of the type that can hold your Bible in the little container at the back, known of course as bible-back chairs. The chairs hung on pegs on the wall, in the same way that the religious Shaker families hung their chairs on the walls of their worship spaces. It was also reminiscent of something you might see in rural parts of American Southern States, where chairs are hung on the outside porch walls of some poorer shack-like homes.

Again I acknowledge there are chairs in so many of the images I create. The black Victorian chairs in *Sweeney*, the single stool in *Pacific Overtures*. In the eleven o'clock number in *The Color Purple* Celie sings, "*Got my chair when my body can't hold out*".[1] That lyric is really why the chairs are there, to support her. The style of chair changed for the New York transfer, but more of that later.

I didn't know what props we would use, I seldom do before rehearsals begin, but I did know there wouldn't be many. I've worked with some terrific prop departments in many theatres and before we start, I apologetically forewarn them that they may have to provide things that will eventually get cut – just like that birthday cake in *Company* or that baby in *Chalk Circle*. This will be no negative reflection on them or their excellent work. However, the props that last the course will be the appropriate props for how we are going to tell the story. My reputation for having a theatrical surgical scalpel goes ahead of me, so these artists usually know what to expect. I hope that none of them take it personally.

Now, the casting. It took a lot of searching for artists with the vocal skills that we needed, but I'm delighted to say that the pool of available people had grown, thanks to drama schools at long last having changed their attitudes. More actors of colour are being trained for the theatre, perhaps not yet in equal proportion, but certainly with significant moves forward. The score of the musical needed great singers. Catherine Jayes was my Musical Supervisor again and we were delighted with how the cast came together. The role of Shug Avery was to be played by the tremendously talented Nicola Hughes, who had headlined many West End shows. Her casting created a "star" precedent for how that role would be cast in the future. We had to find a Celie, the central character whose journey it is. It's an enormous role, hardly ever offstage, and a big sing. I clearly remember it was a rainy Thursday afternoon and we were auditioning in the rehearsal room at the theatre. A young woman came in, small of stature and with a wonderful smile. Having trained at the renowned Royal Academy of Dramatic Art, she had been building a healthy resume. We spoke for a bit, had a laugh or two, and then – she sang! I couldn't quite believe it. I've experienced a few memorable auditions during my career, but this was extraordinary. We *had* to get this girl to play the role. Luckily she said yes! Her name was – Cynthia Erivo.

Cynthia was a wonderful Celie, in every way. She had great success with the role in London, but when we took it to New York, things truly went stellar for her. It was the launch of a remarkable career. We still see each other, and for all the success that she so greatly deserves, for all that it has changed for her in her life, she remains that lovely girl with the big smile who I first met on that rainy Thursday.

We started rehearsals with no thought of a future beyond the Chocolate Factory. We delved into how we were going to tell this epic story with only some chairs. It was a puzzle that needed solving and nothing makes me happier.

I had met with Marsha Norman before rehearsals began. Marsha is a Tony and Pulitzer Prize-winning playwright, and a really classy lady of the theatre. I'd always admired her work and many years before I'd particularly enjoyed directing her play *'Night Mother*. When we met I tentatively shared that I wanted to make a few trims in the piece, particularly in the big Act Two opening, which is set in Africa. She is nothing if not generous and said to do whatever I needed to do! So, I did trim it – well, cut it actually! I took approximately forty-five minutes out of the original. My work is almost always staged in a way in which I cut out all the musical transitions that are usually there between scenes, many of which were put in to cover moving the scenery. Not having much scenery tends to mean no transitions. When Marsha saw the show in a preview performance, she was very approving, and totally okay about the cuts. We only disagreed over one scene, which I wanted to take out and she wanted left in. She won – quite rightly. The cuts we made in London remained, becoming the text for the Broadway revival.

It's interesting, though perhaps not surprising, that much of the imagery I created to tell the story was, in fact, religious. In the original novel, Celie talks to two characters who are no longer with her. She talks to Nettie, her beloved sister, who has gone to be a Missionary in Africa, and she talks to God, the central focus of that Southern churchgoing community that is the background to our story. Celie births a baby. No real baby please! Instead she pulled a white sheet – my granny again? – from under her costume, wrapped it as if it were swaddling clothes to represent the baby, and put it into a basket just like Moses. That sheet is used again, to be the space for a picnic she attends near the end of the show. Easter is a big part of the story, as are the three church ladies who criticise everything. They may have been from Putnam County, Georgia, but they reminded me of childhood churchgoers in the Highlands of Scotland. The musical even starts in church, preacher and all. Yes, the work I described in an earlier chapter, the work with the religious stories, was certainly having an influence on *The Color Purple*. We had a good run in London. In fact it was quite a hit. And so, on to Broadway.

I hadn't thought much about the colour of my skin in the London rehearsal room. Not that I wasn't aware, not that I was being irresponsible or insensitive, but somehow it felt less of an issue there. The actors were certainly generous, but of course they were used to white men directing their stories. Of course, when we did it in London, this wasn't about any of us British people. It was about people from another country, people whose recent ancestors would have been slaves. It's about African-Americans. Our actors' families may have come from Africa, or perhaps they originated from the Windrush generation who, starting in the late 1940s, came to Britain from the Caribbean, but nobody was African-American. When it was decided that *The Color Purple* would return to Broadway, with an American Company, well that was a very different thing.

Two years after it had closed in London, we gathered together for our first day of rehearsals in New York. We were going into the Jacobs Theatre on 45th Street, one of those very nice mid-sized Broadway houses, perfect for the show. We had to move away from the three-sided configuration and it now sat within the proscenium arch. The wooden floor of the set was still the primary visual feature, though with more levels than the flat floor we had in London. I had to create a set that gave a much bigger audience the opportunity to see every part of the action, and the varying levels were the answer. The chairs were this time mounted on a series of very tall wooden panels. The panels were all broken and roughly hewn, probably giving a much more outdoors feel than we had in London, which was very helpful for the storytelling. Those panels went all the way up into the flies, all the way up to God! I should say there were many more chairs, all mounted to create a visual installation on that broken wall. Brokenness had become very much a theme for me. The chairs were no longer bible-backed, but rather a random collection of antique wooden American chairs with an age that covered the duration of Celie's story.

The small band were in a room below the stage, the music piped in. Never my favourite thing, but it did mean that the set could jut out, allowing the cast to really connect with the audience as there was no orchestra pit to worry about. Also I was insistent that unless I could be guaranteed that all the musicians be Black – sadly unlikely at that time – it was best that they not be seen. Wonderful new orchestrations had been created by the highly talented Joseph Joubert, and our Music Director was the excellent Jason Michael Webb. The writers were all now with us. The aforementioned Marsha; the late Allee Willis, one of the lyricists and a true character; Brenda Russell, a very classy African-American singer-songwriter; and finally Stephen Bray, also African-American, known for his collaborations with Madonna and his extensive body of work in the world of popular music. As so often happens when you leave a smaller theatre and go into the large, high-pressure, Broadway environment, there were many more people to wrangle. However, everybody was hugely excited about the musical being given another chance. There were changes in the pool of collaborators. My dear Ann Hould-Ward did new costume designs for Broadway, Jane Cox who had also done the Chocolate Factory did a wonderful job of the lightning, and Charles G. LaPointe took over as Hair

Designer. I cannot stress how wonderful it is for a director to work with familiar collaborators. Whilst I fully appreciate the importance of working with new people, and how necessary that is in order to diversify, it is a complex issue. I deliberately found new opportunities for artists of colour to work at Classic Stage in the director and design categories. In doing so, I hope my own work has grown through working with people who bring different life experiences to the table. As I said earlier, I have done this long enough to see women be given a much greater voice. It may be a slow process, but I know that same voice will be given to artists from the Black community. It can be dangerous to expect too much change too quickly, but we will get there.

Before rehearsals, our producers were concerned that Cynthia was new to Broadway and that nobody would know her. I did say, "*Give it three months*"! For once I'm happy to say "*I told you so*". There was also a little concern about a British girl playing this iconic American role. A debate in itself! This meant we had to find great African-American artists for the other main roles, Shug Avery and Sophia. The former was played by the remarkable Jennifer Hudson. The latter was brilliantly played by the feisty Danielle Brooks, who later went on to reprise the role in the 2023 movie and to be Oscar-nominated for her work. The rest of the cast was terrific, with some of the best singing ever heard on a Broadway stage.

I sat everybody down on the first day of rehearsal and said "*This is your story, not mine. I am here to help you tell your story. I do know where Georgia is, and I know about some of the musical's major themes, poverty, church, God, family, maybe even a little brokenness.*" I told them the story of that bus and how I now sensed that I might be driving it. I now understood what it felt like to be the minority in the room and was humbled by the privilege of being invited in. I wanted the actors to get away from all the stereotypes that were usually expected of them as actors of colour. It challenged them, it certainly challenged me, and it was a joy.

There was the day Oprah Winfrey, one of our lead producers, came to visit. I can still see her now standing around the piano with the company, singing the title song. Oprah has a long relationship with the material, reaching back to the original Steven Spielberg movie. She is an extraordinary human being, committed to making our world a better place.

Then the dream came true. Alice Walker came to a rehearsal. She sat beside me as the company ran through the first act. What I can only describe as true wisdom shines from her. She watched, she smiled, she said little. As she left, she quietly said to me "*The ancestors would be so pleased!*"

The preview period was productive and I had a strong sense that something was happening that was bigger than all of us. I don't wish this to read as arrogant, but I knew it was going to be good, after all it worked in London and now it felt like it had come home. However I had no idea we were making something that would so profoundly touch the audiences who saw it. After Cynthia had sung that great anthem "I'm Here", celebrating the importance of loving self as well as loving others, the audiences were straight on their feet. At the end of the show when the company were singing "*The Color Purple, look what God has done*" those audiences, male, female, Black, white, straight, gay, Christian, Jewish and maybe even non-believer, had their arms in the air praising the Lord. It really was remarkable. It made theatre necessary. It made you glad to be alive.

I had been so concerned that all my John Doyle sheet-birthing sort of theatre might alienate the busloads of church ladies who had booked to come, after all they may have been expecting real trees and authentic recreations of Southern interiors onstage? They may think they weren't getting their money's worth. How wrong I was. We shared the same imagery after all. I also think that the production brought in non-theatregoers. At the end of one show there was a box sitting on the front of the stage, a fried chicken food container. It was almost empty. Some patrons had been having something to eat during the show and had left their trash. Many cast members were furious but I was delighted. These folks came to the theatre and didn't know the rules. They weren't disruptive, just hungry. For me there was a very tangible connection between them and the lady in Portree who called out for *Macbeth* to be killed. It is a great privilege to welcome new audiences into our theatres.

Our show opened and it was a big hit! Great reviews and award nominations aside, the most thrilling thing for me was on Opening Night, when Celie and Mister, the man who had so bullied her in their marriage, were sitting on either side of that white sheet having a moment of true reconciliation. I felt a hand on my shoulder. I didn't need to look. It was as natural as that lady watching

Nicholas Nickleby, except this time I knew the lady. Her gentle hand had made the entire journey worthwhile. The lady was Alice Walker.

Other great actresses joined the company at various stages. The divine Heather Headley took over from Jennifer Hudson and had a huge personal success. And then Jennifer Holliday, one of the first women of colour to be awarded the Tony, for *Dreamgirls*, returned to Broadway as the third Shug Avery. Without her success all those years before, this whole new generation of Black actresses may not have been given the Broadway opportunities now rightly offered to them.

Cynthia won numerous awards, I won a Drama Desk and was nominated for a Tony. The show won Best Revival and the list includes a Grammy and an Emmy. It was in the same season as the arrival of *Hamilton*. If somebody had approached you to say they were writing a musical about Alexander Hamilton, one of the Founding Fathers and the first US Secretary of the Treasury, wouldn't you have said they were quite mad? Especially as it was to be played primarily by actors of colour? It would never take off. There would be no audience for it. Well, Tony Award-winning writer and composer Lin-Manuel Miranda most certainly proved you wrong. It's the perfect example of theatre meeting politics in a highly accessible and entertaining way. I feel sure there will be more *Hamilton*s and the theatre will always be necessary in the national political discourse. Directors need to be encouraged to seek the stories that reflect our societies, writers need to be encouraged to write those stories, and freelance artists need to do all they can to remember that theatre really can help to change the world.

The Color Purple had a terrific fifteen months on Broadway. Life-long friends were made, including, for me, Matthew DiCarlo, another very trusted Production Stage Manager and Associate Director. I'd also like to take a moment to acknowledge my Design Associate David L. Arsenault. Both of these extraordinary young men gave me the safety of complete artistic support, and we continue to enjoy a great deal of laughter together. It came to the last performance. I usually don't attend those as the Protestant in me can't bear all the hugging, but this time I really wanted to be there. The job and the company had meant too much. Before every show, members of the acting company had met in a small room under the stage for what they called "Prayer Circle". It was exactly what it says. They were asking their God to help them give a good telling of the story. I never felt it was my place to join, but on this last occasion, I did. One of the actresses, Carrie Compere, was leading the prayers. She finished by thanking God for the director and said, "*And God, he's a White Man!*" Just as the prayers finished, there was a huge sustained cheer and applause from the auditorium above. I knew the audience would be excited, but this ovation seemed excessive. I went out front to see what was going on. Well, Hillary Clinton had arrived, accompanied by her husband, the ex-President. It was her first public appearance after the election of 2016, when she so devastatingly lost to Donald Trump. The love and support in that auditorium was palpable. When Cynthia reached that last song, the applause went on and on, with the whole audience being on their feet for what must have been five minutes. The first to leap up was former Secretary of State Hillary Rodham Clinton.

On that same day a young man came up to me when he was waiting to go in to see the final show. He approached me and said he wanted to say something to me. I'm usually a little uncomfortable with any intrusion into my personal space, but I smiled at him and he said "*Thank you for The Color Purple.*" I asked him if he'd already seen it and he said, "*Yes. Fifty Six Times.*" I jokingly asked him if he was okay, but in reality I was thrilled. Another young theatregoer on a journey, just like that kid at the Inverness Empire Theatre.

So, a London run, a Broadway run, two years of touring the US playing to packed houses everywhere it went, and the question remains "*Should it have been directed by a middle-aged white man?*" I'm not the person to ask, and certainly not the person to decide. I did ask Hilton Als, highly respected African-American theatre critic, the same question. His response was "*It doesn't matter who does it, as long as it's the right person for the story.*" I've no doubt that the question is by now the subject of somebody's dissertation. I will leave it to be answered by the many thousands of people who saw the production.

"Black Lives Matter" was building a long-overdue powerful voice during our Broadway run. America was experiencing extraordinary social and political change. I had been helming a piece of work that I had no idea would have the profound effect it did have, a piece of theatre mirroring the nature of our society at precisely the right moment. I would now like to take you to another Black show I did, as not so long after *The Color Purple* I decided to do *Carmen Jones* at Classic Stage.

Carmen Jones is an adaptation of the Bizet Opera by Oscar Hammerstein II. He had the vision to adapt it to be performed by a Black cast, and it was first presented on Broadway in 1943, the same season as *Oklahoma!*. Whatever one thinks of the fact that this was created by a white man, we must remember that Hammerstein had written, with the great Jerome Kern, *Showboat*, where there is a White chorus and a Black chorus and where racial prejudice and the mixing of blood are at the centre of the story. I think it's completely fair to say that he was way ahead of his time; after all *Showboat* premiered on Broadway in 1927 and it is arguably the first great American musical. Staging it now may be challenging, but its place in history should never be forgotten. Let's also acknowledge George Gershwin, who, in 1935, wrote *Porgy and Bess*, an undisputed masterpiece. If we look at these choices through a modern lens, they may make you somewhat uncomfortable. However, we need to consider the fact that few other successful writers were creating musical theatre pieces that gave this degree of opportunity for actors of colour. Most Black actors in musicals were at best relegated to the chorus, but more likely were still doing vaudeville. I remember asking my friend and colleague André De Shields, one of Broadway's finest Black actors, if he had started his career as a dancer? His response was "*What choice was there?*"

Ted Chapin was executive director of the Rodgers and Hammerstein Foundation and therefore an enormously powerful man. Ted has always been a good friend, wonderfully encouraging of my work, and when I asked him about acquiring the Rights to *Carmen Jones*, he was hugely supportive. I did, inevitably, want to make changes, to cut it down to one act, and to look at how to make the tone of the dialogue less hokey. So, with Ted's blessing, I set about working on the project. I was trying to find new audiences for CSC. The organisation was seriously looking at what a classic meant to us today, and in particular wanted to build a repertoire that might attract Black audiences. It's very interesting that many people told me I shouldn't do *Carmen Jones*. I was told it was offensive, dated, no longer appropriate, but the interesting thing is that all those who conveyed this message were white. Nobody from the Black community resisted it at all, on the contrary they encouraged it. The film, starring Dorothy Dandridge, had been a big hit with the African-American audience. Remember there had been hardly any opportunity for that audience to see "themselves" on the screen and Dandridge had been nominated in the Best Actress category at the 1955 Oscars.

Because my work was now much more known to actors and actresses of colour, I was able to attract some marvellous performers who had never otherwise been offered opportunities at Classic Stage. Above all, the great Anika Noni Rose played Carmen. Anika is a powerhouse of talent, has a very impressive career in theatre and on screen, is totally fearless, and I felt I had a real partner in making the production. She had a great personal success in the role and I hope we get the opportunity to make more work together.

The adaptation is set in a parachute factory during World War Two, and very much follows the plot of the original Opera, yet somehow the treatment of the story and of the score makes it more sultry and dangerous than the original tends to be. The *New York Times* made our production a Critics Pick and described it as *"primal and breathlessly seductive"*.[2] Audiences flocked to see it and Classic Stage was successful in attracting a more diverse audience than that which usually came through the doors. It was 2018 and our world was going to change during the following couple of years. I do believe though that our production paved the way for re-looking at some of these old-fashioned musicals. If you are interested in doing such work, remain courageous. There will always be people who want to criticise you, maybe hoping you will fail. Years ago in Liverpool, when the going got tough, a fellow director sent me a note. He'd written out the Theodore Roosevelt quote *"The credit belongs to the man who is actually in the arena......"* Every artist should read it. You need the strength to remain brave, maybe bold, and to tell the stories you believe should be told.

Anika is quoted as remembering my saying to the *Carmen Jones* company *"There are culturally things I don't know, so I'm open to whatever you all are bringing."* Her response was *"To have someone say those words makes you feel much safer than someone who steps in feeling like they know everything."* How could I know everything? How could any director know everything? If you aren't going to learn from the project you are doing, why are you doing it?

There is strength in acknowledging that you will always be learning. It certainly makes it worth showing up for work every day.

During all the work at Classic Stage, I had my stage manager Bernita Robinson at my side. Bernita was one of the first African-American stage managers in New York City, and as such she was not only a wonderful source of knowledge, but, for me, a great teacher. On *Carmen Jones* I would check in with her at the end of every rehearsal to ensure that I was never using vocabulary or imagery that might be read as inappropriate. To have a dear friend help you who doesn't share the colour of your skin does mean that you can be vulnerable and open to sharing and to helping make change. I do believe that the only way forward is to learn from each other. I understand the argument of "not doing your work for you", but I believe we have to take mutual responsibility for relearning and rethinking.

So, if approached now to do a production of a Black story, would I do it? If I can connect with that story, if there are parallels between that story and my own life experience, then yes, I probably would. You see I fundamentally believe that theatre is an art form that demonstrates that which makes us the same. I know there will be many who disagree with me, but it is that very demonstration of our "sameness" that gives theatre its central power. When those audiences were crying and yelling for Celie, they weren't crying for her, they were in fact crying for themselves.

As a gay man, do I think straight directors should direct plays that centre on gay stories? Surely it all comes down to sensitivity. Now having said that, when I chose to direct *A Man of No Importance* I knew I wanted to work with a gay actor in the central role. I didn't want to be teaching the unteachable to a straight actor. That is not to say a straight actor can't play a gay role, it was simply that, in this instance anyway, I needed mutual understanding with the actor who was playing the role. When casting the role of Diaghilev in Terrence McNally's play *Fire and Air*, neither Terrence nor I felt the sexuality of the actor mattered, but rather that he be a fine actor with a great classical facility with text. So, we cast the marvellous Douglas Hodge, who was totally convincing as a gay man, particularly as a homosexual of the early twentieth century. Interestingly, in 2010, Doug had won his Tony Award for his portrayal of Albin in *La Cage Aux Folles*. I wonder if he would be cast in the role now?

What we find acceptable creatively must change as society changes. We simply need to be aware of those changes and act accordingly. The danger lies in feeling one must do what is "right". By that I mean don't just follow what is politically correct, but make choices that are the best choices for you at the moment of choosing.

These questions of appropriateness are important. Of course some people are more culturally and socially right for a project, but it is dependent on so many things. We need to be careful that we don't find ourselves creating a panel who sit in judgement over such decisions. Please don't cancel creativity just because you don't agree with it. Can only a murderer play Macbeth? I certainly hope not! Can only a woman direct *The Three Sisters*? That would be sad. Can only a Jewish actor play Shylock? To be absolutely honest, I don't know. I think it comes down to what you are intending to say with the production. If we say that only Black directors can direct Black work does this mean only white directors can direct white work? In doing so we may end up with a Black theatre and a White theatre, and before you know where you are we're back in 1974 at the University of Georgia.

I'm honoured to have been a small cog in the wheel of change of the last fifty years, and I know the changes of the next fifty will be equally complicated but just as fulfilling.

11

From the Met to Sydney Opera House

As I said in an earlier chapter, Opera is a theatrical form that has always intrigued me, although I didn't start directing any until rather a long way into my career. Some directors dedicate themselves solely to working in that field, but I've been very much a theatre director who does some Opera. However, I have learned a great deal from my involvement with Opera singers, Opera Houses and even Opera audiences and I'd like to share some of those observations with you.

My first tentative ventures were with the Young Persons' and Community departments of major companies. I started by doing a project called *Ice*, a new operatic fairy tale, commissioned by the London Symphonia. We worked with residents of the London Borough of Tower Hamlets and performed it at the People's Palace on the Mile End Road, the project being led by two professional Opera singers. One of the wonderful things about making opera within the community is that the participants have no fear of it as an elitist form and therefore approach it with great freedom. I followed that experience with two productions for Welsh National Opera, this time performed solely by young singers. The first was a new Opera called *The Tailor's Daughter*, again based on a fairy tale, and the second, which we performed in Belfast as well as in Cardiff, was *L'Elisir D'Amore* by Donizetti.

Next was another fun and unusual opera project. It was for a tour and starred my old school friend Janis Kelly. It was, believe it or not, a two-woman version of *The Marriage of Figaro*. The two sopranos had devised a condensed version of Mozart's masterpiece and it was created in order to tour throughout the UK, having to be able to pack up and travel in one suitcase. You've heard nothing until you've experienced some of the great Mozart sextettes sung by two feisty sopranos! Delicious madness.

A UK company that I admired very much was called Opera Factory. It was an experimental Opera company under the direction of Australian Director David Freeman. I recall with great fondness a production they made of *Cosi Fan Tutte*, all set on a beach and interestingly Janis was a member of that company. It was described by the *Guardian* critic as one of the *"ten productions that changed British Opera"*. Freeman was influenced by the work of the great Peter Brook. Brook is my theatrical hero, a director who rejected a promising career at the Royal Shakespeare Company and on Broadway in order to be able to dedicate himself to experimenting in theatre with his own company in Paris. His production of *Carmen*, set on a rug, was remarkable. You can probably tell that I am drawn to the smaller-scale, more experimental work, even though most of my own Opera productions have happened in major Opera Houses.

As destiny would have it, the first of these bigger productions was with Scottish Opera, the company whose work introduced me to the form way back during that 1970 school trip to Edinburgh. In 2006 they invited me to direct *Lucia Di Lammermoor*. Now this is an Opera I have been asked to do on more than one occasion, probably because it's set in Scotland and I am, after all, Scottish. This is ironic considering it's written by an Italian, sung in Italian, and doesn't have much about it that's authentically Scottish, still, it makes great theatre! The tragic tale comes from source material by Sir Walter Scott and is in fact a descent into insanity, as the famous "Mad Scene" demonstrates. It was a joy to be back in Glasgow. Walking every day to the rehearsal room along the same streets I had walked as a young student. Described by one critic as *"an essay in austerity"*, there wasn't a hint of tartan in this production. I wanted to explore the bleakness that I knew from growing up in the Highlands. The chorus, who very much understood what I was after, could easily adopt the grey Presbyterian faces I remember from childhood Sundays. Although I rehearsed in a somewhat traditional way, schedule in hand, I still didn't work it all out before I started. Liz Ascroft created a wonderful design, providing a sweeping plateau of steps on which I could tell the tale, the singers being dressed in authentic period costumes, using beautiful dark hues and tones. Design is an essential element in Opera, the visual being a very important tool in a form that is so often sung in an unfamiliar language. We performed the production in 2007 at the beautiful Theatre Royal, Glasgow and I'm happy to say that it was a big hit for the company. The local boy had come home and everybody was very happy.

One of the key differences between directing Opera and directing other forms of theatre is that, as the director, you don't have the final say! You aren't the boss! Who is? The Conductor. You see, it's primarily about the music. Companies do all they can to convince us that they're driven by the story, but I don't think it's quite true. Undoubtedly the powers that be in those companies are trying to give the theatrical element more status, as demonstrated by bringing in Tony-winning directors to make the productions. However, once you're in there, the music still wins the day. I have no problem with this, after all the music is what we remember and the stature of the music is what makes the form unique. The conductor has the daunting responsibility of protecting the authenticity of the musical interpretation and at the same time leading the singers and an often enormous orchestra. In much of the musical theatre work I have done, the tempi are led by the singers themselves, with the Conductor following the singer, if indeed there is a Conductor! However in Opera the Maestro sets the musical pacing of each moment. That's how it has to be or else the whole thing would fall apart. I have been very fortunate in having worked with some terrific conductors, who do care about the story. They collaborate with the singer to find the best possible support for that particular artist's voice, whilst honouring the feelings and intentions of the production. The entire collaboration is wonderful but when push comes to shove, the Maestro is the boss! Yet for some reason the production still seems to be publicly associated with the director. The Anthony Minghella *Butterfly*, the Doyle *Peter Grimes*. Perhaps that's a way of making sure the director ultimately takes the blame? Anyway, I do again need to stress that one of the things I like about directing Opera is that I am the number two. It somehow takes the pressure off and in fact it makes me happy that another one of the cousins is in charge this time!

After its Glasgow success, the Scottish Opera production of *Lucia* was then invited to go to the Mariinsky Theatre, in St Petersburg, Russia. It was to be performed by their resident company and the soprano role was to be taken by the great Anna Netrebko. She was to be going on to sing the role at The Met, a role she had never sung before, so the company were interested in my production being done to provide her with the opportunity of exploring the role. She would do one performance and then another soprano, who had also rehearsed, would take the rest of the run. They offered me a very nice fee and I was happy that our work would be given some extra life. One of the disappointments for a director when making an Opera is that it's given very few performances in the company's schedule. This is probably because they need to provide a wide variety of product in order to sustain their audience attendance figures. Anyway, I awaited my call to fly to St Petersburg to attend rehearsals. We all agreed that my Glasgow Associate Director would re-stage it, but it was assumed that I would be needed to work with the star. The rehearsal call kept being delayed and as we were getting nearer the date of the premiere, I asked my agent to find out what was going on. I was eventually asked to be at the Mariinsky four days before it opened. Now, I knew from experience that singers don't sing for a couple of days leading up to Opening Night, so I was bemused. Did this mean they only wanted me to work with the Lucia for one day? What on earth was I supposed to achieve in that time? Their response was that the diva would only be rehearsing it for that one day so I wouldn't otherwise be needed. My point of sharing this with you is to demonstrate a situation where "process" really didn't matter. Not that it was Ms Netrebko's fault, as I believe she had a huge success with the role, and this sort of situation is not at all uncommon in the world of Opera. However, I found it rather insulting so, for the only time in my career, I took the fee and declined to show up. Nobody cared. I'd probably have been a nuisance anyway!

Next for me was, as they say, something completely different. I was approached by Los Angeles Opera to direct *The Rise and Fall of the City of Mahagonny*. This complex political hybrid of Opera and musical theatre is written by Kurt Weill and Bertolt Brecht, and is absolutely up my street. Even more up my street because it was going to have a cast of both Opera singers and Broadway stars. The wonderful tenor Anthony Dean Griffey, who went on to play *Peter Grimes* for me at The Met, was to be the leading man. My own Patti LuPone and the extraordinary Audra McDonald were the Broadway stars, and you will never see any shine brighter! Smaller roles were to be played by Opera singers and the chorus was, of course, that of the Los Angeles Opera. It was to be performed in the Dorothy Chandler Pavilion right there in downtown Los Angeles. The Dorothy Chandler is huge, in fact it used to host the Oscars, but that didn't matter as the piece itself is epic and would be visually big, much bigger than I was accustomed to.

We rehearsed in West Hollywood. James Conlon was the Maestro, and we had a terrific collaboration. Mark Bailey, from those York Mystery Cycle days, designed the set and of course Ann Hould-Ward did the costumes. She was perfect for it in that she had done huge amounts of Opera and was also used to the requirements of Broadway leading ladies. We set it in a desert landscape and created our own theatrical equivalent of Las Vegas. The three acts of the Opera time-travelled, starting in a Depression-Era wilderness, and ending in a representation of our contemporary world, full of artifice and deeply disturbing. I loved every moment of it, but often ask myself if I really understood it? I think I found an understanding of it, maybe that's the best way to describe how one can react to any piece of art, especially one as complicated as this. I certainly revelled in its political message.

What was really inspiring was to see those singers from a more formal musical and theatrical world learn from the two ladies. The three of us introduced them to our way of working, with much repetition and the desire to keep working on the piece, putting the story first. We wanted to keep rehearsing right up to Opening Night, not the norm in Opera, and it was invaluable in this complex piece, which is really a musical theatre/Opera hybrid. What was also thrilling was that it was the first time I was ever booed! It is traditional for Directors and Designers to take a bow on Opening Night, which I hate but usually feel pressurised into doing. The audience was on its feet, probably desperate to be the first to get to the car park. I walked on to the stage to take my "call" and there was some booing. Not much, just a few people, but enough to make me very happy. I'd upset somebody! Part of the job! I somehow think Bertolt would have been proud. If you'd like to see the production it's available on DVD. Also there is a recording, which I'm pleased to say won two Grammys.

By now it was 2008 and I was at the Metropolitan Opera in New York City. During the Broadway run of *Sweeney Todd* my agent called asking "*Would you take a meeting with Peter Gelb, the General Manager at the Met?*" The phrase "*take a meeting*" has always amused me as it somehow suggests that you're in charge of the situation!

Anyway, off I went for my first visit to the Lincoln Centre. I had imagined I would be one of many directors Mr Gelb would be seeing and was a little surprised not to be sitting in line. He is an intelligent and charming gentleman and during our very nice meeting he asked if I'd been to the Met. I think he meant had I previously worked there? However, I naïvely said, "*No. I've never been able to afford the ticket prices.*" He then said "*Would you like to come here to direct a new production of Benjamin Britten's Peter Grimes?*" I almost fell off my chair. I love that Opera. As I said, Rob and I had lived in the Old Town in Hastings on England's south coast and on stormy nights, perhaps after a couple of drinks, we would walk down to the Harbour Arm and give our own unique rendition of one of the Opera's great Finales. Here I was going to be doing it for real! Peter Gelb had seen my work on Broadway, somehow seeing beyond that tiny show and decided I could do this enormous piece at one of the world's finest Opera Houses. My colleague and friend Scott Pask designed the set and we worked closely to find the imagery with which we would tell the story. Down near our house in Hastings there were tall fishermen's net-huts, which look truly ominous on a bleak day. Scott created a set from representations of those huts. It turned into a giant wall, with doors built into it at numerous levels, just as the net-huts have. This wall could magically move up and downstage and the side walls of our dark box could close in, so that the playing space could be made very large or much smaller by some very elegant stage technology. It was hugely effective. The designer builds a scale model to look like the set, then that model goes to the Met Studios, where it is taken to a larger scale. Our first experience of the actual set was many months before rehearsals began, in fact during the previous summer. I walked out onto the Met stage for the first time and found myself standing in our finished set. I'll be honest and tell you I could feel myself starting to choke up. There it was, this giant idea, fully finished and I was standing on it looking out to that extraordinary auditorium! We were due to go into rehearsal in January of

2008, and this was the summer of 2007. Yes, we had to start technical rehearsals for the Opera in August – six months before the actual rehearsals began. Believe me, this is a very unusual situation. You are given a full week of tech, working out all the set moves and basic lighting cues, and are even provided with twenty-four actors to stand in for the company. For somebody like me, none of this sat easily, however, I do have to reluctantly admit that we got a lot done. The reason for the pre-rehearsal tech is because once the season starts, it's very difficult to stop and start the repertoire. These are enormous pieces of art, and getting from Opera to Opera in the season is a major task which has to be carefully worked out. After all, as Moliere said, "*Of all the noises known to man, opera is the most expensive.*" Here it was again, economics guiding art. Usually your show rehearses in the morning, probably until around 2.00pm, then the crew turn it around to the set for the evening performance of another Opera. If you're ever offered the opportunity to watch a turn-around rehearsal at the Met, take it! An army of some 200 stage-hands, perfectly drilled, achieve it all in a few hours in order that lights can be checked, costumes and wigs put in place and everything be ready for the evening performance. Another remarkable thing at the Met is the costume department. Nothing is too much trouble. Now bear in mind there were 100 chorus members to be costumed in period clothing, as well as a large principal cast. Everybody is wigged, with jewellery and accessories made to perfection. A very long way from the Watermill Theatre, Newbury.

We had a wonderful Conductor, Donald Runnicles, a fellow Scot, and a remarkable cast led by Anthony Dean Griffey, Patricia Racette, Teddy Tahu Rhodes and the famous British mezzo-soprano, Dame Felicity Palmer. We had a worryingly short rehearsal period, three weeks in the studio before going into tech. Opera rehearsal periods are notoriously short and even then it can be hard getting your singers all of the time. I was only given the chorus for six pre-tech rehearsals and I had to fight to get that number. It's no wonder Opera is often accused of being static – just try getting 100 people on and off stage in a reasonable manner. It can take a long time. Principal singers are often doing double duty by travelling to do performances or concerts at the same time, meaning you have to carefully plan your rehearsal schedules to accommodate their pre-negotiated absences. What people don't appreciate is that Opera singers very seldom get paid to rehearse, their payments coming as fees on a per performance basis. Deep down then, there is no financial incentive to devote all of your time to a rehearsal period and they have to earn their living elsewhere. Fortunately we had a very committed company, who didn't miss many rehearsals and I very much enjoyed working with them, for all my frustration over not having enough time with the chorus. I fondly remember Felicity being very excited one day because I referred to them as "*actors*" and not "*singers*"!

I was rather surprised one day to look at a rehearsal call sheet to see "Music with Maestro Runnicles" and next to it "Staging with Maestro Doyle". Not only was I amused to be called Maestro, but I was somewhat bemused to see my function as doing "staging". There is the root of the challenge. It didn't say "acting with" or "scene study with", both of which suggest some degree of a psychological search for truth and tone, but rather "staging". Making pictures. Bardini back in Georgia used to say that it was only the British and the Americans who used the word "blocking" or "staging" when referring to the putting together of a play or musical. "Blocking", a word that means placing, but can also mean stopping, like a barrier. For all the Opera I have done since, I still think it's hard to get Opera companies to understand that there is a lot more to it than staging!

We left the rehearsal room and started onstage rehearsals. You usually get a couple of days that are known as "Stage and Piano", meaning the director can work on the set with the company but still with a piano accompaniment. These are the directors' rehearsals. Then the schedule usually allows for a couple of days off (or in the case of the Met chorus, days of doing other shows), and you gather again to do a couple of days called "Stage and Orchestra". Those days belong to the Conductor. Woe betide the director who goes anywhere near the stage on those rehearsals! The reason for splitting it in this way is obvious. The management doesn't want the orchestra there all the time, after all orchestras are made up of a large number of musicians, making them very expensive. The chance for the singers to repeat the material over both sets of rehearsals can be very useful. However, with some singers, you only truly hear their performance for the first time at the "Stage and Orchestra". You may have thought they sounded loud before but now you hear them actually "sing out". Not only that, but the "singing out" can mean that their bodies start to contort in order to produce the sound, and all the work you did on naturalism can vanish in one afternoon. I was aware that our production was going to be filmed in front of a live audience and so worked hard to get the cast to understand the need to be simple and natural in front of the camera. I was pleased to be invited to attend the filming of the Opera, which you can now see on DVD. I was asked to go to the "truck" where they control what the cameras are doing. I duly showed up, nobody asked who I was, I was totally ignored and eventually I slipped away into the night. The theatre is a never-ending pattern of insulting, even personally humiliating situations and I've learned that the best way to manage them is to simply ignore them and walk away.

In many senses I have sympathy with Opera singers. They have the critical voices of their coaches and teachers in their heads. They even have dialect coaches in the rehearsal room, constantly correcting them on the sounds. I had to put a stop to that when I discovered that the dialect coach for "Grimes" was in fact Italian – a very nice person, but not with the most convincing example of an East Anglian accent. I admire singers for their commitment to the work, for the stamina they need to get through a performance and for the open-mindedness and flexibility they must have. I say the last because the likelihood is that a singer in one of the trickier roles may have sung it in many productions. Some operatic characters have very few singers who can sing that role, either because of its vocal range or the way it is "set" in the voice. Let me give you the example of the tenor in the Scottish Opera production of *Lucia* who had done the role in seventeen other productions. It was hard for him to make the necessary prop adjustment from a knife to a gun, which was totally understandable. However, whenever a gun was pointed and he had to respond, his right hand reached for an imaginary blade that just wasn't there.

Peter Grimes was quite successful. Audiences liked it. They were even a little shaken up by it. I left for a short vacation after the Opening. A couple of days later I had a phone call which deeply disturbed me. To give you some context, there was what we as a creative team felt was an important moment at the end of the production. The dark walls all moved away and we were left in a large white space with a structure at the back. On the structure stood some actors dressed in modern black clothes, as a parallel to the Victorian-clad community who were standing below. The story examines the possible abuse of a young Victorian boy and the witch-hunt that follows. I wanted to say that there are those who still take advantage of our young and that, for right or for wrong, communities still carry out their own witch-hunts, taking the law into their own hands, and declaring unproven judgements. After the final chorus, and the usual Opera bows, the cast left and what remained was this modern image with today's boy standing on the structure looking out to the audience as they left the theatre. It was a way of asking us to take responsibility for our actions. Anyway, the person on the phone, from the Management of the Metropolitan Opera House, was telling me that they intended to cut that final image, saying, if I recall correctly, that it was too expensive to build the new set for each performance. If that was the case, why wasn't that voiced all those months before when we first did those technical rehearsals for the piece? I would have understood, after all I've run enough theatres to understand the constraints of a budget. I would have found another no-cost way of making the same point. This felt like the censorship of a core idea and was deeply hurtful and upsetting. To this day I don't know why it happened or indeed if the image was actually cut. I do know I was given no choice in the matter. Maybe a Board Member didn't like it? A rather potent example of bringing in artists to refresh the repertoire and then reverting to what you know and what makes you feel safe. I get it. I've run a theatre. However, it's surely our job to be brave?

That experience made me question whether I would do any more Opera. Then I was invited to direct a series of pieces over various seasons with a UK company that I very much admire. The admirable Wasfi Kani is the highly successful Artistic Director of Grange Park Opera, who work out of a beautiful Opera House just south of London. Her Executive Director is the terrific Bernard Davies, who takes all the pressure away from the artists he works with, which is in itself a wonderful skill. The theatre is in the grounds of an English Stately Home and is quite beautiful. My first production for the company was *Madama Butterfly* by Puccini. I have also done *The Carmelites* for them, one of my all-time favourite productions. It had a simplicity and serenity that made me very happy. The ending of that Opera is extraordinary. The nuns of the story, which is set during the French Revolution, are sent to the guillotine. They leave the stage one by one during the score's beautiful closing hymn. Poulenc, the composer, has left empty bars to allow each execution to be individually heard. Chilling, and pure theatre. I recently did a production there of a piece called *Werther* by Massenet, a rather lovely Opera with seven principals and six children – bliss. My relationship with the company has been very special to me. It's wonderful to be asked my opinion on who might play a role, bearing in mind that the singers are often booked years before the director. This ongoing commitment between Opera House and director is very rare and much appreciated.

Well, *Lucia di Lammermoor* came back around. This time in the form of a new production to be shared between three theatres, Houston Grand Opera, Venice's La Fenice and the famed Sydney Opera House. This was one of those dream jobs, on paper anyway! An interesting example of the same production making for three very different experiences. Part of the deal was that after the first production in Houston, I would go to each of the two venues and rehearse it with a new company each time. Hardly a hardship, after all La Fenice has to be one of the most beautiful European Opera houses, and Sydney Opera House is iconic, one of the architectural wonders of the modern world. So, we started in Houston. The company was, at that time, led by Anthony Freud, who I knew when he was head of Welsh National Opera. He was hugely collaborative and a joy to work with. I was excited to have another try at an Opera I now knew so well, after all the world is always a new place whenever you make work and so your influences are forever changing. The soprano role was to be sung by a remarkable young Russian by the name of Albina Shagimuratova. It was her first time singing it, which is always quite a feat as it is one of the great demanding coloratura roles, set very high in the human voice and very challenging vocally. The set and costumes were again to be designed by Liz Ascroft and although we were understandably influenced by the Scottish Opera production, this was even bleaker, with walls of painted sky that rose and lowered, once again expanding and contracting the acting area – a bit of a personal theme I suppose. I was very pleased with the work we made and Albina had a great personal success.

Next La Fenice. Well, there is nothing quite like crossing St Mark's Square to go to work in the morning. Nothing like seeing your set floating down a canal on a gondola, ready to be loaded into the door at the back of the theatre. However, the rehearsal period was challenging. As I said the Opera is sung in Italian, but almost all of the company were in fact Eastern European and few of them spoke Italian. They spoke even less English. There was a translator, but she could hardly deal with all the challenges facing her. Some days it felt like directing in semaphore! Thankfully the soprano was Australian, so at least we could have some exploration of the role and how she might play it. Her name was Jessica Pratt and I really enjoyed our collaboration. I truly believe that it is a director's responsibility when working with different artists on a role, in the same production, to be as flexible as possible. I re-rehearsed *The Color Purple* when Heather Headley took over the role from Jennifer Hudson, after all they are two very different people, different acting styles, different bodies. I then did the same thing when Jennifer Holliday took over from Heather. In the case of Lucia, Jessica wasn't Albina and so it was an altogether different interpretation, which was very satisfying. However, much of being at La Fenice wasn't satisfying. Things got behind schedule onstage. It's a cliché to say that Italians always leave to tomorrow what they could have done today, but in this case the cliché was dangerously true. Not only that, but you could never quite believe what you were being told in terms of planning, et cetera, so it made the job very frustrating. My dear friend Ellen Burstyn came to see the Opening in Venice. She was a little upset when I got a few boos at the curtain call. Robert correctly told her not to worry as "*John would be delighted*"! I regret to say it, but I was equally delighted to float out of Venice.

The Sydney Opera House. First class flights to the other side of the world. Being provided with an apartment that overlooked Sydney Harbour and that iconic bridge. Rehearsing with a new company and a new Maestro. The most wonderful thing though was working with Emma Matthews, the acclaimed Australian soprano who was to play Lucia. All the ladies who played the role were a joy to work with, but somehow Emma took things to a whole new level. She was a highly experienced actress, terrific to work with, really understood what rehearsal meant, and was also the mother of a young family so everything was in proportion. I will never forget the first time we rehearsed the famous Mad Scene together. She had to bathe herself in the blood that was in a bowl central to her long wedding table. Most actresses would be working out the best way to use the blood without actually getting it in their hair or anywhere too uncomfortable. Not Emma. She was fearless. She covered herself in it. This seemingly balanced human being somehow understood madness enough to totally immerse herself in that gory mess. She also understood her own voice enough to be unafraid of not always sounding beautiful. Believe me she sounded great, but was always in character. The singing and the acting blending perfectly together. One thing about Sydney I remember with less joy. The enormous set had by this time been to Italy and then again travelled across the world. I don't know if it was simply exhausted but on the Opening Night it ceased to function. Not for long, probably not noticeable to anybody who didn't know the production, but enough to devastate both myself and Liz. Anyway, I do look back on Sydney with pleasure and maybe even disbelief. From the Inverness Opera Company to Sydney Opera House? Somewhat ridiculous really. It's interesting to note that my production in Sydney was replacing a much-loved one that had famously starred the late, great Dame Joan Sutherland. Quite a responsibility. Sutherland passed the baton to Emma and I liked that some years after Emma's success, they brought the production back into the repertoire and cast Jessica, who had done it in Venice. Again, an Australian soprano handing the role to another. I didn't need to go back to Sydney to rehearse it, primarily because the soprano knew the production. I was relieved. I didn't need any more *Lucia*! Though it is certainly a privilege to be sitting in your house in the UK while audiences are watching your work on the other side of the world.

I referred to it earlier, but I did do my very own actor-musician adaptation of *Carmen*, not the *Carmen Jones* of New York City, but a production that started at the Watermill and then went to the Linbury Theatre at the Covent Garden Opera House. It was so exciting and so audacious! I do recall after one performance being asked to deal with an audience member in the foyer who was furious with me. I said to him I was sorry he was so upset and I didn't set out to trash Bizet's score in order to offend. He stopped me and said "*I'm not upset by the changes, I'm upset because it's so real.*" I drew his attention to the final images of the production. The actress playing Carmen was standing in a bucket of water, playing a trumpet. Real? Really? Somehow though I did appreciate what he meant. It was visceral. Interestingly we went on to repeat this production elsewhere and each time I rehearsed it I cut more and more stuff until we were down to a few things and an audience sitting in a circle. What goes round comes round.

Finally I would like to share with you a production of *Porgy and Bess* I made for the Danish Opera Company in Copenhagen. They have a beautiful and very impressive new Opera House there and this time we daily travelled to and from work on a water-taxi. My friend and trusted colleague Nikki Woollaston choreographed, again Liz did the set and also the costumes, and the terrific Joanna Town designed the lighting. We worked in a large, beautiful rehearsal studio in the Opera House. It is interesting to note that this production in 2011 was the first time *Porgy* had been performed in Copenhagen since 1943, with that having been the first time it had been performed outside of the US. In 1943, Denmark was under Nazi occupation, and Hitler banned the production. So, this new Danish production felt like quite a responsibility. We gathered singers from London, Germany, Africa and New York. There wasn't an abundance of Black faces in Copenhagen, and so our company become quite celebrated locally. It was a really fun rehearsal period. The Opera is sung in English so there was none of that problem of understanding or misunderstanding. The material is much loved within the Black community so our singers sang it with great relish. From the beautiful *"Summertime"* to *"It Ain't Necessarily So"*, music for many of the songs had been in that childhood piano stool.

The facility of that Opera House was extraordinary. I mentioned earlier how the repertoire often means changing sets daily, which can sometimes impede upon the work of a new production. However, in this case, you could rehearse onstage in the morning on the full set, then, at the press of a button, that set could move upstage, large metal doors opened and it glided into the rehearsal room, which allowed you to continue working with the singers on the set all afternoon. An absolutely wonderful way of creating the very best work possible and proof of the power of State-subsidised theatre. No rich Board members to bother you this time. The Queen of Denmark came across in her boat to watch our Opening. Porgy was back in Copenhagen after all these years. George Gershwin got the better of Adolf Hitler after all!

So, Opera is indeed a wonderful art form. It is unique but one into which a director should tread with caution, being ready to learn from all who are involved. It won't always be plain sailing, but it's worth it. There's nothing quite like being in a rehearsal room with the Metropolitan Opera Chorus as they sing the Act Three Finale of *Peter Grimes*. Nothing like being at the Sydney Opera House with a great singer-actress rehearsing the Mad Scene from *Lucia Di Lammermoor*. Nothing like being at the beautiful Danish Royal Opera House making a new production of *Porgy and Bess*. The list goes on.

12
Opening Doors

This book is titled "*Opening Doors*", which makes me wonder what doors I've opened, if any? When you win the Tony Award you're expected to give an acceptance speech. I recall very little of mine, but I do remember that I made reference to doors. The doors that are so often shut to you, the doors you knock throughout your career that are never answered. I was fifty-four years of age and wanted to use the opportunity to encourage all those artists who were staring at unanswered doors to just keep knocking! I was living proof that a door would eventually open. So, let me take the opportunity of concluding this book by recollecting moments when doors opened for me or when I may, hopefully, have opened a door for somebody else.

OPENING DOORS to the storytelling of politics in the theatre

When I was little we were always told never to talk about three things – sex, religion and politics – as these were the three subjects that always caused arguments within a family. It's been a lifelong challenge for me as those three themes are fundamental to storytelling in the theatre. I defy you to find one Shakespeare play that doesn't include at least one, if not all, of these subjects. Tell me one good story that doesn't have passion and sex somewhere at its core? I've already written about the subject of religion both in the history of the theatre and in its methods today. So, I'd like to take a little time here to focus on how politics have influenced the choices I have made in making theatre and in the stories I have wanted to tell. Politics have always been important to me, in particular the telling of political stories in theatrical form and how storytelling can have an influence upon political thinking. A play called *When the Wind Blows* in those early Worcester days, which somewhat delightfully deals with the fear of a nuclear war that has been terrifying two ordinary people. *Whose Life Is It Anyway?*, again at Worcester, a brilliant play about our right to personal choice in assisted dying. *Sarcophagus*, that play in Liverpool about the Chernobyl Disaster. These were all examples of plays that were dealing with the hot topics of their time and all of which were hugely satisfying to direct. Let me spend some time though with a production that means a lot to me and that I hope was successfully impactful.

As you will by now have gathered, Brecht has been a constant theme. He wrote "*The worst illiterate is the political illiterate, he doesn't hear, he doesn't speak, nor participates in the political events.*" His political courage and his style of making theatre have always influenced me and inspired my work. That LA Opera production of *The Rise and Fall of the City of Mahagonny* is a perfect example. However the play that I'd like to focus on is a production I made at Classic Stage – *The Resistible Rise of Arturo Ui*. In writing about it, I will refer to the lead character as *Ui*. As I said previously, it was written in 1941 and is a satire on the rise of Adolf Hitler and the Nazi party prior to World War Two. However, it's set in a fictional Chicago, with *Ui* portrayed as a mobster. The play is full of references to Shakespeare, and *Ui* is explicitly compared to *Richard III*. Indeed there is a wonderful central scene where a Shakespearean actor teaches *Ui* how to walk, talk, indeed how to present himself in every way – terrifying really. He gives *Ui* what is unfortunately referred to today as a "Brand" and the walk becomes the infamous goose-step.

I set the action of the play in a cage, the type that immigrants are detained in at the US border. It had a metal-framed door which clanged like a prison when slammed shut, the sort of slam I recalled so well from that prison experience outside Coventry. I used almost no furniture, except a couple of folding metal tables and some matching chairs, again very typical of that utilitarian environment. The lighting was basic and very bold. The costumes were totally modern and primarily in black, like a Nazi-inspired Greek Chorus. There were only eight actors, two African-Americans, two Asian-Americans, one Hispanic, one Middle Eastern, one Caucasian woman and one Caucasian man. The actors each played more than one character, but if you knew the German archetypes they were portraying you would recognise Hermann Göring and Joseph Goebbels. The central character was majestically played by Raul Esparza, yes the same actor who had played Bobby in *Company*. He has such a visceral energy as an actor and I cannot imagine having made this play with anybody else. Casting is a very important part of the job, finding people you want to make work with and who can illuminate the work you are making.

In 2018 when we made the production, we were slap bang in the middle of President Trump's first term. I don't think it's unfair or irresponsible to say that so much of his language was easily interpreted as echoing Germany in the 1930s. The language of Fear. Now, Raul doesn't look like Donald Trump, so we weren't setting out to create any form of impersonation. However, when our *Ui* went to the podium and started the last great speech of the play it was terrifyingly reminiscent of the world around us, a mirror up to the incessant rhetoric we saw on our television screens. As our *Ui* ranted, we played a recording of a crowd gradually building the Sieg Heil chant of those 1930s rallies. I asked the sound designer to slowly mix in the sound of a modern Trump rally. This time the German chant merged in with the MAGA chant of "*Lock Her Up*". The merging of the sounds was very slow but by the crescendo of the Act there was nothing subtle about it. I didn't want it to be subtle. I wanted it to be an assault. We need waking up! As Brecht says at the end of the play,

> *If we could learn to look instead of gawking,*
> *We'd see the horror in the heart of farce,*
> *If only we could act instead of talking,*
> *We wouldn't always end up on our arse.*
> *This was the thing that nearly had us mastered;*
> *Don't yet rejoice in his defeat, you men!*
> *Although the world stood up and stopped the bastard,*
> *The bitch that bore him is in heat again.*[1]

Many people accused me of rewriting the play, and suggested that I'd taken liberties in order to make a political point. I am putting it on record that I rewrote nothing. It was all Bertolt Brecht. This is a classic play, one that makes us face our reality. I will forever be grateful for making some people rather angry.

On a personal note, during late rehearsals I had a call to tell me that my elderly mother had passed away. So, I set about doing the technical rehearsals of the play, was there for some early previews, and then flew back to Scotland to carry out the rituals. My mother was a rather politicised woman and I think deep down she would have approved of *Arturo Ui*. She came from a generation devoid of "trigger warnings". They could face the uncomfortable aspects of what make us human. I have great reservations about warning the audience of what they are going to experience. Isn't that raw experience the point of the theatre? Perhaps to disturb really is part of the job. I don't in any way want to suggest that we shouldn't be concerned over how our audiences might react and for their safety in doing so. However, I recall a student at Princeton being upset with me because I'd asked them to read Strindberg's *Miss Julie* without giving trigger warnings. My response is simple – why read, see or do the play if you've been warned that it may upset you? It's *meant* to upset you.

OPENING DOORS to "essentialism" in theatre-making

I'd like to circle back to that first production of *Caucasian Chalk Circle* in Liverpool. The one with the pillow-baby. It contained a couple of moments that stand out as landmarks in my theatremaking journey. First was the final rehearsal in the studio. All our props and furniture had moved over to the theatre space and we were left with a rather empty rehearsal room. I decided we should do a run-through of the play anyway, even in this virtual emptiness. What those actors did was thrilling and had I been a little braver I would have asked that we discard the set and do our play in this thrilling way. However, too many people had made too many creative contributions to the production by that point, and it may have been professionally disrespectful. I have a hunch that I might be a little braver now, after all, as Shakespeare said, "*The Play's The Thing*". Then there was the day when our lighting designer Wayne Dowdeswell came to watch a rehearsal. Wayne was a resident lighting designer with the Royal Shakespeare Company and we've done many shows together. We were in the rehearsal room when he said to me, "*So, how do you want it to look?*" I gestured toward the room and said "*Like this.*" "*You mean with fluorescent lights?*" "*I think so, yes.*" And so, that's what he did. He stripped most of the sophisticated lighting equipment out of the theatre and lit the show with the glaring boldness of fluorescent tubes. It made the space hard and strong visually. What I love about this story though is his lack of ego. He wasn't interested in the lighting design looking beautiful and therefore reflecting well on him. Rather he wanted to serve the play, serve the work we had made in the rehearsal room. Another powerful experiment in theatremaking. There are so many examples of discovering what is "essential" in how I make my work. Too many to list here. Suffice it to say that in whatever I do, I aim to discover the essence, uncover what I want to say, and to get out of the way of the story itself. The intention should never be "*What makes me look good?*" But rather, "*What makes the play look good?*"

Throughout my career, critics and audiences have tried to label or define my work. "*He's a minimalist.*" I'm perhaps the only person who hasn't attempted a definition. Yes, I'm interested in how we make theatre in a unique way. Interested in how we only use that which is "*essential*" in the telling of a story. Interested in giving the stage back to the actor. You see, I think the only truly essential part of theatremaking is the actor. We need to return the theatre to them. We need to remind our audiences of what theatre really is. Theatre is people. Two people in conversation. If the conversation is rich and stirring, you really don't need anything else. We need to abandon unnecessary and often empty spectacle and return to the essence of what theatre is. People in dialogue. People in conflict. People in love. The great Peter Brook writes about these themes so brilliantly in his extraordinary but very simple treatise on the theatre, *The Empty Space*.

There is a distinction – for me – between Minimalism and Essentialism. As I just said, I've never called myself a minimalist, and productions like *Peter Grimes* and *Mahagonny* visually support that. Minimalism suggests to me a need to work with as little as possible. Essentialism however is somehow more productive, more alive. It takes a little courage to explore the kind of theatremaking where you only allow yourself to work with that which is essential. The essential chair, the essential prop, the essential coat. My work wasn't always like that, as I believe I've already indicated. However, now I'm only interested in making theatre using that which is truly essential, and I hope I may have opened or re-opened doors to others to do the same.

OPENING DOORS to those who have not been given a fair opportunity

Let's start with women. When I began in the theatre, it was so much harder for women than it was for men, even though more women were being trained in drama schools. So few female directors – remember Ann Stutfield at Ochtertyre: so few plays that focussed on stories about women and so few truly popular female playwrights – think of all these classical plays by all those dead white men. There were almost no television series that centred on women and it was even unusual to see a woman have reporting or anchoring jobs in the news media. To this day most of our great National Events are fronted on TV by men!

Allow me to focus on a few actions I took to help further the female story, starting with a production of a one-woman play called *Female Parts*, written by Dario Fo and Franca Rame. Dario Fo was a highly prolific Italian playwright. His most famous plays include *Accidental Death of an Anarchist* and *Can't Pay, Won't Pay*, and his extraordinary body of work won him the Nobel Prize for Literature in 1997. *Female Parts* is a collection of short plays, originally performed in 1977 by his wife Franca Rame. I directed a production in the studio theatre in Worcester in the early 1980s. The actress was the terrifically versatile Eliza McClelland, and after the Worcester run we took the plays to the famous King's Head pub theatre in Islington followed by a transfer to the Arts Theatre in London's West End. The plays are all performed by the same woman and all focus on the stories of women who are trapped, either by their work, or by men, or by childbirth, or by the society around them. It was a journey into feminism in the theatre. In those days we didn't ask questions like "*Should this be directed by a man?*" Eliza and I worked hard to have the work seen by as many audiences as possible, in the belief that the message of the plays needed to be heard. It's interesting that there were then many companies focussing on feminist theatre. One such was *Monstrous Regiment*. Their name came from the Scottish Protestant Minister John Knox's sixteenth-century pamphlet entitled *The First Blast of the Trumpet Against the Monstrous Regiment of Women*. You can see what his point of view was! *Monstrous Regiment* produced work from 1975 to 1993. This was only one of many such companies and I highlight it to give an example of those collectives of female artists who really were influencing the theatre, all with a strong political point of view. Many of today's great female theatre directors emerged under the influence of those trailblazers. It makes me happy to realise that I have actively encouraged female directors, including Phyllida Lloyd, Marianne Elliott, Shariffa Ali, Victoria Clark, Sarna Lapine – to name but a few. A humble contribution to a changing and enriching theatre.

Giving opportunities to artists of colour. I hope I've already demonstrated how important this is, both to me personally and to the arts at large. We inhabit a rich and diverse world and the theatre should reflect that. I'm not saying it's easy to make collaborations with people who don't look like you, or who come from very different cultural backgrounds and experiences. However, it is more enriching than I care to say. I stopped, listened and learned from Shariffa Ali when she was making *Mies Julie* at Classic Stage. I stopped, listened and learned from every company member of *The Color Purple*. I will be totally honest and say that I was scared when I first started working with artists of colour in those early Liverpool days. Would I say the wrong thing? Would I cause offence? I'm sure I did both but I hope that by remaining vulnerable and not pretending to have all the answers, I made my colleagues aware that I was listening and learning. Then the thrilling dynamic of working with actors of Asian descent during *Pacific Overtures*. It may be a cliché, but those actors were more polite, quieter, perhaps held more to themselves. That didn't stop us sharing our experiences on a daily basis. Learning from each other. Listening to each other. I do believe it's as easy and as complicated as that, and I hope some of the examples I have set out have opened doors to others, have in some way encouraged new ways forward. The great Alexander Solzhenitsyn entitled his Nobel Speech *One Word of Truth*. In the speech he expands to say "*one word of truth outweighs the whole world*". That's all we have to do. To tell the truth. To each other in the rehearsal room. To our audiences. To the world we live in. That truth will finally outweigh the lies and falsehoods we are fed on a daily basis. Telling our truth in a rehearsal room is a vulnerable act, and has to be handled with great care. It should never be indulgent, but giving everybody in the room the chance to be heard is essential, complex as it may be. To ask questions to which we do not know the answer. To learn.

OPENING DOORS to collaborating with artists from different cultures

As I indicated earlier, Liverpool was a city where politics and socialist thinking were very much at the forefront of the mind. In response to this, I programmed two Soviet-era plays to be done next to each other, with the same company of actors.

The first was *Sarcophagus* by Vladimir Gubarev, which examined the aftermath of the Chernobyl disaster, focussing on nine victims arriving at a radiation clinic for the terminally sick. Gubarev was not only a playwright but he was also science editor of Pravda, one of Russia's most influential newspapers. The second was *Victory Celebrations* by Solzhenitsyn. It centres on a Soviet battalion having a banquet in a devastated Eastern European mansion at the end of World War Two. He wrote the play in 1953 in the Ekibastuz Labour Camp. He had no pencil or paper so he wrote the play in verse in his memory, writing it down on his release. Verse was easier to memorise than prose, but it is still a remarkable feat.

Authenticity in artistic choices was not the focussed topic that it is today, but I knew that I wanted to get some authentic Russian input into the productions and so, as I said earlier, I wrote to the Moscow Art Theatre. The artistic director, Oleg Yefremov, generously invited me to Moscow to experience the work of the company and to develop the two productions. In so many ways, it was a life-changing experience. Russia had always seemed very far away, so I was surprised to be on a flight that wasn't going to last more than a few hours. I came down the airplane steps hearing my grandmother's voice in my head, "*Better Dead than Red*"! I stayed in a tall hotel near the Kremlin and lost seven pounds in the first week. It was hard to find food, the bread lines long and the black market rife. I remember one long evening meeting at the theatre, accompanied by copious amounts of vodka. *Sarcophagus* is not approved of in Moscow and so we had to be very careful of how and when we spoke about the play. I went to Gubarev's ominously luxurious apartment and he, my designer and I were protected by armed guards outside the door. Solzhenitsyn was the enemy in Russia. He had defected to Vermont in the United States. His compulsion to tell the truth obviously got him into terrible life-threatening trouble. It seems to me we need him and his like again. Discussing his play really had to be done very carefully, especially as this was to be a World Premiere.

My strongest memories though are personal. First there was the day when Yefremov took me to the Novodevichy Cemetery to see the grave of Anton Chekhov. The padlocked site was unlocked to allow us to pass the graves of Dmitri Shostakovich and Sergei Prokofiev in order to get to our destination. There it was! Alongside that of his wife, the actress Olga Knipper, for whom he had written many of his greatest roles. Quite nearby is the grave of the great Konstantin Stanislavski, one of the most seminal theatre teachers and directors of the twentieth century, who had a major influence on naturalistic acting styles, an artist who absolutely believed in telling the truth onstage. It was a beautiful day, and we were surrounded by cherry trees. It was a great personal gift to take me there. Then there was the evening when Sasha, my previously mentioned designer, invited me to his apartment for supper. It consisted of one room which I believe he shared with his wife, herself a highly respected actress, with his small daughter, and with his mother-in-law. The latter had been standing in line all day to find food for us, which included the much-prized caviar. I don't like any form of sea-related edibles, but I wasn't going to be disrespectful, so I swallowed and kept smiling. His car was outside the apartment and, like many, he removed the tyres every night, bringing them all indoors so that it wouldn't be stolen. He gave me a gift of a set of Babushka dolls to take home to my daughter. These were very special people. When he came to England to work on the plays, I wanted him to meet my daughter,

Beccy. When there, her rather well-fed cat crossed the room. He smiled his wry smile and said "*Ah, Capitalist Cat!*" When he left the UK I asked him what Beccy and I could give him for his daughter, as we wanted to return his kindness. His response? "*Bananas.*" His daughter had never seen a banana!

The Berlin Wall came down when I was in Moscow. 9 November 1989. My birthday. I had gone to see a play at the Arts, and came out afterward into a cold November night. I heard rumbling and, right there in front of me, along came a seemingly endless procession of tanks making their way to Red Square. Out of the top of each tank sat a young Russian soldier holding a billowing red flag. It was an extraordinary demonstration of military power, the likes of which I had never seen and I hope will never see again. All this against a backdrop of a changing Europe.

The plays were successful in Liverpool and I really think the questions they posed had an impact on the company and audience alike. During the rehearsal period the actors and I made a day-trip to Sellafield, the large multi-function nuclear site on the coast of Cumbria. I clearly recall the charming tour guide, who turned every awfulness of that place into some kind of positive. "*We are fortunate to be taking other people's nuclear waste, after all it balances our economy!*" Terrifying!

Oddly, nuclear waste seems to have been a theme in a couple of the pieces I've made. The movie I shot, *Main Street*, was set in Durham, North Carolina. Durham had been one of the centres of the tobacco industry in the US and as such had been very wealthy. However almost all the tobacco had gone, and the movie was looking at the effect this had on a dying community. It tells the story of a man who persuades an elderly lady, played by the brilliant Ellen Burstyn, to rent him the tobacco warehouse that her family had owned. It was standing empty, and she needed the money. What she then found out was that the man, Gus Leroy, played to perfection by Colin Firth, was storing nuclear waste in the warehouse, putting the community at risk. The scary thing is that nuclear waste does in fact travel around the US at night, in yellow barrels, waiting for places to store them until dumping sites are ready. As Shakespeare rightly says in *A Midsummer Night's Dream*, "*Lord what fools these mortals be!*"

OPENING DOORS to William Shakespeare

Shakespeare really says everything that needs to be said. I feel saddened when I hear of certain reputable universities no longer being prepared to teach his work because his politics and his view of human beings, in their opinion, have ceased to fit with what they would like the students to hear. Shakespeare is being cancelled! Has anybody ever verbalised love as well as him? In *Twelfth Night*, "*Love Sought is Good but Given Unsought is Better.*" Or grief, "*When he shall die, take him and cut him out in little stars, and he will make the face of heaven so fine, that all the world will be in love with Night, and pay no worship to the garish Sun*" in *Romeo and Juliet*. Plays like *Macbeth*, or *Richard III*, are deeply political, and were written for strategic reasons, often complimenting the monarch of the day. I've been fortunate in that I've directed almost half of the Canon and learnt from those plays at every opportunity. Now are there some that are a little questionable today? Please never expect me to direct *The Taming of the Shrew*. Though I have directed *Kiss Me Kate*, the musical version of the play, which portrays women in a somewhat more powerful light.

One way I have contributed to creating accessibility in Shakespeare is by co-writing *Shakespeare for Dummies*, part of the world-famous series of *Dummies* books. I was visiting my old Georgia friend Charlotte Headrick in Corvallis, Oregon, who was, by this time, Chair of the Theatre Department at Oregon State University. I agreed to lead some workshops and give some talks during my otherwise casual visit. I remember one of these being an evening talk to the wider community, about how to make Shakespeare acceptable for non-theatre audiences. After the talk a gentleman came up and asked if I would be interested in writing a book with him. I asked what the subject would be? He said "*Shakespeare*" and I politely declined, saying that there really were enough books on the subject to last us all a lifetime and what is there to say that's new? He persevered and said "*It would be a Dummies book*." I had heard of the *Dummies* series, the most famous of which were *Windows for Dummies* and *Internet for Dummies*. So, we met for coffee the following morning.

Ray Lischner, in his wonderfully positive American way, had connected with the publisher of the books. He was primarily a scientist, and felt he needed a practitioner to collaborate with him – which is where I came in. Anyway, to cut a long story short, the publishers liked the idea and we started writing the book. Now, this was in the 1990s, when not so many people had the Internet. Ray was on the West Coast of America and I was on the South Coast of England. At that point I had never even sent an email. So, I bought my first computer and set up the technology. Ray, on the telephone, taught me how to use the device, and from those early moments we wrote a book! We did it all via the Internet, never met in person and had very few telephone calls. Because of the time difference I was awake when he was asleep and vice versa, and so we wrote the book in record time, Ray provided the factual information and I provided the fun that is to be had in learning about Shakespeare. Take a look, you might enjoy some of the games we set up to encourage people to enjoy speaking verse, or to understand the sometimes complicated prose. I'm happy to say that the book was a big success, selling massively worldwide. I often meet people who have read it and who are bemused that I co-wrote it. I've even taught university courses around it, always surprised that the students didn't take offence at the word "Dummies"!

OPENING DOORS to rethinking cast-sizes and methods of casting

It all began way back in those early days in the Highlands where we couldn't afford to do plays or musicals with large casts and so those choices were pragmatic. However that seven-person production of *Macbeth* was certainly good early practice in exploring what's possible. It's interesting that in fact I'm almost always drawn to doing Shakespeare with eight people. Four men and four women. I have no problem with women playing men's roles, but am more questioning over having men play women's roles. Men get plenty of opportunities in the classics, women less so. Surely it is the responsibility of a modern director to do all they can to redress that balance. It also seems important that the casting reflects the strength of women and as an example I would cite the wonderful Mary Beth Peil, who played King Duncan in my most recent production of *Macbeth*. She brought a strength and yet an appropriate gentleness to the role that actually reflected who she is as a human being. I understand why some directors choose to make productions with all-male companies. We know that's how it was done in Shakespeare's day. Let's remember though that there were no actresses in his day. We live in a different time and should surely cast accordingly. I do draw a distinction regarding Phyllida Lloyd's all-female productions. I don't mean to belittle them, but these are excellent experiments and are an important part of a journey toward giving women more powerful roles to play. After all, women are just as powerful as men in our Western societies.

Going back to my eight-some productions, the truth is I really love working out the puzzle. *Gondoliers* in the West End had eight people, *Sweeney Todd* nine. Sometimes I hit a stumbling block, for example if there are more speaking roles in a scene than I have actors available, but those situations usually lead me to asking what is most important in the scene, can any lines be attributed to another character, and what is really vital to the clarity of the storytelling? I already mentioned the *Dream*, where the characters are split into three groups, the Court, the Mechanicals and the Lovers. The fun comes in giving each actor three roles, one from each grouping. I even enjoy the challenge of doing that "trebling" without changing costumes or putting on false beards! Indeed in that York production the actors didn't change costume, but rather used their costumes in different ways to go from character to character. Of course this takes many conversations with the costume designer to help figure it out. In fact, I don't believe you can or should go into rehearsal with everything worked out, but rather you need to have a carefully considered notion which the actors then help you explore and manifest. I like the puzzle and I like the scary unknown involved in not having it perfectly drawn out. It's in the unknown that art can happen.

Most of my shows at the Watermill Theatre had reduced cast sizes, mainly because the dressing room didn't hold many people, just like at Classic Stage. I say this with a smile, but I do believe that if you passionately want to tell a story you will find a way. Pragmatism really does lead to creativity. Even the big companies who once did large cast shows are now having to find ways to rethink their casting options and the scale of work they make. The financial climate of our modern theatre is challenging, so producers and audiences alike have to meet those challenges.

It's a long time since the colour of somebody's skin has affected my casting choices. I have no problem with a Black woman playing a white man's daughter. There is no question that we find this less challenging in Classical theatre, and even a little easier in musical theatre. Perhaps it's more complex in straight plays? I fully understand that, but I believe it important to cast Black actors in positions of strength and not to sideline them into always playing the servile roles, or always playing the bad guys. I recall casting the excellent New York actor Eddie Cooper in one of the roles in *Arturo Ui*, a character who was the ultimate thug. I very much wanted to work with Eddie and so I asked him if he was comfortable playing the baddie? He needed to understand that I wasn't looking to be in any sense stereotypical. Eddie had no problem with the notion and we have worked together many times since. All it took was an honest conversation, without which a fruitful artistic collaboration may never have existed. We have to recognise where we sit in our responsibility to the development of modern theatre. I don't mean we have to be blind to colour as I know that is terminology that upsets many people. However, we have to do all we can to represent and represent well.

OPENING DOORS to the next generation of theatre artists

As I've already indicated, I've always taught alongside my work as a professional theatre maker. There was that term at the Royal Scottish Academy, not long after I'd graduated, teaching voice to my near contemporaries. When I was Artistic Director at Worcester and Cheltenham, I taught workshops and masterclasses at many of the London drama schools. Something I always enjoyed was teaching courses at the Actors Centre, a London school for professional actors who wanted to continue with active study. In Liverpool, as I've already mentioned, there was a large education component attached to our work. Called the Hope Street Project, its aim was to teach drama to local young people who had tough backgrounds and who weren't coping in traditional education. There were two units, one called "Acting Up", which as the title suggests was for students starting in drama, but who had perhaps been "acting up" in social situations. The other unit was called "Acting Out", for students who were a little further along on their journey, learning skills that could be transferrable when they went "out" into the field. It was a privilege to be able to work with those students alongside the work of the professional company.

I think it fair to say that leading the activities of any rehearsal room requires a strong element of good teaching. Not "telling" but rather, "enabling". Almost everywhere I've been Artistic Director I've encouraged the forming of a Youth Theatre, where these enabling skills really come into their own. There were huge teaching elements to the work on all the productions of the *Mystery Plays*. Indeed if teaching isn't a component in directing those community projects, then there is something lacking in the process. When I was at Classic Stage in New York, there was a small education department working within what was an already small organisation, not small in aspiration but certainly small in staff resources. "Teaching Artists" came in from the community to work alongside many of our productions, facilitating school matinees, workshops et cetera. I think the idea of a Teaching Artist is a wonderful one, putting teaching at the centre of our art form. I have always enjoyed mentoring, and particularly enjoy the interaction this allows with young theatre directors. Throughout the last few years, I've tried to regularly have meetings with young directors. At one point, I was spending an hour with one person per week, which was a thoroughly uplifting experience. I'd tell each one of them that I wouldn't be looking to employ them, but simply wanted to be a sounding board in what I know can be a lonely profession. "*Where do I start? How do I survive? Can I have a life and be in the arts?*" All questions that faced me again and again. I don't necessarily have the answers, but I do know that it's a helpful resource to have somebody who will listen.

When I first gave up running UK theatres, I took some longer residencies, including at Rose Bruford College, directing and teaching on their newly formed Actor-Musician course. I taught on three occasions at Western Kentucky University, leading a course and directing a production on each occasion. Even in the dark days of the pandemic, I taught courses on Zoom, at many schools such as the renowned Bristol Old Vic. However the most fulfilling and meaningful passage of my teaching life was at Princeton University.

I met a wonderful woman called Professor Stacy Wolf, and we arranged to get coffee together. We met in a little café on Manhattan's 9th Avenue, and Stacy asked me if I would be interested in doing some teaching at Princeton, where she was a Faculty Member. I hadn't started at Classic Stage and, whilst enjoying my freelance life, I was seeking something of that familial feeling that comes with being attached to an institution, either theatrical or educational. Stacy is most certainly a woman of her word, and so began a ten-year residency that was enriching and uplifting. The Theatre Department at Princeton doesn't offer a "Major", so they are not aiming to train young professionals. It isn't a Conservatoire. They offer a "Certificate" in theatre, meaning that the student has followed a series of courses and finished with creating an appropriate project or presentation. This usually meant that one was working with students who had a broad educational focus, many of them planning to be economists, politicians, scientists, mathematicians. However they all had a very sincere interest in the theatre. It was wonderful to teach a room of students who most definitely could, and perhaps will, change the world. Most of the classes have a maximum number of twelve participants and so you could really connect and hopefully make a difference. I taught many courses, including *The History of the American Musical*, *The Nature of Theatrical Reinvention* and of course the first *Actor-Musician* courses in the United States of America. During my time there, the Directorship of the course changed and it was led by my lighting designer colleague and friend, Jane Cox. Jane and I enjoyed so many wonderful conversations about the place of study within the theatre. There we were, in her Princeton office every Monday morning, still planning to change the world. Thank goodness that one remains a student.

I am of course often asked "*How do I get work?*" I never respond with things like "*Write Letters*", "*Send emails*". After all, I've never done those things myself. However, I do say "*Be focussed. Be you. Don't get in your own way. You are enough.*" However I think the best advice of all is "*Be decent*". It may not get you the first job, but it will almost certainly mean you'll get invited back.

OPENING DOORS to the rehearsal room

Leading a room full of creative artists is a huge privilege and an awesome responsibility. You have to maintain a high degree of safety, both physical and emotional. Rehearsal is, by its very nature, a private activity. I'm never totally comfortable with people observing my work, perhaps because I'm not sure of what's going to happen from one moment to the next. As I said, I do still follow a schedule, but it has a flexibility that makes my aims achievable. It may say "Morning: Work on the dinner scene". I don't write down what aspects of the "dinner scene". I simply work into the scene, carving away with the actors until we get somewhere near the possibilities that the scene offers. I don't have an aim, or a plan to demonstrate what I think the scene is about. I hope I wouldn't know what the scene was about, after all the aim is that the actors will help me find the answer. There is also an enormous amount of repetition. Doing the scene again and again until it becomes simpler and less self-conscious. As you can imagine, there is a good deal of conversation going on. I will tell the room stories of how the scene relates to my own story. Should they wish to, they can contribute their own stories. Everything is valuable. However, this is only if they are comfortable and I would never exert a "*now you tell*" pressure. We all matter in the rehearsing of a story. Ask your stage manager what they think. Bring your designers into the process. Don't do it by yourself, as it's simply not going to be interesting enough. To give these thoughts a focus, let me take you into the rehearsal room of one particular production:

The Three Sisters, by Anton Chekhov, in a new adaptation by the wonderful American Playwright, Sarah Ruhl. We primarily rehearsed in New York City in readiness for a production in Cincinnati. The play is usually set in the rather grand residence of the Prozorov family, home to the three sisters Olga, Masha and Irina. I was interested in setting it in that home but post the advent of communism, after Czarism. I wanted it to look like a once elegant room that was now boarded up and broken, very much like many of the spaces I saw, and indeed worked in, on my trip to Moscow. Scott Pask designed a wonderful bleak environment, quite perfect for what I wanted to say. Irina, the youngest sister, is having her birthday in the play. Our Irina was an attendant in the office that had once been the drawing room of her childhood home, as if it had been taken over by the regime and she now had a humble job there. I was interested in a world where the middle-classes had been eradicated. None of this was on the page of Sarah's wonderful adaptation, but the way she had chosen words took me in this direction. When rehearsals began I didn't know where we would end up. Irina opened the one birthday card of her past, the same one she opened every year, and her family returned to her, as if in a memory. I've always been interested in how a small onstage action can open the floodgates to an entire story. The box of photographs in *Fiddler on the Roof*. In writing this I realise that bringing family back together is a recurring theme in my work. The characters were again dressed as they would become – broken, torn, just like *Fiddler*. We started rehearsal with that amount of information. I cast a terrific group of actors. However the usual preconception of Chekhov is of a world that is rather faded and sad but in a wistful beautiful environment, perhaps with falling leaves and a chaise longue. So the first task was to challenge that preconception. We had racks of old clothing in the room, all of which Ann Hould-Ward and I had selected from a Manhattan Salvation Army clothing depositary. Not in a field this time. We had selected numerous items that we felt might be appropriate for the characters. Once we got them to the rehearsal room, I asked the actors to choose from these rags the things they would like to use to represent the last remnants their characters would have worn. Ann then built the designs around these choices. I will be honest and say that the ideal way for me to work would be to have a long rehearsal period, and with nothing pre-designed. The finances of contemporary theatre don't allow for that, but that shouldn't stop you finding ways of challenging that somewhat failing system.

Every day the actors came in and got into those clothes. They rehearsed in them, and were even to be seen in them on 8th Avenue during the lunch break! I took the same process with any props they might use, as if those also were remnants of the items they may have owned. If we found something was redundant, or not helping the story, it was, as usual, discarded. For a week we rehearsed in a darkened room, partly to break down any sense that the actors were being watched and therefore likely to perform, but also to try to find the reality of how we truly behave, encouraging them simply to "be", just like Romeo and Juliet in John Reich's imaginary prison cell. What goes on in the darkness that can occupy our minds? It took courage, but was never threatening. I usually find myself in the scenes with them, rather than sitting at the front watching them. I remember one day stopping them and asking "*Why do you all sound like you're trying to be British?*" A response was "*Well, it's Chekhov!*" I said, "*But he was Russian! It's a translation, an adaptation. His characters* weren't British. Can't you simply sound American?" Some actors went pale. It went against all their training! But they gave it a try, and we started to build a world that was so much more authentic to the actors in the room.

As we built the characters, we always left the staging free. Of course there were some moments that "set" themselves – an entrance, an exit, standing up, sitting down. But never quite the same twice. Always seeking freshness, spontaneity. It felt like a bringing together of so many of the things I had been exploring in theatremaking over so many years. I always work on a basis of *"less is more"*, and hope that actors trust that impulse. The root of *"less is more"*, though, lies in the fundamental belief that *"you are enough"*. It's not an easy notion to own, I don't find it easy for myself, but it's vital if you are going to tell theatrical truth. If, after I am gone, actors can still remember me saying *"you are enough"*, and maybe pass it on to somebody else, I will be relatively happy in eternity.

We never "staged" or "blocked" the play, but some of the key moments became theatrically memorable. Corey Stoll as Vershinin and Laila Robins as Masha, looking out the window of the set, her saying she *"will get to Moscow"* even though that's probably a futile hope. It was made more potent by the fact that the window was blocked up by concrete blocks, allowing no light out or in. It was as you might find in a condemned building and of course, there was no view. There was no hope! Another image is of the late Lynn Cohen, one of America's finest actresses, rummaging through onstage refuse bins to find things to help keep her character warm, representing the fight to survive that we have in us all. Lynn always said I had spoiled her forever after that rehearsal period. I hope she meant it in a good way!

So, did audiences like it? I have no idea. If I am totally honest, I don't care. "Liking" is not in my area of concern. I try to get the actors not to "like" but rather to experience, explore, be bewildered, feel something. I try not to say I "liked" something, as that can mean it gets repeated again and again to maintain my approval. I feel exactly the same about the audience. I hope that they feel involved and stimulated but I can't legislate for "like". Usually audiences either love my work or they hate it. I'm OK with those extremes – save me from the mediocrity of the middle road.

I am a little questioning over the need to have an "Intimacy Director" in the room. Of course I do understand where the need for this post came from, and

I'm not for a moment deeming it unnecessary. However, I recently did a musical where the theatre insisted I have an Intimacy Director. Now it's worth saying at this point that intimacy has never been a prevalent feature in my work. I did say to the management of the theatre that this may be an unnecessary budgetary consideration, especially as there won't be any intimacy. They still felt that the role should be present in the room. There was, of course, no intimacy, and so time and money were wasted. Taking care of people is fundamental to a good director's process.

I hope I've given you a small sense of what it's like in that room. It's about process, not product. It's usually fun and it aims to be challenging. It's about being caring and being careful. The job is ideally never finished.

OPENING DOORS through music

Some years ago, Lyn Gardner in the *Guardian* newspaper identified me as an *"unlikely revolutionary"* and *"the saviour of the Broadway musical"*.[2] I am flattered by Lyn's observations but I do question their validity. No, the real revolutionary of the American Musical is the man my work is most associated with, Stephen Sondheim. Steve was the saviour of the Broadway musical, and I was simply fortunate to find myself caught in his slipstream.

As I've already said, music has been at the heart of everything for me. The childhood piano, the vocal lessons at the Royal Scottish Academy and the singing in the bingo hall. I've been interested in the musical since all those years ago at the Inverness Empire Theatre. I love a good old-fashioned Broadway musical, even though I'm highly unlikely to be invited to direct one. I am so fortunate that I was able to cut my teeth on all those musicals in regional theatre, leading to my need to find a way of doing them that uniquely worked for me. Nothing makes me happier than being in a rehearsal room with music. I get excited by the power of the human voice in song and am fascinated by how the sound of differing instruments will change the effect of a piece of storytelling.

The development of actor-musicianship is, of course, my calling-card. That's what people recognise me for. Yes, I hope my body of work may have opened doors to new ways of doing musicals. Not just carrying a tuba around, though, but also getting to the heart of the musical itself. I've built myself a reputation for doing revivals of musicals. I was surprised when I started working in the US and realised that "revival" tended to mean "copy". I have no interest in copying the original, rather I'm interested in finding new ways to tell old stories, just as I would do with Shakespeare. However, it does make me happy to see that since my Broadway production of *Sweeney Todd*, there have been more radical revivals occurring. Daniel Fish did a complete rethink on *Oklahoma!*. Michael Arden a new *Once on This Island*. Seeing this "revivifying" makes me feel that, though I may not have revolutionised the American Musical Theatre, I may have given it a little bit of a nudge.

My life has been haunted by Stephen Sondheim's lyrics, all the way back to that *Side by Side* and maybe even back to *West Side Story* in the piano stool. I'd like to take a moment to investigate a lyric from *Sunday in the Park with George*.

"*Stop worrying if your vision is new. Let others make that decision – they usually do.*"[3] I'm lucky that I have been doing this for so long that I no longer care what people think of my work. People say that the same images appear again and again. That's right, they do. That's all I have. It interests me that in a painter, the repeated imagery the artist uses is defined as a "period" – for example *Picasso's Blue Period*. In the theatre though, such repeated imagery can be seen as a lack of imagination. Well, I encourage all young directors to allow themselves to repeat. Through that repetition you will find what is uniquely you. Have no worries about whether it's "*new*". It will be work that is made by you, not by somebody else, and so, in that sense, it will be "*new*".

I admired and still admire Hal Prince. My greatest inspiration is the work of Peter Brook. My theatrical hero was Steve Sondheim. They are all gone now, so I have to be a bridge to aid the passing of the torch. There is new music being written, there are new songs being sung, we just have to be as brave as those three remarkable gentlemen. They resisted the urge to be definable, they pushed on regardless of whether they were getting public approval. They were the epitome of true artists!

OPENING DOORS to myself

When all the intellectualising is done and all the essays have been written, one thing is sure. My work is who I am. My work is where I come from. Quite recently Robert and I took a road trip round the Highlands of Scotland. Surveying that bleak, sometimes barren, sometimes lonely, always beautiful landscape, I saw the source of my own work. I saw why light matters to me in the theatre, with those glorious sunsets and bleak skies. I saw the colours that I repeat again and again in my design work, brown and blue and grey. It was all there, all the time.

In writing this Memoir I do want to make it clear that I'm still working. I'm not sure if it will ever totally end, although I am enjoying a little more time in my beloved Scotland. You see I'll probably always be helping people into the sand-box. Always be the boy who doesn't want to join in but loves the event of the other children playing. Always taking responsibility for the professional "cousins" and encouraging them to walk and talk and be, somehow, better! I'm still searching for the simplest, clearest, least cluttered and perhaps least expensive way of telling the story. I'm still in that bedroom with the faces on the wardrobe, and still with my mother when she proudly purchased the single ball of wool.

I'm still back there, where it all began.

Notes

Preface

1 Stephen Sondheim, "Merrily We Roll Along" from *Merrily We Roll Along*, 1981 used with permission.

5 Thinking Out of the Box

1 Alice Walker (2013), "The World Has Changed: Conversations with Alice Walker", p.298, The New Press
2 Ben Brantley (2011), '*Ten Cents A Dance*: Music, Memories and Regret', *New York Times*, 16 August. Available online: https://www.nytimes.com/2011/08/16/theater/reviews/ten-cents-a-dance-at-williamstown-theater-festival-review.html (accessed 6 May 2025).

7 Then Along Came Steve

1 Terry Teachout (2005), 'Fresh Blood on Broadway', *The Wall Street Journal*, 4 November. Available online: https://www.wsj.com/articles/SB113105939612187812 (accessed 6 May 2025).
2 Stephen Sondheim, George Furth, *Merrily We Roll Along*, 1981 used with permission.
3 Ben Brantley (2005) '*Grand Guignol, Spare and Stark*', *New York Times*, 5 November. Available online: https://www.nytimes.com/2005/11/04/theater/reviews/grand-guignol-spare-and-stark.html (accessed 6 May 2025).

8 Building the Box Set

1 Stephen Sondheim, "With So Little to Be Sure of", *Anyone Can Whistle*, 1964 used with permission.

9 Give My Regards to Broadway

1. Patricia Cohen (2020), 'The Forerunners: *Sweeney Todd* (2005 Revival)', *New York Times*, 13 April. Available online: https://www.nytimes.com/interactive/2020/04/13/t-magazine/sweeney-todd-revival.html (accessed 6 May 2025).
2. Ibid.
3. Stephen Sondheim, "Another Hundred People", *Company*, 1970 used with permission.

10 Now I Was Driving the Bus!

1. Stephen Bray, Brenda Russell, Allee Willis, "I'm Here", *The Color Purple*, 2005. used with permission
2. Ben Brantley (2018), 'Review: Bad Girl Makes Good in a Glorious *Carmen Jones*', *New York Times*, 27 June. Available online: https://www.nytimes.com/2018/06/27/theater/review-carmen-jones-anika-noni-rose-john-doyle.html (accessed 6 May 2025).

12 Opening Doors

1. Bertolt Brecht, *The Resistible Rise of Arturo Ui*, translated by George Tabori (Methuen Drama, 2013)
2. Lyn Gardner (2008), 'The amazing Mr Musicals', *Guardian*, 24 January. Available online: https://www.theguardian.com/stage/2008/jan/24/theatre.musicals (accessed 6 May 2025).
3. Stephen Sondheim, Sunday in the Park With George (Four By Sondheim, Applause Libretto Library, 2002) used with permission.

Bibliography

Brecht, Bertolt, *The Resistible Rise of Arturo Ui*, translated by George Tabori (Methuen Drama, 2013)

Brantley, Ben (2005) '*Grand Guignol, Spare and Stark*', *New York Times*, 5 November. Available online: https://www.nytimes.com/2005/11/04/theater/reviews/grand-guignol-spare-and-stark.html (accessed 6 May 2025)

Brantley, Ben (2011), '*Ten Cents A Dance*: Music, Memories and Regret', *New York Times*, 16 August. Available online: https://www.nytimes.com/2011/08/16/theater/reviews/ten-cents-a-dance-at-williamstown-theater-festival-review.html (accessed 6 May 2025)

Brantley, Ben (2018), 'Review: Bad Girl Makes Good in a Glorious *Carmen Jones*', *New York Times*, 27 June. Available online: https://www.nytimes.com/2018/06/27/theater/review-carmen-jones-anika-noni-rose-john-doyle.html (accessed 6 May 2025)

Bray, Stephen, Brenda Russell, Allee Willis, "I'm Here", *The Color Purple*, 2005

Cohen, Patricia (2020), 'The Forerunners: *Sweeney Todd* (2005 Revival)', *New York Times*, 13 April. Available online: https://www.nytimes.com/interactive/2020/04/13/t-magazine/sweeney-todd-revival.html (accessed 6 May 2025)

Eliot, TS, *Four Quartets* (Faber and Faber, 2001)

Gardner, Lyn (2008), 'The Amazing Mr Musicals', *Guardian*, 24 January. Available online: https://www.theguardian.com/stage/2008/jan/24/theatre.musicals (accessed 6 May 2025)

Sondheim, Stephen, "Another Hundred People", *Company*, 1970

Sondheim, Stephen, George Furth, *Merrily We Roll Along*, 1981

Sondheim, Stephen, "Merrily We Roll Along" from *Merrily We Roll Along*, 1981

Sondheim, Stephen, "With So Little To Be Sure Of", *Anyone Can Whistle*, 1964

Teachout, Terry (2005), 'Fresh Blood on Broadway', *The Wall Street Journal*, 4 November. Available online: https://www.wsj.com/articles/SB113105939612187812 (accessed 6 May 2025)

Walker, Alice (2013), "The World Has Changed: Conversations with Alice Walker", p.298, The New Press

Shows by Chapter

Chapter 1

FINIAN'S RAINBOW	Empire Theatre, Inverness. Actor.
MACBETH	Inverness Royal Academy. Actor.
DIDO AND AENEAS	Inverness Royal Academy. Actor.
THE CHILTERN HUNDREDS	Inverness Royal Academy. Actor.
COSI FAN TUTTE	Inverness Royal Academy. Actor.
GUYS AND DOLLS	Inverness Little Theatre. Actor.
THE PYJAMA GAME	Inverness Little Theatre. Actor.
THE GLASS MENAGERIE	Royal Scottish Academy
THE PRIME OF MISS JEAN BRODIE	Inverness Little Theatre
CAUCASIAN CHALK CIRCLE	Conservatory Theatre, San Francisco.

Chapter 2

NO EXIT	University of Georgia, USA
THE RESISTIBLE RISE OF ARTURO UI	University of Georgia, USA. Actor.
WALTZ OF THE TOREADORS	University of Georgia, USA. Actor.
THE EXORCIST	Geffen Playhouse, LA
BAREFOOT IN THE PARK	Ochtertyre Theatre, Perthshire. Actor.
THE LION IN WINTER	Ochtertyre Theatre, Perthshire. Actor.
SWEETER THAN ALL THE ROSES	Ochtertyre Theatre, Perthshire
A SOLDIER'S TALE	Ochtertyre Theatre, Perthshire
ON THE ROAD TO AVIZANDUM	Perth Festival of the Arts
JOCK	Edinburgh International Festival
KNOX	Edinburgh International Festival
THE SCOTS GUIDE TO THE ARTS	Edinburgh International Festival

Chapter 3

THE SPIRIT OF SCOTLAND	Tie-Up Theatre Company
TOAD OF TOAD HALL	Tie-Up Theatre Company
CINDERELLA AND THE MARVELLOUS MICE	Tie-Up Theatre Company
THE STORY OF ANNE BONNEY	Tie-Up Theatre Company
THE BRAHAN SEER	Tie-Up Theatre Company
THE MARVELLOUS MICE ON THE MOON	Tie-Up Theatre Company
THE GLASS MENAGERIE	Tie-Up Theatre Company
A MAN FOR ALL SEASONS	Tie-Up Theatre Company
THE OWL AND THE PUSSYCAT	Tie-Up Theatre Company
THE WIZARD OF OZ	Eden Court Theatre, Inverness
COWARDY CUSTARD	Eden Court Theatre, Inverness
THE PRIME OF MISS JEAN BRODIE	Eden Court Theatre, Inverness
THE HOLLOW CROWN	Eden Court Theatre, Inverness
THE IMPORTANT OF BEING EARNEST	Eden Court Theatre, Inverness
SAILOR BEWARE	Worcester Repertory Theatre
BLYTHE SPIRIT	Worcester Repertory Theatre
JACK THE RIPPER	Worcester Repertory Theatre
THE MIKADO	Worcester Repertory Theatre
A TALE OF TWO CITIES	Worcester Repertory Theatre
CABARET	Worcester Repertory Theatre
AFTER LIVERPOOL	Worcester Repertory Theatre
SIDE BY SIDE BY SONDHEIM	Worcester Repertory Theatre. Actor.
UNCLE VANYA	Worcester Repertory Theatre
GYPSY	Worcester Repertory Theatre
DAMES AT SEA	Worcester Repertory Theatre
BORN IN THE GARDENS	Worcester Repertory Theatre
CALIFORNIA SUITE	Worcester Repertory Theatre
ANNIE	Worcester Repertory Theatre
SWEET CHARITY	Worcester Repertory Theatre
PIAF	Worcester Repertory Theatre
JUDY	Worcester Repertory Theatre
CROWN MATRIMONIAL	Worcester Repertory Theatre
FEMALE PARTS	Worcester Repertory Theatre
EDUCATING RITA	Worcester Repertory Theatre
FORTY YEARS ON	Worcester Repertory Theatre
JUST BETWEEN OURSELVES	Worcester Repertory Theatre
JUST JEROME	Worcester Repertory Theatre
SIMPLY SIMON	Worcester Repertory Theatre
MISS JULIE	Worcester Repertory Theatre
SUMMIT CONFERENCE	Worcester Repertory Theatre
PINOCCHIO	Worcester Repertory Theatre
POSTMAN PAT	Worcester Repertory Theatre

THE DRESSER	Worcester Repertory Theatre
THE WIZARD OF OZ	Worcester Repertory Theatre
VESTA	Worcester Repertory Theatre
TRAFFORD TANZI	Worcester Repertory Theatre
LAST OF THE RED HOT LOVERS	Worcester Repertory Theatre
WAY UPSTREAM	Worcester Repertory Theatre
KNOTS	Worcester Repertory Theatre
THE STRONGER	Worcester Repertory Theatre
DUET FOR ONE	Nottingham Playhouse
BODIES	Watermill Theatre, Newbury
MOVE OVER MRS MARKHAM	Watermill Theatre, Newbury
JUST BETWEEN OURSELVES	Watermill Theatre, Newbury
LAST OF THE RED HOT LOVERS	Watermill Theatre, Newbury
A CRIMINAL SUGGESTION	Cheltenham Everyman Theatre
ALADDIN	Cheltenham Everyman Theatre
MY FAIR LADY	Cheltenham Everyman Theatre
PEER GYNT	Cheltenham Everyman Theatre
HEDDA GABLER	Cheltenham Everyman Theatre
GHOSTS	Cheltenham Everyman Theatre
TOM AND VIV	Cheltenham Everyman Theatre
AFTER LIVERPOOL	Cheltenham Everyman Theatre
AN ITALIAN STRAW HAT	Cheltenham Everyman Theatre
ANYONE CAN WHISTLE	Cheltenham Everyman Theatre
THE COUNTRY WIFE	Cheltenham Everyman Theatre
WEST SIDE STORY	Cheltenham Everyman Theatre
CRIMES OF THE HEART	Cheltenham Everyman Theatre
CINDERELLA	Cheltenham Everyman Theatre
EDUCATING RITA	Cheltenham Everyman Theatre
GUYS AND DOLLS	Cheltenham Everyman Theatre
THE PROSPERO SUITE	Cheltenham Everyman Theatre
'NIGHT MOTHER	Cheltenham Everyman Theatre
PRIVATE LIVES	Cheltenham Everyman Theatre
SLEEPING BEAUTY	Cheltenham Everyman Theatre
A STREETCAR NAMED DESIRE	Cheltenham Everyman Theatre
SWEENEY TODD	Cheltenham Everyman Theatre
THE CRUCIBLE	Cheltenham Everyman Theatre
TOMFOOLERY	Cheltenham Everyman Theatre
THE KING AND I	Cheltenham Everyman Theatre
DRIVING MISS DAISY	Vienna & Zurich
GYPSY	Gaiety Theatre, Dublin
BELLS ARE RINGING	Greenwich Theatre, London

Chapter 4

THE TROJAN WOMEN	Liverpool Everyman
'TIS PITY SHE'S A WHORE	Liverpool Everyman
ALICE AND WONDERLAND	Liverpool Everyman
CAUCASIAN CHALK CIRCLE	Liverpool Everyman
DR FAUSTUS	Liverpool Everyman
LOVE AT A LOSS	Liverpool Everyman
MEDEA	Liverpool Everyman
SCHOOL FOR SCANDAL	Liverpool Everyman
THE WHITE DEVIL	Liverpool Everyman
WAITING FOR GODOT	Liverpool Everyman
THE MAN IN THE MOON	Liverpool Everyman
WIZARD	Liverpool Everyman
MRS MOON PLAY	Liverpool Everyman
TOM JONES	Watermill Theatre, Newbury
CHARLEY'S AUNT	York Theatre Royal
WHERE'S CHARLEY?	New York City Centre Encores
TRAVELS WITH MY AUNT	York Theatre Royal
THE RIVALS	York Theatre Royal
TOM JONES	York Theatre Royal
BEDROOM FARCE	York Theatre Royal
THE WAY OF THE WORLD	York Theatre Royal
THE MADNESS OF GEORGE III	York Theatre Royal
A VIEW FROM THE BRIDGE	York Theatre Royal
PASSION	Classic Stage Company, NYC
ALLEGRO	Classic Stage Company, NYC
PEER GYNT	Classic Stage Company, NYC
DEAD POETS SOCIETY	Classic Stage Company, NYC
WINGS	Second Stage, NYC
STOP THE WORLD I WANNA GET OFF	NYC Workshop
UNMASKED	NYC Workshop
THE CRADLE WILL ROCK	Classic Stage Company, NYC
FIRE AND AIR	Classic Stage Company, NYC
DRACULA	Classic Stage Company, NYC. Designer.
FRANKENSTEIN	Classic Stage Company, NYC. Designer.

Chapter 5

CANDIDE	Liverpool Everyman/UK Tour
GHOSTS	Northlands Festival
MOLL FLANDERS	York Theatre Royal

CABARET	York Theatre Royal
PAL JOEY	York Theatre Royal
INTO THE WOODS	York Theatre Royal
PETER PAN	Oxford Playhouse
MOLL FLANDERS	Salisbury Repertory Theatre
TOM JONES	Watermill Theatre, Newbury
CABARET	Watermill Theatre, Newbury
SINBAD	Watermill Theatre, Newbury
BEAUTY AND THE BEAST	Watermill Theatre, Newbury
IRMA LA DOUCE	New York City Centre Encores
IRMA LA DOUCE	Watermill Theatre, Newbury
CINDERELLA & THE ENCHANTED SLIPPER	Watermill Theatre, Newbury
AND A NIGHTINGALE SANG	Worcester Repertory Theatre
SINBAD	Watermill Theatre, Newbury
FIDDLER ON THE ROOF	Watermill Theatre, Newbury
A STAR DANCED	Watermill Theatre, Newbury
ONLY A MATTER OF TIME	Watermill Theatre, Newbury
LAST DAYS OF THE EMPIRE	Watermill Theatre, Newbury
WIZARD OF OZ	Watermill Theatre, Newbury
PIAF	Watermill Theatre, Newbury
PINAFORE SWING	Watermill Theatre, Newbury
MACK AND MABEL	Watermill Theatre, Newbury
MERRILY WE ROLL ALONG	Watermill Theatre, Newbury
AMADEUS	Wilton's Music Hall, London
TEN CENTS A DANCE	Watermill Theatre & Cardiff Festival
TEN CENTS A DANCE	Williamstown Festival, USA
AUGUST RUSH	Paramount Theatre, Chicago
OKLAHOMA	Chichester Festival Theatre
GONDOLIERS	Apollo Theatre, London
MACK AND MABEL	Criterion Theatre, London

Chapter 6

WORCESTER PAGEANT	Worcester Cathedral
YORK CYCLE OF MYSTERY PLAYS	York Theatre Royal
COVENTRY CYCLE OF MYSTERY PLAYS	Coventry Cathedral
COVENTRY CYCLE PRISON PROJECT	Coventry Cathedral
THE NATIVITY	Liverpool Everyman & Tour
GREENWICH PASSION PLAY	Greenwich Park, London
THE 12	Goodspeed Theatre
SALVATION ARMY CONCERTS	Royal Festival Hall & Royal Albert Hall

Chapter 7

SWEENEY TODD	Watermill Theatre & UK Tour
SWEENEY TODD	New Ambassadors, London
SWEENEY TODD	O'Neill Theatre, Broadway & US Tour
MERRILY WE ROLL ALONG	Cincinnati Playhouse
A BED AND A CHAIR	New York City Centre
SONDHEIM 80th BIRTHDAY GALA	New York City Centre
THE LADIES WHO SING SONDHEIM	Lincoln Centre, NYC

Chapter 8

ROAD SHOW	Public Theatre, NYC
PACIFIC OVERTURES	Classic Stage Company, NYC
ASSASSINS	Classic Stage Company, NYC
CLASSIC CONVERSATIONS	Classic Stage Company, NYC

Chapter 9

COMPANY	Barrymore Theatre, Broadway
A CATERED AFFAIR	Walter Kerr Theatre, Broadway
THE VISIT	Lyceum Theatre, Broadway

Chapter 10

THE COLOR PURPLE	Menier Chocolate Factory, London
THE COLOR PURPLE	Jacobs Theatre, Broadway & US Tour
CARMEN JONES	Classic Stage Company, NYC
PORGY AND BESS	Danish Royal Opera
A MAN OF NO IMPORTANCE	Classic Stage Company, NYC

Chapter 11

ICE	City of London Symphonia
THE TAILOR'S DAUGHTER	Welsh Opera

L'ELISIR D'AMOUR	Welsh Opera
CARMEN	Linbury Theatre, ROH
FAST FORWARD FIGARO	UK Tour
LUCIA DI LAMMERMOOR	Scottish Opera
RISE AND FALL OF MAHAGONNY	Los Angeles Opera
PETER GRIMES	Metropolitan Opera, NYC
MADAMA BUTTERFLY	Grange Park Opera
THE CARMELITES	Grange Park Opera
WERTHER	Grange Park Opera
DAUGHTER OF THE REGIMENT	Grange Park Opera
LUCIA DI LAMMERMOOR	Houston, Venice & Sydney Opera House

Chapter 12

WHEN THE WIND BLOWS	Worcester Repertory Company
WHOSE LIFE IS IT ANYWAY?	Worcester Repertory Company
ARTURO UI	Classic Stage Company, NYC
FEMALE PARTS	Arts Theatre, London
SARCOPHAGUS	Liverpool Everyman
VICTORY CELEBRATIONS	Liverpool Everyman
MAIN STREET	Movie
MUCH ADO ABOUT NOTHING	Western Kentucky University
A MIDSUMMER NIGHT'S DREAM	Western Kentucky University
THE WINTER'S TALE	Western Kentucky University
MACBETH	Classic Stage Company, NYC
AS YOU LIKE IT	Liverpool Everyman
OTHELLO	Liverpool Everyman
MUCH ADO ABOUT NOTHING	Liverpool Everyman & Tour
MACBETH	York Theatre Royal
RICHARD III	York Theatre Royal
HENRY IV, Parts One, Two & Three	York Theatre Royal
TWELFTH NIGHT	York Theatre Royal
A MIDSUMMER NIGHT'S DREAM	York Theatre Royal
AS YOU LIKE IT	Classic Stage Company NYC
MACBETH	Tie-Up Theatre Company
A MIDSUMMER NIGHT'S DREAM	Regents Park Open Air Theatre
ROMEO AND JULIET	Worcester Repertory Theatre
TWELFTH NIGHT	Cheltenham Everyman Theatre
HAMLET	Co-Producer
KISS ME KATE	Stratford Festival Theatre, Ontario
SHAKESPEARE FOR DUMMIES	Co-Author
MACBETH	Worcester Repertory Theatre

ANTONY AND CLEOPATRA	Co-Producer
TWELFTH NIGHT	Classic Stage Company. Designer.
TROJAN WOMEN	Birmingham Theatre School
YOU'RE GONNA LOVE TOMORROW	Palace Theatre, London
RING ROUND THE MOON	Webber Douglas Academy
MAN OF LA MANCHA	Rose Bruford College at Battersea Arts Centre
THE THREE SISTERS	Cincinnati Playhouse
ALFRED HITCHCOCK PRESENTS	Bath Theatre Royal

Index

A BED AND A CHAIR Sondheim/ Marsallis/Doyle New York City Center 125
A CATERED AFFAIR, Fierstein/ Bucchino Old Globe Theatre, San Diego & Walter Kerr Theatre, NYC 154–6
A MAN OF NO IMPORTANCE McNally/ Ahrens/Flaherty Classic Stage Company, NYC 71, 176
A MIDSUMMER NIGHT'S DREAM Shakespeare York Theatre Royal 23, 48, 62–3, 207
A STAR DANCED Doyle/Travis Watermill Theatre, Newbury 89
AHRENS, Lynn 71
ALI, Shariffa 69, 201
ALLEGRO Rodgers/Hammerstein Classic Stage Company, NYC 82
AMADEUS Shaffer Wilton's Music Hall, London 90
AMERICAN CONSERVATORY THEATRE, San Francisco 15
ANDREWS, Julie 161
ANGELSON, Lynn 65
ANYONE CAN WHISTLE Sondheim/ Laurents Everyman Theatre, Cheltenham 48
ARDEN, Michael 215
ARSENAULT, David L. 172
ARTS COUNCIL 31, 35, 46, 55, 59, 80, 164
AS YOU LIKE IT Shakespeare Everyman Theatre, Liverpool 58, 104
ASCROFT, Liz 180, 189, 192

ASSASSINS Sondheim/Weidman Classic Stage Company, NYC 6, 79, 117, 125–6, 135–42
AUSTIN, Right Rev. George 98–9

BABANI, David 132, 163–4
BAILEY, Mark 99, 183
BAKER, Becky Ann 124
BARDINI, Aleksander 24–6
BARLOW, Ginni 43
BENNETT, Michael 151
BERG, Neil 105
BERLINER Ensemble 25, 27
BERNSTEIN, Leonard 59, 76
BERRY, Stephanie 69
BLITZSTEIN, Marc 70
BOROVSKI, Alexander 57, 202–3
BOWERS, Nadia 69
BOWMAN, Ian 9
BRANTLEY, Ben 91, 122
BRAY, Stephen 169
BRECHT, Bertolt 24–5, 27, 58, 182, 196–8
BREWSTER, Yvonne 55
BROOK, Peter 57, 180, 199
BROOKS, Danielle 170
BUBBLE THEATRE COMPANY, London 77–9
BUCCHINO, John 155
BURSTYN, Ellen 28, 190, 204

CABARET Kander/Ebb Worcester, York & Newbury 45, 83, 85
CAMPBELL, Mary-Mitchell 79, 131, 148, 151

CANDIDE Bernstein Everyman Theatre, Liverpool & UK Tour 59, 76–81
CARIOU, Len 125
CARLTON, Bob 77
CARMEN Bizet Watermill Theatre, Newbury & Linbury Theatre, Covent Garden. 82, 191–2
CARMEN JONES Bizet/Hammerstein Classic Stage Company, NYC 174–6
CASTLE, Matt 151
CERVERIS, Michael 114, 117–22, 125, 130, 146
CAUCASIAN CHALK CIRCLE Brecht Everyman Theatre, Liverpool & American Conservatory Theatre, San Fransisco 58, 151, 188–9
CHAGALL, Marc 84, 99
CHAMBERLAIN, Richard 28
CHANNING, Carol 143–4
CHAPIN, Ted 174
CHARLEY'S AUNT Thomas York Theatre Royal & New York Encores. 61
CHAYEFSKY, Paddy 155
CHEKHOV, Anton 203, 211–13
CINCINNATI PLAYHOUSE IN THE PARK 124, 147–53
CITIZEN'S THEATRE, Glasgow 15, 34
CLARK, Victoria 70, 201
CLASSIC STAGE COMPANY, New York 63–72, 135–42, 174–6
CLINTON, Hillary 140, 173
CLOSE THEATRE CLUB, Glasgow 63
COHEN, Lynn 213
COHEN, Patricia 146
COMPANY Sondheim/Furth. Cincinnati Playhouse in the Park & Barrymore Theatre, NYC. 79, 91, 125, 128–9, 147–54
COMPERE, Carrie 183
CONLON, James 183
COOPER, Eddie 208
COSI FAN TUTTE, Mozart 9, 180
COVENTRY CYCLE OF MYSTERY PLAYS 101–3

COX, Jane 131, 169
CRADLE WILL ROCK Blitzstein Classic Stage Company, NYC 70
CUERVO, Alma 130
CUTHBERTSON, Iain 31

DANIELE, Graziela 159
DANISH Opera Company 192–3
DAVIES, Bernard 188
DAVIS, Toni 65, 139
DEAD POETS SOCIETY Schulman. Classic Stage Company, NYC 68
DEE, Janie 89
De SHIELDS, Andre 174
DiCARLO, Matthew 172
DOBELL, Linda 55
DOUGLAS, Timothy 69
DOWDESWELL, Wayne 198–9
DOYLE, Patrick 74

EATON, Bob 77
EBB, Fred 39–40
EDGAR, Kate 79–80
ELDER, Claybourne 130
ELICE, Rick 160
ELIOT, TS 1, 49–50
ELLIOTT, MARIANNE 125, 201
ELVIDGE, Marcia 28
EMPIRE THEATRE, Inverness 10, 12, 14
ERIVO, Cynthia 167–74
ESPARZA, Raul 148, 151, 153, 197
EUSTIS, Oskar 128, 132
EVERYMAN THEATRE, Cheltenham 45–51, 60
EVERYMAN THEATRE, Liverpool 28, 53–60, 63, 76–7, 80–1, 95–6

FARROW, Mia 125
FEDERAL Theatre Project 70
FELCIANO, Manoel 116
FEMALE PARTS Fo/Rame Worcester, Islington & Arts Theatre, London. 200–1
FERRARI, Elena 78

FIDDLER ON THE ROOF Bock/Harnick/
   Stein Watermill Theatre, Newbury
   87–8, 100
FIERSTEIN, Harvey 77–8
FINIAN'S RAINBOW Harburg/Lane/
   Saidy. Empire Theatre, Inverness
   11–12
FIRE AND AIR McNally. Classic Stage
   Company, NYC 70, 176
FIRTH, Colin 204
FISH, Daniel 215
FLAHERTY, Stephen 71
FOOTE, Horton 74
FORD, Ruth 97–8
FOSSE, Bob 44, 157–9
FRANKEL, Richard 121, 153
FRASER, Jill 84–91, 123
FREUD, Anthony 189
FURTH, George 128, 147–54

GALLIE, Kay 30
GALLO, David 148, 155
GALLOWAY, Jenny 80
GARDNER, Lyn 214
GELB, Peter 184
GELBART, Larry 127
GEMIGNANI, Alexander 116, 130, 148, 165
GETS, Malcolm 91, 124
GHOSTS, Ibsen 74–5
GOLDMAN, James 29, 127
GONDOLIERS Gilbert/Sullivan/Doyle/
   Travis Watermill Theatre, Newbury &
   Apollo Theatre, Shaftesbury Avenue 87,
   207
GRANGE PARK OPERA 188–9
*GREENWICH PARK 2000 MYSTERY
   PLAYS* Doyle 103–5
GRIFFEY, Anthony Dean 182
GRIFFIN, Gary 165
GROVES, John 15
GUBAREV, Vladimir 202–3
GUTHRIE, Tyrone 23
GUY'S HOSPITAL OLD OPERATING
   THEATRE, London 109, 132

HAMILL, Kate 69
HAMMERSTEIN, Oscar 127
HARRISON, Jeremy 83, 100
HARRISON, Tony 95
HART, Larry 91
HAVERGAL, Giles 15
HEADLEY, Heather 172, 190
HEADRICK, Charlotte 28, 105, 205
HEDDA GABLER, Ibsen 49
HEGARTY, Paul 109
HELLMAN, Lillian 76
HERMAN, Jerry 89–90, 143
HODGE, Douglas 70, 176
HOLLIDAY, Jennifer 172, 190
HOPE STREET PROJECT, Liverpool
   208–9
HOULD-WARD, Ann 131, 153, 155, 169,
   183
HOWCROFT, Michael 108
HUDSON, Jennifer 170, 190
HUGHES, Nicola 167
HUMPHRIES, Barry 154
HUNTER, Adam 119–20, 160
HUNTER, Russell 30
HUNTLEY, Paul 118–19

IBSEN, Henrik 29, 74
ICE London Symphonia People's Palace,
   City of London 179
ILLG, Roberta 28
INTERNATIONAL SALVATION ARMY
   103
INTO THE WOODS Sondheim/Lapine
   York Theatre Royal 84
INVERNESS OPERA COMPANY
   10–12
IRMA LA DOUCE. Monnot/Norman/
   Moore Watermill Theatre, Newbury &
   City Center, NYC 88–9

JACKSON, Rebecca 100, 109
JACOB, Stephanie 109
JACOBS, Amanda 29–31, 34–6
JACOBY, Mark 116, 119
JARRETT, Greg 79

JAYES, Catherine 45, 55, 78–9, 90, 167
JENKINS, Daniel 124
JENKINS, Rebecca 108
JOE ALLEN'S, New York 48, 117
JONES, Elizabeth 60
JONES, Richard G. 119
JOUBERT, Joseph 169
JUSTMAN, Amy 151

KANDER, John 90, 156–60
KANI, Wasfi 188
KAYE, Judy 145
KEITH MURRAY, William 28
KELLY, Janis 9, 179–80
KENWRIGHT, Adam 113
KENYON, Sam 109
KESLER, Jackson 28, 98
KIRDAHY, Tom 156
KUHN, Judy 64, 138
KULICK, Brian 64

LANGE, Jessica 154
LANSBURY, Angela 48, 154
LAPINE, James 64, 128
LAPINE, Sarna 201
LAUCHLAN, Iain 17–18
LAURENTS, Arthur 127–8
LAWRENCE, Taylor Pope 25
LaPOINTE, Charles G. 169
LISCHNER, Ray 205–6
LIVERPOOL ANGLICAN CATHEDRAL 53, 96
LIVERPOOL METROPOLITAN CATHEDRAL 53, 96
LLOYD, Phyllida 45, 48, 201, 206
LOUD, David 118, 125
LUCIA DI LAMMERMOOR Donizetti Scottish Opera, Glasgow Theatre Royal 180–1
LUCIA DI LAMMERMOOR Houston, Venice, Sydney 189–91
LUCIA DI LAMMERMOOR Mariinsky Theatre, St. Petersburg 182
LuPONE, Patti 88, 114, 117–22, 145–6, 154, 161, 183

MacARTHUR, Edith 29
Macbeth Shakespeare Inverness, Cawdor & Classic Stage Company, NYC 9–10, 37–8, 69, 206
MACK AND MABEL Herman/Stewart Watermill Theatre Newbury & Criterion Theatre, London 89–90
MAIN STREET, Foote 204
MANN, Karen 43, 109
MARSALIS, Wynton
MASON, Marsha 70
MATCHAM, Frank 46
MATTHEWS, Emma 190–1
MAZZIE, Marin 70
McCLELLAND, Eliza 200–1
McDONALD, Audra 183
McKECHNIE, Donna 44, 91, 151, 160
McNALLY, Terrence 70, 127, 156–60, 176
MENDES, Sam 129
MERMAN, Ethel 144
MERRILY WE ROLL ALONG Sondheim/Furth Watermill Theatre, Newbury & Cincinnati Playhouse in the Park 91, 101, 121, 124, 148, 150
MIRANDA, Lin-Manuel 172
MOLL FLANDERS Stiles/Leigh York Theatre Royal 82–3
MOSCOW ART THEATRE 57, 60, 202

NETREBKO, Anna 182
NEW YORK TIMES 64, 91, 146, 175
NICHOLAS NICKLEBY Dickens/Edgar 62, 157–8
NICOLL, Harry 9–10, 19, 99
NORMAN, Marsha 167–8
NORRIS, Rufus 45
NORTHERN MEETING PARK, Inverness 12
NORTHERN MEETING ROOMS, Inverness 8
NOVODEVICHY CEMETERY, Moscow 203
NUNN, Trevor 41, 158

O'BRIEN, Michael 26, 28, 72
OCHTERTYRE THEATRE, Perthshire 28–31
OPERA FACTORY, David Freeman 180
OREGON STATE UNIVERSITY, Corvallis 28, 105, 205

PACE UNIVERSITY, New York 158
PACIFIC OVERTURES Sondheim/Weidman Classic Stage Company, NYC 44, 135–42
PALMER, Felicity 185
PANTER, Howard 113
PAPP, Joe 128
PAPPAS, Rick 125
PARKER, Dorothy 76
PARSONS, Jim 71
PASK, Scott 124, 159, 184, 211
PASQUALE, Steven 138
PASSION Sondheim/Lapine Classic Stage Company, NYC 64, 128
PEER GYNT, Ibsen 47–8
PEIL, Mary Beth 206
PETER GRIMES Britten. Metropolitan Opera, NYC 184–8
PETER PAN Doyle/Travis Oxford Playhouse 84–6
PETERS, Bernadette 90, 114, 125
PRATT, Jessica 190–1
PINAFORE SWING Doyle/Travis Watermill Theatre, Newbury 88–9
PORGY AND BESS Gershwin Danish Royal Opera, Copenhagen 192–3
PRINCE, Faith 155
PRINCE, Hal 50, 110, 123, 129, 136
PRINCETON UNIVERSITY 21, 64, 81, 209–10

RACETTE, Patricia 185
RADCLIFFE, Alan 44
RADIO CITY MUSIC HALL, New York 161
REDINGTON, Christine 34–6
REES, Roger 157–60
REICH, John 23–4

REINHARDT, Max 23, 27
REMICK, Lee 48
RHODES, Teddy Tahu 185
RICARDO-PEARCE, David 108
RICH, Frank 132
RICHARDSON, Ralph 47
RIVERA, Chita 44, 157–60
ROAD SHOW, Sondheim/Weidman. Public Theatre, NYC & Menier Chocolate Factory, London 128–42, 163
ROBBINS, Jerome 87–8, 157
ROBINS, Laila 213
ROBINSON, Bernita 176
ROCKWELL, David 67
RODGERS, Richard 91, 127
ROMEO AND JULIET, Shakespeare Swan Theatre, Worcester 24, 42–3
ROSE BRUFORD COLLEGE, Sidcup 81, 100, 209
ROSE, Anika Noni 175
ROTARY CLUBS OF AMERICA 18–20
ROTH, Jordan 156
ROYAL SCOTTISH ACADEMY OF MUSIC AND DRAMA/ROYAL CONSERVATOIRE OF SCOTLAND, Glasgow 13–16, 34, 74, 81, 214
RUHL, Sarah 211
RUNNICLES, Donald 185
RUSSELL, Brenda 169
RUSSELL, Willy 54
RYE, Ann 30

SANDERS, Scott 164–5
SARDI'S, New York. 143–4
SARTRE, Jean-Paul 27
SCHENKKAN, Robert 105
SCHREIER, Dan Moses 83, 119, 132
SCOTTISH CHAMBER ORCHESTRA 31
SCOTTISH SOCIETY OF PLAYWRIGHTS 31
SCOTTISH OPERA 9
SHAFFER, Peter 90
SHAGIMURATOVA, Albina 189

SHAKESPEARE FOR DUMMIES Doyle/ Lischner 205–6
SHAKESPEARE, William 1, 55, 69, 73, 205–6
SHEVELOVE, Bert 127
SHIELDS, Brooke 28
SIDE BY SIDE BY SONDHEIM Swan Theatre, Worcester 43–4
SKYE GATHERING HALL 38
SIMON, Neil 29, 42–4, 71, 117
SMITH, W. Gordon 30–1
SOLZHENITSYN, Alexander 201–2
SONDHEIM, Stephen 6, 48, 50, 63–4, 76, 81, 90, 107–26, 127–42, 145–53, 215
SOUL, David 89
STEIN, Joseph 88
STERN, Ed 147–8, 153
STOLL, Corey 69, 213
STRATFORD THEATRE FESTIVAL, Ontario 23, 165
STRINDBERG, August 70, 198
STRITCH, Elaine 114, 123, 160
STUTFIELD, Ann 29, 200
SUDEIKIS, Jason 68
SWEENEY TODD Sondheim/Wheeler Watermill Theatre, Newbury, Trafalgar Studios & New Ambassadors, London. Eugene O'Neill Theatre, NYC 10, 12, 50, 79, 88, 90, 100, 107–24, 145–6, 148–9, 151, 164, 215
SWEET CHARITY Coleman/Simon. Swan Theatre, Worcester 44
SWEETER THAN ALL THE ROSES W.Gordon Smith Ochtertyre Theatre, Perthshire 30–1
SWENSON, Will 138

TAKEI, George 136
TALAWA THEATRE COMPANY 55, 164
TEACHOUT, Terry 107
THE COLOR PURPLE. Bray/Norman/ Russell/Willis. Menier Chocolate Factory, London & Barrymore Theatre, NYC 106, 160–1, 163–74

THE EMPTY SPACE Brook 199
THE EXORCIST Pielmeier Geffen Playhouse, LA 28
THE NATIVITY Harrison Everyman Theatre & both Liverpool Cathedrals 95–6
THE RESISTIBLE RISE OF ARTURO UI Brecht Classic Stage Company NYC 25, 196–8
THE RISE AND FALL OF THE CITY OF MAHAGONNY Brecht/Weill LA Opera 25, 182–3
THE TAYLOR'S DAUGHTER Irvine/ Cullen Welsh National Opera 179
THE TROJAN WOMEN Euripides Everyman Theatre, Liverpool 55
THE THREE SISTERS Chekhov/Ruhl Cincinnati Playhouse in the Park 148, 211–13
THE VISIT Kander/Ebb/McNally Williamstown Theatre Festival & Lyceum Theatre, NYC 91, 156–60
THE WARS OF THE ROSES Shakespeare York Theatre Royal 61–2
THE 12 Schenkkan/Berg Goodspeed Opera House 105–6
TEN CENTS A DANCE. Rodgers/Hart/ Doyle Williamstown Festival Theatre & McCarter Theatre, Princeton 91
THATCHER, Margaret 53–6, 59–60, 75, 92
THOMAS, Ben 104–5
THOMPSON, Mark 41
TIE-UP THEATRE COMPANY 33–9
TIFFANY, John 91
TOM AND VIV Hastings Everyman Theatre, Cheltenham 49–50
TOWN, Joanna 192
TRAVIS, Sarah 79, 87–8, 107, 119, 145
TUNICK, Jonathan 131–2, 137, 155
TWELFTH NIGHT Shakespeare Everyman Theatre, Cheltenham 50

UNIVERSITY OF GEORGIA, Athen, Georgia. 17–28, 49, 72, 116

VERDON, Gwen 44
VIDAL-HALL, Clare 122

WAKEFIELD, Colin 109
WALE, Terry 43
WALFORD, Glen 54, 77
WALKER, Alice 82, 164, 170
WALSH, Barbara 148
WATERMILL THEATRE, Newbury 63, 84–91, 101, 107–13, 119, 149
WEBB, Jason Michael 169
WEBB, Rema 106
WEIDMAN, Jerome 129
WEIDMAN, John 128–42
WEILL, Kurt
WELLS, Orson
WESTERN KENTUCKY UNIVERSITY 28, 209
WHEELER, Hugh 127

WHITE, Helena 26–7
WHITE, Sue 100–1
WHITEHALL THEATRE, London 12
WHITING, Liz 44
WILLIS, Allee 169
WINFREY, Oprah 165, 170
WINNINGHAM, Mare 71
WOLF, Stacy 209–10
WOOLLASTON, Nikki 192
WOPAT, Tom 155
WORCESTER CATHEDRAL 94–5
WORCESTER REPERTORY COMPANY, Swan Theatre 39–45

YEFREMOV, Oleg 202–3
YORK THEATRE ROYAL 59–63, 82
YORK CYCLE OF MYSTERY PLAYS
    Lochead York Theatre Royal 61, 96–100